Virtual Voyages

Anthem Studies in Travel

Anthem Studies in Travel publishes new and pioneering work in the burgeoning field of travel studies. Titles in this series engage with questions of travel, travel writing, literature and history, and encompass some of the most exciting current scholarship in a variety of disciplines, with research representing a broad range of geographical zones and historical contexts.

Editorial Board

Charles Forsdick, University of Liverpool
Mary B. Campbell, Brandeis University
Steve Clark, University of Tokyo
Claire Lindsay, University College London
Loredana Polezzi, University of Warwick
Paul Smethurst, University of Hong Kong

Other Titles in the Series

Travellers to the Middle East from Burckhardt to Thesiger: An Anthology
Edited by Geoffrey Nash

Travel Writing in the Nineteenth Century: Filling the Blank Spaces
Edited by Tim Youngs

Creating Irish Tourism: The First Century, 1750–1850
William H. A. Williams

Related Titles from Anthem Press

Russia's Penal Colony in the Far East: A Translation of Vlas Doroshevich's "Sakhalin"
Translated and with an Introduction by Andrew A. Gentes

Govind Narayan's Mumbai: An Urban Biography from 1863
Edited by Murali Ranganathan, with a Foreword by Gyan Prakash

America Magica: When Renaissance Europe Thought it had Conquered Paradise, 2nd edn
Jorge Magasich-Airola and Jean-Marc de Beer,
Translated by Monica Sandor, with a Foreword by David Abulafia

What I Saw in America
G. K. Chesterton, with an Introduction by Simon Newman

Virtual Voyages

Travel Writing and the Antipodes 1605–1837

Paul Longley Arthur

ANTHEM PRESS
LONDON · NEW YORK · DELHI

Anthem Press
An imprint of Wimbledon Publishing Company
www.anthempress.com

This edition first published in UK and USA 2011
by ANTHEM PRESS
75-76 Blackfriars Road, London SE1 8HA, UK
or PO Box 9779, London SW19 7ZG, UK
and
244 Madison Ave. #116, New York, NY 10016, USA

Copyright © Paul Longley Arthur 2011
http://www.paularthur.com

The moral right of the author has been asserted.

Extracts from *Fragmens du dernier voyage de La Pérouse [Fragments from the Last Voyage of La Pérouse]* [1797], trans. John Dunmore, 2 vols (Canberra: National Library of Australia 1987), are reproduced with the permission of the National Library of Australia.

Cover design by John Douglass, Brown Cow Design, Western Australia
Cover features detail of: The first map of Australia, from Nicholas
Vallard's atlas (1547), National Library of Australia, Call no. MAP RM 2393;
and Vincenzo Coronelli's 'Marly' terrestrial globe (c. 1683) featuring
a map of New Holland, displayed at Bibliothèque Nationale François Mitterrand
in Paris (reproduced under a Creative Commons Attribution-Share
Alike 3.0 license). Photographic image and license details available at
http://commons.wikimedia.org/wiki/File:Globe_Coronelli_Map_of_New_Holland.jpg.

All rights reserved. Without limiting the rights under copyright reserved above,
no part of this publication may be reproduced, stored or introduced
into a retrieval system, or transmitted, in any form or by any means
(electronic, mechanical, photocopying, recording or otherwise),
without the prior written permission of both the copyright
owner and the above publisher of this book.

British Library Cataloguing-in-Publication Data
A catalogue record for this book is available from the British Library.

Library of Congress Cataloging-in-Publication Data
The Library of Congress has catalogued the hardcover edition as follows:
Arthur, Paul Longley.
Virtual voyages : travel writing and the antipodes 1605–1837 / Paul Longley Arthur.
p. cm.
Includes index.
ISBN 978-1-84331-800-2 (hardcover : alk. paper) – ISBN 978-1-84331-839-2 (ebook)
1. Voyages, Imaginary–History and criticism. 2. Europe–History, Naval. 3. Europe–Discovery
and exploration. 4. Australia–Description and travel. I. Title.
G560.A78 2009
809'.9332–dc22
2009047631

ISBN-13: 978 0 85728 408 2 (Pbk)
ISBN-10: 0 85728 408 8 (Pbk)

This title is also available as an eBook.

the affinity of dreams is vision
crossing into distant harbours searched for
in an incomplete cartography or
on the vessels of a secret mission
an inventory registered as birth.

for to exist is knowledge mapped in mind
where greed and recognition join to find
the revelations of a double earth
hosting antipodes of otherness,
light's counter shadows casting their dark sun,
a world beyond within the world that is:
black swans, snow summers, opposites as one.
collecting images to climb the shore
which houses them in rock and arid ground
when memory returns to where it found
the source of all the life it lived before.

– Manfred Jurgensen, *Shadows of Utopia* (1994)[1]

TABLE OF CONTENTS

List of Illustrations	ix
Acknowledgements	xiii
Editorial Note	xv
Introduction	xvii

Chapter 1: Real and Imaginary Voyages — 1

    Colonial Vision — 5
    Reality Effects — 7
    Utopian Worlds — 9
    Literary Criticism — 11
    Robinsonades and Gulliveriana — 15

Chapter 2: Blank Spaces for the Imagination — 19

    Antipodean Inversions and Reversals — 21
    Joseph Hall's *Mundus alter et idem* (1605) — 28
    Gabriel de Foigny's *La Terre Australe connue* (1676) — 36

Chapter 3: Exoticism and Romanticism — 47

    The Colour of Truth — 53
    Robert Paltock's *The Life and Adventures of Peter Wilkins* (1750) — 56

Chapter 4: Finding Paradise and Utopia in the Pacific — 79

    The Disappearance of La Pérouse — 84
    Fragmens du dernier voyage de La Pérouse (1797) — 85
    The Life of La Perouse, the Celebrated and Unfortunate French Navigator (1801) — 97

Chapter 5: Australia's Mythic Inland		**107**
Australia in the Antipodes		108
The Dead Heart		117
Account of an Expedition to the Interior of New Holland (1837)		123
Conclusion		133
Notes		143
Index		181

LIST OF ILLUSTRATIONS

Figure 1. Map showing the projected southern continent. From Ambrosius Macrobius, *Dream of Scipio* (c. 1560). National Library of Australia. Call no. MAP Ra 277. xviii

Figure 2. [Anon.]. 'Geai, pare des plumes du Paon' [hand-coloured engraving] (c. 1802). Mitchell Library, State Library of New South Wales, Australia. Call no. SV/151. 3

Figure 3. Images of 'Antipode', 'Sciapod' and 'Blemmyae' [woodcut engravings]. From Hartmann Schedel, *Liber Chronicarum* [*Nuremberg Chronicle*] (Nuremberg: Anton Koberger 1493). Blat XII. National Library of Australia. Call no. mfm 455. Roll 362, item 3. 21

Figure 4. Theodor de Bry. Detail of 'Descriptio Hydrographica' [map] (Frankfurt am Main: 1599). National Library of Australia. Call no. MAP RM 2748 Tile a2. 23

Figure 5. Pierre Desceliers. Detail of 'La Terre Australle' [map] (1550). This reproduction of the original map by Brisbane Sunmap Centre. © The State of Queensland (Department of Environment and Resource Management) 1980. National Library of Australia. Call no. MAP G8961.S1 1550. 25

Figure 6. Benito Arias Montanus. Detail of 'Pars Orbis' [map] (first published in the Antwerp Polygot Bible by Christopher Plantin in 1571). Reproduction of the original map in *Remarkable Maps of the XVth, XVIth, and XVIIth Centuries* (Amsterdam: Frederik Muller 1894–1899). Plate [parts 2–3] 1. National Library of Australia. Call no. MAP Ra 199 [part 2] plate 1. 26

Figure 7. Cornelis de Jode. 'Novae Guineae Forma, & Situs' [map]. From *Speculum Orbis Terrae* (Antwerp: Gerard de Jode 1593). National Library of Australia. Call no. MAP RM 389. 27

Figure 8. Page 214, showing detailed footnotes. From [Joseph Hall], *The Discovery of a New World, or, A Description of the South Indies,*

	Hitherto Unknowne, by an English Mercury, adapted into English by John Healey (London: For E. Blount & W. Barrett 1609). National Library of Australia. Call no. RB MISC 1874.	31
Figure 9.	Map of the fictional southern land. From [Joseph Hall], *Mundus alter et idem siue Terra Australis ante hac semper incognita longis itineribus peregrini Academici nuperrime lustrate* (London: Printed by Humphrey Lownes 1605). Between pages 18 and 19. National Library of Australia. Call no. mfm 1314.	32
Figure 10.	Title page. From [Joseph Hall], *The Discovery of a New World, or, A Description of the South Indies, Hitherto Unknowne, by an English Mercury*, adapted into English by John Healey (London: For E. Blount & W. Barrett 1609). National Library of Australia. Call no. RB MISC 1874.	33
Figure 11.	Julia Ciccarone. 'The Urgs' [oil on canvas] (1995). Reproduced with permission of the artist. © Julia Ciccarone 1995. National Library of Australia. Call no. N 759.994 C568.	43
Figure 12.	Julia Ciccarone. 'Birth of the Australian' [oil on canvas] (1995). Reproduced with permission of the artist. © Julia Ciccarone 1995. National Library of Australia. Call no. N 759.994 C568.	44
Figure 13.	Julia Ciccarone. 'Birth of the Europeans' [oil on canvas] (1995). Reproduced with permission of the artist. © Julia Ciccarone 1995. National Library of Australia. Call no. N 759.994 C568.	45
Figure 14.	Justus Danckerts. 'India quae Orientalis' [map] (c. 1690). Reproduction of the original map in R. V. Tooley, ed., *Early Maps of Australia: The Dutch Period* (London: Map Collectors' Circle 1965). Plate XXI [no. 49]. © Map Collectors' Circle 1965. National Library of Australia. Call no. MAP s 016.911 MAP.	49
Figure 15.	Vincenzo Coronelli. 'Nuova Guinea' [map]. From *Isolario* (Venice: Vincenzo Coronelli 1697). Plate 148. National Library of Australia. Call no. MAP NK 1564.	50
Figure 16.	Melchisédech Thévenot. 'Hollandia Nova' [map]. From *Relations de divers voyages curieux* (Paris: J. Langlois 1663). National Library of Australia. Call no. MAP RM 689A.	51
Figure 17.	Emanuel Bowen. 'A Complete Map of the Southern Continent'. From John Harris, ed., *Itinerantium bibliotheca, or, A Complete Collection of Voyages and Travels* (London: 1744). This reproduction of the original map by the Department	

LIST OF ILLUSTRATIONS

	of Lands and Survey, Melbourne 1886. National Library of Australia. Call no. MAP RM 2055.	52
Figure 18.	Louis-Philippe Boitard. 'A Glumm Swimming' [engraving]. From [Robert Paltock], *The Life and Adventures of Peter Wilkins* (London: Printed for J. Robinson & R. Dodsley 1751). Vol. 1, between pages 184 and 185. National Library of Australia. Call no. mfm 1651, reel 2897, no. 3.	65
Figure 19.	Louis-Philippe Boitard. 'A Gawrey Extended for Flight' [engraving]. From [Robert Paltock], *The Life and Adventures of Peter Wilkins* (London: Printed for J. Robinson & R. Dodsley 1751). Vol. 1, between pages 156 and 157. National Library of Australia. Call no. mfm 1651, reel 2897, no. 3.	66
Figure 20.	Louis-Philippe Boitard. 'The Use of ye Back flap when ye Glumm flyes' [engraving]. From [Robert Paltock], *The Life and Adventures of Peter Wilkins* (London: Printed for & R. Dodsley 1751). Vol. 1, between pages 158 and 159. National Library of Australia. Call no. mfm 1651, reel 2897, no. 3.	67
Figure 21.	Louis-Philippe Boitard. 'Nasgigs Engagement with Harlokins General' [engraving]. From [Robert Paltock], *The Life and Adventures of Peter Wilkins* (London: Printed for J. Robinson & R. Dodsley 1751). Vol. 2, between pages 122 and 123. National Library of Australia. Call no. mfm 1651, reel 2897, no. 3.	68
Figure 22.	Julia Ciccarone. 'Youwarkee: Flying Woman' [oil on canvas] (1995). Reproduced with permission of the artist. © Julia Ciccarone 1995. National Library of Australia. Call no. N 759.994 C568.	69
Figure 23.	Julia Ciccarone. 'Half-Caste' [oil on canvas] (1995). Reproduced with permission of the artist. © Julia Ciccarone 1995. National Library of Australia. Call no. N 759.994 C568.	70
Figure 24.	Julia Ciccarone. 'Peter Kills Harlokin' [oil on canvas] (1995). Reproduced with permission of the artist. © Julia Ciccarone 1995. National Library of Australia. Call no. N 759.994 C568.	71
Figure 25.	Julia Ciccarone. 'Hero' [oil on canvas] (1995). Reproduced with permission of the artist. © Julia Ciccarone 1995. National Library of Australia. Call no. N 759.994 C568.	72
Figure 26.	Robert de Vaugondy. 'De l'Australasie' [map]. From Charles de Brosses, *Histoire des navigations aux Terres Australes*	

	(Paris: Chez Durand 1756). Vol. 2, map IV. National Library of Australia. Call no. MAP T 1002.	80
Figure 27.	Giovanni Maria Cassini. 'La Nuova Zelanda' [map]. From Giovanni Maria Cassini, *Nuovo atlante geografico universale delineato sulle ultime osservazioni* (Rome: Presso la Calcogr. Cameral 1798). Vol. 3, plate 35. National Library of Australia. Call no. MAP T 289.	93
Figure 28.	Giovanni Maria Cassini. 'La Nuova Olanda' [map]. From Giovanni Maria Cassini, *Nuovo atlante geografico universale delineato sulle ultime osservazioni* (Rome: Presso la Calcogr. Cameral 1798). Vol. 3, plate 36. National Library of Australia. Call no. MAP T 288.	94
Figure 29.	Compilation of eight illustrations [engravings]. From [Anon.], *Bysh's Edition of The Voyages and Adventures of La Perouse, to Which is Added The Life of Hatem Tai, or, The Generosity of an Arabian Prince* (London: Printed for J. Bysh 1829). Frontispiece and opposite pages 12, 17 and 20 (two illustrations per page). National Library of Australia. Call no. FERG/7208.	99
Figure 30.	Franz Swoboda and Martin Hartl. 'Generalcharte von Australien' [map] (Vienna: J. Riedl 1815). National Library of Australia. Call no. MAP RM 586.	113
Figure 31.	'Sketches of the Coasts of Australia and of the Supposed Entrance of the Great River' [map]. From Thomas J. Maslen, *The Friend of Australia, or, A Plan for Exploring the Interior and for Carrying on a Survey of the Whole Continent of Australia, by a Retired Officer of the Honourable East India Company's Service* (London: Hurst & Chance 1830). Folded map. National Library of Australia. Call no. NK4422.	120

ACKNOWLEDGEMENTS

Many people have generously helped me in researching and writing this book, through sharing their ideas, supporting applications for research funding, commenting on drafts, and offering other kinds of valuable advice. I am particularly grateful to Gareth Griffiths and Judy Johnston at the University of Western Australia. I also thank Geoffrey Bolton, Ian Donaldson, Ihab Hassan, Iain McCalman, Richard Nile and Paul Turnbull. Greg Dening read early drafts of the book and inspired me with his approach to writing history. At Anthem Press, Tej Sood, Janka Romero and series editor Charles Forsdick oversaw the publication process professionally from start to finish. Philippa Tucker, whose own research interests include early modern conceptions of the antipodes, copy-edited the manuscript, and I am grateful for her many helpful suggestions.

My interest in visions of the antipodes, travel literature and the early novel began in the 1990s when I was a PhD candidate in the Department of English at the University of Western Australia. Research fellowships at Murdoch University (2004–7) and Curtin University (2007–9), Western Australia, enabled me to do further research and complete the writing of the book. I gratefully acknowledge the long-term support of these institutions.

Until relatively recently much of the primary print material of the seventeenth and eighteenth centuries had not been digitized or was not readily accessible online. The most memorable aspect of the research process was travelling to libraries in Australia, New Zealand, England, France, Portugal and North America, to examine and handle documents that in some cases had received little attention for hundreds of years. Each rare book I discovered added to a growing picture, showing new patterns, disrupting others – ultimately shaping the ideas and arguments presented here. These visits were made possible with the financial assistance of university grants and through short-term scholarships and fellowships, all of which I acknowledge with gratitude. In 1996 I received the University of Western Australia Graduates Association Postgraduate Research Travel Award. Between 1996 and 1998 I was a Visiting Scholar at the Australian National University (ANU) on three occasions – at the Research School of Pacific and Asian Studies, the Humanities Research Centre and the Centre for Cross-Cultural Research. In 1998 I participated in the Writing Voyages and Encounters seminar at ANU convened by Greg Dening, Bronwyn Douglas, Jonathan Lamb, Vanessa Smith, Nicholas Thomas and Paul Turnbull – an intensive month-long residential program that took my thinking in new directions. In 2004 I was Helen and John S. Best Research Fellow at the American Geographical Society Library (University of Wisconsin–Milwaukee). The visit was also supported by an Australian Academy of the Humanities Fieldwork Fellowship. In 2006 I was a Visiting Research Fellow at the Humanities Research Centre at ANU and was an Adjunct Research Fellow of the newly formed Research School of Humanities from 2007–9, which led to further visits to Canberra for conferences and for research. In 2007 I was an inaugural Research Fellow at the Centre for Historical Research at the National Museum of Australia and a residential fellow at Manning Clark House, Canberra. I finished work on the manuscript in 2009 while a visiting fellow at two research centres – the Center for Cultural Analysis at Rutgers University, USA, and HUMlab, the digital humanities centre at Umeå University, Sweden. I learned a great deal from the exceptional people I had the privilege to meet during these visits.

Most importantly, I thank my parents, Kateryna, Neville and Richard, my wife Sarah and children Mila and Felton, who have contributed to and shared in the writing of this book.

I have published a number of journal articles and book chapters in which the arguments presented here were first developed in different forms. These include: 'Fictions of Encounter: Eighteenth Century Imaginary Voyages to the Antipodes', *The Eighteenth Century: Theory and Interpretation* 49, no. 3 (2008): 197–210; 'Antipodean Myths Transformed: The Evolution of Australian Identity', *History Compass* 5, no. 6 (2007): 1862–78; 'Capturing the Antipodes', in *Comedy, Fantasy and Colonialism*, ed. Graeme Harper (London: Continuum 2002), 205–18; 'Imaginary Conquests', *Journal of Australian Studies* 23, no. 61 (1999): 136–42; and 'Fantasies of the Antipodes', in *Imagining Australian Space: Cultural Studies and Spatial Inquiry*, ed. Ruth Barcan and Ian Buchanan (Nedlands: University of Western Australia Press 1999), 37–46.

EDITORIAL NOTE

The term 'antipodes' is used throughout this book, along with the related concept of the 'great south land'. While other terms, such as '*Terra Australis*' and 'South Seas', were popular in the eighteenth century, 'antipodes' emphasized qualities of oppositeness and otherness associated with the southern hemisphere since ancient times. It also highlighted the connection between metropolitan centre and colonial periphery and lent itself to utopian literary treatment.

Voyages of exploration led to discoveries of various kinds, and the term 'discovery' itself can be used in several ways. In 1815, the *Monthly Review* claimed that a 'first discoverer' is 'the European who finds a land which before was unknown to Europeans'.[1] Alternatively, discovery can suggest the transmission of new knowledge, 'bringing some hitherto unknown place to the notice of others, particularly geographers and cartographers'.[2] It can also mean to 'take notice for the first time of a piece of the surface of the earth for one civilization', that is, it can start before physical contact.[3] Discovery can go on after the initial events, in a dialogic relation with past knowledge, 'fitting new knowledge together with the old in evaluating what was seen'.[4] In colonial contexts, discovery and exploration made 'the "other" a foil against which to see the "objectivity", "rationality" and "universality" of western scientific representations'.[5] It also involved a denial of Indigenous knowledge of the lands found.[6] The history of geographical discovery is often thought of as a process that exposed reality, dispelled uncertainty and did away with the old myths that preceded firm knowledge. However, discovery here is understood in the broadest possible way, as a much larger and more complex activity than simple revelation or initial observation and reporting of new worlds.

In quotations from primary sources, some typographical errors have been corrected and spelling has been altered from the original only insofar as to change the long 's' to its modern form and to substitute the lettering of 'i' with 'y' and 'u' with 'v' (and vice versa). The many changes to place names that have occurred over the past four centuries have also been standardized. According to explorer Matthew Flinders, the term 'New Holland' began to displace the earlier term '*Terra Australis*' and variations of the 'great south land' some time after Abel Tasman's second voyage in 1644.[7] Before the name of Australia gained acceptance early in the nineteenth century, the landmass had been labelled on maps variously as *Terra Incognita, Terre Australe* or *Terra Australis*, and New Holland, *Nouvelle Hollande* or *Hollandia Nova*.[8] Here Australia is generally used instead of New Holland when the context is geographical rather than historical. References to place names in the Pacific follow the same rule.

The terms 'Europe' and 'Europeans' are applied from the sixteenth century onwards, even though there was only a sketchy conception of a unified Europe at that time. These terms are used in a very general manner, without always making distinctions between divergent approaches to colonialism, nor between the literary and scientific traditions of individual nations. This apparent simplification is accurate in the sense that a collective geographical conception of Europe as 'the north' was fundamental to thinking about the antipodean region as 'the south'. This was also a conflation routinely made in the stories of imaginary voyages that are the focus of this book, in which the travellers are often referred to simply as 'the Europeans'.

INTRODUCTION

> The Meridian of the Antipodes is likewise passed; every league, thanks to our good fortune, which we now travel onwards, is one league nearer to England. These Antipodes call to mind old recollections of childish doubt & wonder. Even but the other day, I looked forward to this airy barrier as a definite point in our voyage homewards; now I find it & all such resting places for the imagination are like shadows which a man moving onwards cannot catch.
> – Charles Darwin, diary entry, 19 December 1835, on the *Beagle*[1]

Born out of an ancient geographical theory of balance, the term 'antipodes' was first used to refer to the vast uncharted underworld of the southern hemisphere from a northern perspective. The principle behind this belief, as described in the *Quarterly Review* in the nineteenth century, was 'that all the land, which had till then been discovered in the southern hemisphere, was insufficient to form a counterpoise to the weight of land in the northern half of the globe'.[2] The idea of the antipodes as a counterbalance, though now remembered only as a peculiar, discredited theory, has been surprisingly influential as an imaginative concept. An antipodean expectancy filled minds, maps, novels and utopian plans, laying the foundation for perceptions of Oceania and Australasia that continue to impact on how this part of the world is seen from a distance as well as from within. The region of the antipodes has been occupied by European settlers and their descendants for a relatively short time. And yet, this brief period is set against a backdrop of one of the longest recorded histories of imagining prior to geographical discovery. It is little wonder, then, that the antipodes provided the setting for a curious battle to be played out – between discovery and invention, fact and fiction, historical experience and fantasy, science and faith – within the literary genre of the 'imaginary voyage' that is the focus of this book. For more than two centuries this once popular form of travel fiction, now all but forgotten, made use of the shifting boundaries between these sets of binaries. In doing so, it contributed to the course of literary history and also to the history of colonialism.

xviii   VIRTUAL VOYAGES

A giant southern continent featured in the classical imagination as early as the fifth century BC, with the landmass once thought to fill much of the southern half of the globe.[3] In his commentary on Cicero's *Republic*, the *Dream of Scipio* (c. fifth century AD), Ambrosius Macrobius included a map showing Europe, Africa and Asia in the northern hemisphere separated from a southern continent by a great ocean. A version of this map from a sixteenth-century edition of the *Dream of Scipio* (c. 1560) is reproduced here (Figure 1). Similar schematic maps were produced over this 1,000-year period, based on theories informed by classical geography. On many of these maps the equatorial region was portrayed as a burning torrid zone, following the beliefs of Pythagoras.[4] As the discoveries of voyagers gradually filled in the blanks on world maps and edged into the

Figure 1. Map showing projected southern continent, from Ambrosius Macrobius, *Dream of Scipio* (c. 1560).

antipodean space, the geographical parameters of the antipodes subtly shifted. The boundaries were never fixed, clearly defined or neatly drawn. They were mobile because early voyagers' mapping was partial and contradictory but also because the idea of the antipodes began as a means of speculating about a geography that could not yet be described.[5] As parts of this southern world were named, mapped and integrated into a northern worldview, the antipodes of the imagination diminished in area by stages until, during the course of the seventeenth century, it came to rest over present-day Australia, New Zealand and the South Pacific. The 'great south land' theory was not finally abandoned until the second voyage of James Cook in 1772–5.[6] In place of the anticipated solid landmass, paradoxically, explorers found the Pacific Ocean – dotted with its more than 25,000 islands – the planet's largest single geographical entity, making up approximately one third of the earth's surface and covering an area greater than all the earth's landmasses put together. This was one of the last remaining parts of the globe for European explorers to chart, and the final missing segment in a historical jigsaw puzzle that had taken centuries to piece together.[7]

At no time, however, has the antipodes been solely a spatial reference. We know from the earliest writings and illustrations that the mythological world of the antipodes took myriad forms, with the region portrayed in striking and bizarre ways that revealed fascination and curiosity as well as frustration at a lack of knowledge. Antipodes literally means both 'opposite-footed' and 'opposite-footers', referring to the place and to the people or creatures who might live there – making this 'an archetypal Other', arguably 'the first in Western literature'.[8] Mythic concepts can also be thought of as gestures of control. The idea of the antipodes proposed symbolic power over a distant and unknown space, and in this context visions of the antipodes can be thought of as an important early component in the formation of European imperial discourse.[9] Even when the classical concept of the antipodes started to be accompanied by the geographically more specific *Terra Australis*, the antipodes retained a powerful symbolism.[10] In the eighteenth century the antipodes continued to refer not so much to a geographical place as to a symbolic space that embodied the enigma of all that was beyond reach. The way the region was imagined and represented was influenced by the notion that travelling away from Europe was akin to travelling back in time: the more remote the place, the more backward the culture.[11] Indigenous peoples of the Atlantic and the Pacific were often viewed as 'embryonic civilizations' and analogies were made with ancient Mediterranean societies.[12] Illustrations in a neo-classical style, accompanying travel accounts and embellishing maps, were common. While Indigenous peoples could be viewed negatively, as uncivilized, they could also be viewed positively, as uncontaminated. In this way, the antipodes provided fertile ground for utopian writing and for literary satire.

A southern continent remained largely a figment of European imagination until Dutch discoveries in the early seventeenth century, at which point fantasy was brought face-to-face with an emerging reality. It was within this confused arena that the first contemporary examples appeared of imaginary voyages set in the antipodes. Over the next two centuries writers used the literary form to dramatize the confrontation between myth and reality being played out by European explorers. It provided an ideal vehicle for articulating and reflecting upon Europe's imagined sense of itself in relation to the new worlds it was discovering. Colonial ambition and cross-cultural contact were recurring themes. Using a utopian, satirical mode, these writers also made veiled attacks on political figures and practices.

The imaginary voyage is a literary form with a very long history. Writers have always set stories where geographical frontiers have provided creative openings, and fictional journeys are found in the earliest recorded myths and stories of the world's ancient cultures. Imaginary voyages set in the antipodes, however, took a particular form. Published mainly in Britain and France from the beginning of the seventeenth century to the early nineteenth century, their production came to a peak in the era of major discoveries, colonization and settlement in the second half of the eighteenth century – at a time when one might have expected interest to wane in the face of competition from first-hand documentary accounts of the region. Colonial and utopian themes are interrelated in complex ways in many of these texts. Visions of utopia were overlaid on increasingly real settings in the antipodes. These were no longer 'no-places', as the term would indicate. Imaginary voyage writing evolved from being a vehicle for traditional utopian expression to a well-developed mode of realist fiction utilizing an empirically known setting.[13] The two most well-known works in the imaginary voyage tradition are Daniel Defoe's *Robinson Crusoe* (1719)[14] and Jonathan Swift's *Gulliver's Travels* (1726).[15] The places that Gulliver purportedly visits are in the Pacific region and off the coast of the Australian continent. *Robinson Crusoe* is not set in the antipodes, but it followed the form of seventeenth-century examples that were.[16] While imaginary voyages were set in other locations, there are a number of reasons that can be suggested for why the antipodes proved so popular. First, the antipodes had come to stand for the lure of the unknown. Second, long-held associations of a terrestrial paradise in the southern region continued to offer a framework for imagining ideal societies in the antipodes. And third, even as exploration brought new knowledge, the antipodean world remained tantalizingly *partly* mapped and *partly* known, its ever-changing map full of gaps and holes and extrapolations. The antipodes offered one of the last places on earth where one could dream of a different, better world that had not yet been entirely ruled out as a possibility.

Literary critics since the nineteenth century have argued for and against recognizing the imaginary voyage as a distinct genre. Many agree, however, that the imaginary voyages of the seventeenth and eighteenth centuries were unique in the way they closely – sometimes confusingly – simulated the narrative conventions of genuine voyage accounts. Unless otherwise stated, when I use the term 'imaginary voyage' in this book I am referring to works produced from the seventeenth to the early nineteenth century. In that era it is not surprising that stories of adventures to distant locations were sometimes accepted as authentic documents chronicling real discoveries. Before modern science, and with so many gaps remaining in the world picture, boundaries between fact and fiction were fluid.

This book sketches a history of imaginary voyage writing in the context of changing European literary traditions and tastes and increasing travel and discovery in the antipodes, over two centuries leading to the modern colonial era. It gives detailed readings of six selected imaginary voyages, spanning the years 1605–1837. Three of these have attracted some critical comment, but the remaining three are almost totally unknown. The examples are chosen to illustrate popular themes that run through the literature of imaginary voyages in the era of discovery. Presented as true accounts, these examples tell a remarkably similar story, despite the influence of changing historical, literary and national contexts over a period of more than 200 years. A male traveller, alone or leading a group, leaves Europe to discover a new part of the distant region of the antipodes, explores it, braves dangers, survives attacks, lives there for an extended period of time and ultimately influences the cultures encountered in profound ways. Indigenous populations are portrayed as it might have been convenient to find them in real life: passive, intrigued by the visitors, and pleased to follow their example. That imaginary voyage writing continued to thrive alongside documentary accounts of actual voyages to the antipodes is a sign of the enduring appeal of this literary formula.

Such formulaic depictions of a distant cultural other can be understood as social constructions staged in an elaborate drama of Europe casting itself in a superior role in relation to the unknown, as the 'right side up' (balanced, knowledgeable and enlightened) rather than as 'upside-down' (distorted, mute and uncivilized).[17] As in the case of the many better-known examples of European literature produced in the period of British and French imperial dominance, imaginary voyages played a role in helping to foster a social acceptance of colonial expansion by modelling cross-cultural contact on European terms as natural, beneficial and welcomed by the Indigenous peoples of the antipodes.[18] While the mixing of fact and fiction undoubtedly produced confused understandings for readers, it was the same hybridity that gave these literary works a special kind of power that has not been sufficiently recognized.

That was the power to mask the transition between historical reality and wishful vision and thus to capture people's political acquiescence in the very process of capturing their imagination. This is not to say that imaginary voyages *set out* to do this. It is more likely that they were simply capitalizing on the interest aroused by real voyages of discovery. However, there is no doubt that these texts would have influenced people's attitudes to their expanding empires in the process of expanding their imaginative horizons.

A parallel can be drawn between imaginary voyage writing and speculative cartography in that both freely mixed fact and fiction – and ultimately sometimes deceived their audiences by creating convincing truth effects. Indeed, imaginary voyages are often supported by captivating fictional maps and illustrations. Both modes cast European entry into the elusive spaces of the southern world as a smooth narrative journey, incorporating, transforming and filling in the unknown, with a naturalness that mirrored and promoted the extension of empire.

Colonial themes and imagery are prevalent in many imaginary voyages. Even so, the same texts can also be thought of as modes of critique, satirically exposing and questioning the assumptions and processes of colonialism. Some works, such as *Gulliver's Travels*, include explicit critiques of colonialism.[19] However, they are the exception rather than the rule in the wider body of imaginary voyage literature. In the majority of examples discussed in the following chapters there are only occasional, if sometimes striking, moments that invite counter-colonialist readings – such as those where the hero's wisdom, kindness and valour are exaggerated beyond plausibility. In these cases the figure of the European traveller in a strange, faraway world is parodied, rather than colonialism itself. At the very least this produces 'curious undertones which sometimes subvert their more overt meanings'.[20] One of the functions of parody in satirical literature is to hold open competing views in the mind of the reader, and the results can be unpredictable. As Simon Ryan puts it, parody 'tends to reproduce, even honour, that which it criticises'.[21] In the case of imaginary voyages, this ambivalence has been amplified across the centuries. Another book could be devoted to counter-colonialist interpretations of imaginary voyages. While this is not the focus here, extracts from contemporary periodicals and other sources are included selectively to give a sense of the many facets of debates on colonialism,[22] and to suggest how it might have felt for readers at the metropolitan centre of empire in the first truly global era of voyaging and discovery.[23]

The main texts discussed are exclusively British and French, with the French examples in English translation. Although imaginary voyages were written in other languages, published in other countries, and translated between languages, no other nations produced them in the numbers that Britain and

France did. Despite the rivalry between these countries, and also as a result of that rivalry, works were translated quickly between the two languages. Numerical production in Britain and France was similar, and it is not surprising that they had the strongest traditions of imaginary voyage writing.[24] They were recognized as the dominant European colonial powers of the eighteenth century. The topic of cross-cultural encounters in the distant antipodes had relevance and appeal to writers and readers.[25] With both nations beginning to produce stories fictionalizing these encounters at the very time they were setting their sights on settling that region, real and imaginary voyages became the subject of intense interest.

The imaginary voyage genre deserves attention not only for literary–historical reasons, but also because it offers such a rich store of wonderful stories. With interest in the age of antipodean exploration running high following the 400th anniversary in 2006 of the voyages of Willem Jansz, and of Pedro Fernández de Quirós and Luis Váez de Torres,[26] with numerous replicas of original sailing vessels retracing their courses through the antipodes,[27] and with a greater public awareness than ever of the complexity of colonial history and its legacy, the time is right to revisit the phenomenon of the imaginary voyage. In the process of my research, as I turned the pages of rare books and pamphlets in special collections in libraries in Australia and New Zealand, Europe and North America, I was repeatedly struck by their imaginative exuberance. Playing at the extreme limits of reader tolerance and credulity, the writers took great risks. It is as though they were aware that this point in history provided a final, fleeting and rapidly diminishing opportunity for imaginative revelry in the antipodes – the very last chance for the antipodes to be exploited for their magic and mystery before being domesticated, absorbed and integrated into the scientific and political systems of modern Europe.

Virtual Voyages

Chapter 1
REAL AND IMAGINARY VOYAGES

The fact that there are rarely more than a handful of texts catalogued under the Library of Congress subject heading 'Voyages, Imaginary' in major libraries around the world is not, as it may seem, evidence that relatively few imaginary voyages or works relating to imaginary voyages now exist to be catalogued, although many texts are now rare. Rather, it indicates an anomaly in classification and a lack of interest in the literary form as a recognizable genre. Even when the imaginary voyage has been thought of as a distinct genre, literary critics and historians have tended to marginalize or overlook it on the grounds that these texts had limited truth value when compared with genuine travel accounts. On this basis, imaginary voyages have been seen as fanciful accompaniments to documentary accounts of travel, and as displaced by them. Apart from interest in several well-known works, a small number of critical studies and a general acknowledgement in library classification schemes, the literary form has been largely forgotten, along with hundreds of lesser-known examples. Ironically, the prominence of the iconic eighteenth-century imaginary voyages, *Robinson Crusoe* and *Gulliver's Travels*, has drawn attention away from other works.

There is a further reason, I would suggest, for the lack of critical attention. In terms of genre, imaginary voyages – especially those in the setting of the antipodes – trod a delicate path: being neither history nor romance but a strange marriage of the two, they reflected and exploited a particular moment in the history of maritime exploration when the edges of the known world were being extended and European readers were willing to suspend disbelief and participate vicariously in the process of discovery.[1] When that moment had passed, imaginary voyages lost the connection with the real-world setting that had served them so well, but had not gained a sufficiently strong identity purely as fiction to claim lasting critical recognition.

Antipodean imaginary voyages belong to a broader body of seventeenth- and eighteenth-century imaginary voyage literature that was set in many different locations. In turn, these works can be seen as a link in the chain of a much longer tradition, stretching back to very early forms of travellers' tales, literary romance and utopian projection and forward to nineteenth-century science fiction and fantasy.² All these diverse literary forms make use of the motif of travel and adventure, which has proved to be one of the most appealing, versatile and re-workable in Western literature. The imaginary voyage has been known variously as the '*voyage imaginaire*', 'extraordinary voyage', '*voyage extraordinaire*', 'fabulous voyage', 'fantastic voyage', 'fictitious voyage', 'marvellous voyage' and 'wonderful voyage'. These terms have tended to be used to refer to the literary texts themselves rather than to the voyage as a narrative element. The same rule applied in the seventeenth and eighteenth centuries for the words 'voyages' and 'travels', which typically referred to the written account of a voyage rather than to the actual voyage. The earliest British and French imaginary voyages set in the antipodes appeared from the beginning of the seventeenth century. They include Joseph Hall's *Mundus alter et idem* (published in Latin in 1605 and adapted into English in 1609)³ and Gabriel de Foigny's *La Terre Australe connue* (published in French in 1676 and translated to English in 1693).⁴ These works, which are both discussed in Chapter Two, were written more than 70 years apart and they are stylistically very different. Hall's narrative is highly satirical whereas Foigny's aims to resemble a true account. In this sense they represent two alternative modes that, in later imaginary voyages, tend to be subtly combined. Despite their differences, these seventeenth-century examples helped to establish a range of common themes and a standard narrative structure. However, the greatest numbers of imaginary voyages were published in the second half of the eighteenth century. Phillip Gove lists 130 examples from this period, mainly British and French, in his definitive bibliographical study, *The Imaginary Voyage in Prose Fiction* (1941).⁵ Many of these were set in imagined worlds in the region of the antipodes.

Some critics have claimed that these outright fictions were almost as popular, in their time, as genuine voyage accounts.⁶ But to readers today they seem curious stories, removed in time, place and worldview. What exactly were these 'imaginary voyages'? Their critical reception since the late eighteenth century, discussed in this chapter, gives some clues. These writings were often overtly political. Even the examples that hid their political orientation can be understood as a form of indirect social commentary. Many titles were published anonymously or pseudonymously. Some texts had a mercurial existence, raided and reworked by later editors and compilers. Editorial practices, which were largely driven by financial concerns, left their mark on all kinds of accounts of voyages, real and imaginary. A playful French cartoon, 'Geai, pare des plumes du Paon' (c. 1802) parodies the speed of production and dubious quality of voyage accounts published at the turn of the nineteenth century, a time when travel literature in its many forms had reached a new peak of popularity (Figure 2). The sketch, which alludes to La Fontaine's well-known fable about plagiarism, has Geai cutting up John Pinkerton's *Geography* and riding a donkey-like Pegasus that excretes money.

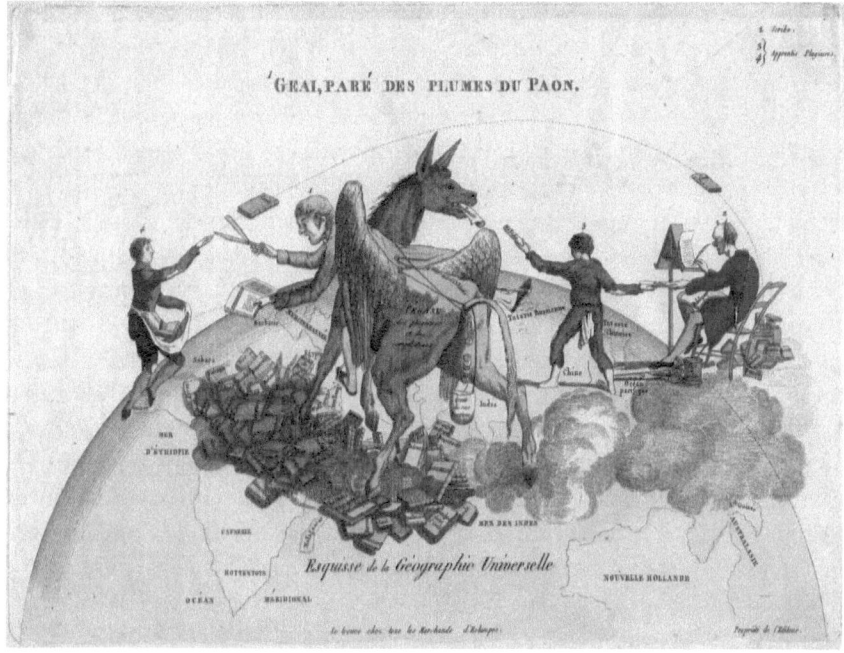

Figure 2. 'Geai, pare des plumes du Paon' (c. 1802).

Strewn in a pile below are reports of voyages undertaken by famous explorers such as Jean-François de Galaup de La Pérouse and Bruny d'Entrecasteaux, and James Cook's voyage account is being thrown to a scribe.[7] The humorous scene is set on top of a globe that clearly shows Australia, labelled as *Nouvelle Hollande*.

Imaginary voyages are fascinating imaginative supplements to historical narratives and there is a danger in missing their significance by limiting the critical focus to aspects such as style, aesthetic qualities, authorial intention or reader response. Looking back over the huge corpus of imaginary voyages from a postcolonial perspective we can see larger themes and commonalities that connect their writing to the events and preoccupations of the period in which they were produced. The parallel process they represent, of imaginative projection, needs to be read against and with the records of real voyages in early modern European culture. The genre casts light on the development of literary realism and especially on the interplay of fact and fiction that continues to challenge historians, anthropologists and literary critics to this day. It also opens up questions of the nature of the relationship between fiction and history, and myth and reality. In the colonial context, it raises the issue of the extent to which observation was influenced by received traditions and fantasy.

The blurring of fact and fiction was not unique to imaginary voyages. It was mirrored in all kinds of contemporary travel literature. Writers of fiction would refer to explorers and explorers would refer to myths perpetuated by the fiction of exploration. In order to validate their fictions, writers would weave facts into their fantasies and, confusingly, in order to explain what they observed, explorers routinely forced reality back into the domain of the mythical by appealing to or framing their own responses in terms of long-held, familiar myths. In the most basic sense, this meant that explorers would look for some things and not others because they were attuned to seeing in particular ways.[8] Situational factors played their part in influencing initial responses to new lands. These included the effects of debilitating physical conditions such as scurvy, the notorious sailors' disease caused by vitamin deficiency. Scurvy was known to result in heightened sensual awareness and make contrasts seem more extreme (such as the difference between pain and pleasure). The disease would leave its victims in unpredictably altered states, often delirious and highly sensitive to visual stimulation, a state of 'scurvied rapture' that also amplified attraction or repulsion.[9] When sailors finally arrived, they were often ill, sometimes terminally. The significance of fertile land capable of replenishing supplies and facilitating healthy recovery understandably took on mythical proportions. In turn, this meant that readers of travel accounts were not in a position to distinguish reliable information from unbridled enthusiasm.

There were also other, more conscious, distortions. Financial imperatives often drove writers to make exaggerated claims and there were political reasons to favour particular images of newly discovered lands. Influential official accounts were usually crafted at least in part to justify subsequent voyages, routinely hiding, for example, the extent and details of conflict with Indigenous peoples. Events would be framed to prove that a voyage had been successful on terms set out by its financiers. There was also the related obligation to hide certain features in order not to advertise the best aspects of the southern world to rival nations. It could be said that travel accounts were not only referring to what was actually *there* in the antipodes but to what was required of an imperialist discourse in order to construct the land, the native, the encounter, in a way that would justify and give meaning to European arrival and actions. Readers, too, would need to interpret texts within the limits of received notions of remote places and cultures.[10] Complicating further the many influences on first-hand perception was the process of writing itself. Explorers' accounts usually began as diaries kept during voyages, but the final published product was almost always written up much later, sometimes by a professional writer (perhaps even a romance writer as in the famous case of Marco Polo) who, typically, did not have the opportunity themselves to travel to get a taste for the world about which they were writing and would be even more likely to be influenced by stylistic and financial considerations to slant or embellish.[11] Manuscripts would later be scrutinized and modified by editors who were well aware of the wide market to be netted by sensational descriptions of faraway places.[12]

It is interesting to note that of the dozen or so German terms that were used to describe imaginary voyage literature, 'only three unmistakably denote fiction', according to Gove.[13] Confusing overlaps between fact and fiction were also produced when voyage account anthologies sometimes unwittingly included fictional accounts; genuine travel accounts, likewise, were mistakenly included in collections of fictional travel literature.[14] In some cases a romanticized discourse of discovery produced inconsistencies;[15] equally, these could simply be hoaxes.[16]

Colonial Vision

The earliest critics to give recognition to the genre of the imaginary voyage from the late eighteenth century tried, almost fanatically, to separate out fact from fiction as they saw it.[17] They also categorized examples in relation to canonical works and absorbed them into more mainstream literary forms such as the utopian tract or robinsonade. Most were not concerned exclusively with imaginary voyages set in the antipodes. As they were primarily interested in literary categorization, the field they discussed was broad. Twentieth-century critics have considered imaginary voyages in relation to the history of modern European prose satire, as part of a longer tradition of utopian portrayal, and for their archetypal images of male dominance that are more typical of nineteenth-century adventure writing. The same literary works have also been approached simply as bibliographical curiosities. Indeed, when handling original editions in library reading rooms, I was intrigued to find that they were so different from one another. Some are illustrated, decorated pamphlets, others are plain and not so aesthetically pleasing, some are large, some small, and like many old documents, many are now delicate or rare.

My key interest in imaginary voyages is in the surprisingly consistent depictions of colonialism and cross-cultural contact that feature in examples set in the antipodes. Similar colonial themes are also found in imaginary voyages set in other locations from the seventeenth century onwards. While there were different treatments, variations and exceptions to the rule, the general consistency is remarkable given that these imaginary voyages were written over a period of more than two centuries and in different language traditions.

The typical format can be described in the following way. A European traveller, alone or leading a group, leaves Europe by ship. He reaches the margins of the known world and then, in a severe storm, by shipwreck, through pirate attack or by some other dramatic natural event, is transported to an imagined world. Writers utilized the imaginative hooks provided by the often tragic occurrences of actual sea voyages as a pivotal organizing element, one that masks a transition from the accepted realities of the known world to the fictionalized spaces of the antipodes. John Dunlop – one of the earliest critics to recognize the genre in his *The History of Fiction* (1814) – described writers of imaginary voyages as 'seizing the advantages presented by shipwrecks and pirates',[18] as though the writers themselves were pirates plundering the cargo of genuine voyage accounts. The reader travels with the protagonist from the familiar world into the elusive and exotic antipodes, traversing a distance that becomes symbolic of difference and displacement to arrive at a space that threatens to overwhelm with its strangeness. As Dunlop put it, the author of imaginary voyages 'throws his characters on some inhospitable shore' where 'the fancied distance entitles him to people it with all sorts of prodigies and monsters'.[19] Typically, the chosen idiom remains the same, and even if the imagined world is highly unbelievable (with the appearance of improbable creatures, for example) the traveller describes them as though they were real. In many examples of imaginary voyages, a 'halfway house', which 'forms a relay or springboard', is also visited on the way to or from the region of the antipodes.[20] As a narrative device, this helps to facilitate the transition from one world to another.

The common destination of the fictional journey is a southern world that is already populated, providing a setting for cross-cultural contact and for social negotiations. Upon entering, the traveller is received in a variety of ways. Sometimes he needs to prove that he is not an enemy before being accepted. Often he acts as though he were what we would now call an anthropologist, chronicling the history and distinctive cultural traditions of the societies encountered, for the benefit of European knowledge. A common trait is that the traveller discusses the differences between the new world and his home world with a learned leader or council open to philosophical debate on the relative merits of different ways of living. Satire and utopian themes are developed through such discussions and observations. The traveller usually arrives powerless in the new world but slowly begins to exert an influence. If the antipodean inhabitants are persuaded by the traveller's arguments in support of the value of European culture, he is often given the role of negotiator or instigator of change. This varies greatly between individual examples, ranging from the traveller simply offering advice, to introducing European language, religion, political and legal systems, and formal education. In some cases he is elevated to the position of an influential leader and he effectively takes control of the antipodean society. In extreme cases, this can involve the traveller recommending and overseeing the use of European weapons to settle disputes between rival communities and so disturbing an existing power balance. Sometimes the result is devout hero worship, with the visitor either revered for his actions or, if the narrative includes an instance of prior European contact, he may be seen as a founding father figure.

In contrast to the reality of colonial conquest – which often followed a pattern that 'began with embraces, continued in abuse, and ended in bloodshed'[21] – the fictional traveller is frequently cast as a peacekeeper. The imposition of European values and of colonial control in its various forms is often by invitation rather than by force. It is helpful to compare Mary Louise Pratt's concept of the 'seeing-man', protagonist of the imperial encounter, with the heroic character of the typical imaginary voyage. Emphasizing the patriarchal aspect along with the imperial, the seeing-man facilitates what Pratt calls 'anti-conquest' – defined as 'the strategies of representation whereby European bourgeois subjects seek to secure their innocence in the same moment as they assert European hegemony'.[22] Pratt refers to the figure of the naturalist to demonstrate how authority can be projected despite apparent innocence and even vulnerability.[23]

Finally the traveller returns to Europe with the intention of telling his tale or publishing an account. Often he puts a manuscript in the able hands of a friend or stranger to have published at a later date. It is also common for the traveller to die during the voyage home, on arrival or soon afterwards, but a text is delivered in some form or another. When read as utopian fiction, this signals the closure of the 'utopian circle', allowing social comparisons to gain full significance.[24]

To help illustrate the typical narrative progression in the imaginary voyages discussed in the following chapters, I take the same approach to each text by using the subheadings 'I' (relating to strategies for verisimilitude), 'II' (describing the traveller's entry to the antipodean world and impressions of place and people), and 'III' (focussing on cross-cultural encounters and colonial themes). The recurrent colonial themes in imaginary voyages may seem simplistic and facile – there is no avoiding the fact that these stories are projections of colonial superiority. And yet, as noted earlier, the apparent simplicity obscures a rhetorical complexity linked with satire and parody. The same works can alternatively be understood as a kind of critical commentary on colonialism.

Reality Effects

Whether individual examples of imaginary voyages were received by readers as genuine accounts is now very difficult to assess. While not all hide the stamp of their fictionality to such an extent that readers would have mistaken them as such, most use similar techniques to create an illusion of authenticity. Verisimilitude in imaginary voyage literature relied upon a 'hyper-empiricism', which provided the evidence necessary to make a narrative seem as though it were dealing with real places, events and experiences.[25] This was the 'secret of producing an interesting account by ingeniously multiplied and adjusted detail',[26] a strategy to 'minimize its sense of originality' by being 'rendered in the most "responsible" prose'.[27]

The starting point for readers is often an elaborate preface, which sets out, sometimes in laborious detail, the historical context in which the work is said to have been written. This can include meticulous biographical details, including of the traveller's extended family, as well as navigational information.[28] A supposed editor may offer explanations for how they obtained the manuscript. This is sometimes by accident, sometimes as a favour or as an act of goodwill towards a sick or dying traveller. It is common for the alleged author to have disappeared or not be able to bring himself to have the work published. All these elaborate devices are included to persuade the reader of the story's authenticity, in spite of the unusual circumstances of its publication.[29] In keeping with literary conventions of this period, long and detailed titles sustain the illusion of authenticity.[30]

The story then follows the format of a traveller's report, letter or diary, describing events and scenes at first hand. As in genuine voyages of discovery, the passage from familiar territory to the imagined world usually involves sea travel but it can also include an expedition over land. The traveller's fictional journey is a framework within which events can take place sequentially, unfolding as though they had happened in real time and space. The world discovered is often positioned with conventional bearings (which mark out an exact space but one that, in reality, is yet to be discovered) or by association with known geographical reference points that relate to European nations or their colonies. Fictional maps are used in many examples of imaginary voyages to enhance realism by visually linking the geography of the imagined world with that of the known world. Complex Indigenous languages are often encountered, and they are usually deciphered in the course of the story.[31] Historical connections are also introduced to create links between the imagined new world and the old world. The setting may be familiarized further by being associated with myths, with earlier reports of unexplained sightings of uncharted land, or with purported prior contact between Europeans and the people of the southern world. Puzzling evidence is often found of European influence from centuries past, a mystery that is ultimately solved. In the same way that geographical coordinates physically locate the imagined world, past contact gives it a temporal dimension that already includes Europeans, as though they had a rightful place in the antipodes. These related strategies have the effect of layering European modes of understanding over the lands discovered.

Maps, like imaginary voyages, could blur the line dividing empirical knowledge from speculation by adding in imaginative elements. They could also help to instil a mental attitude towards the possession of faraway places, by laying them out as provisionally discovered and provisionally claimed. The 'ability to circumscribe geography, by enclosing, defining, coding, orienting, structuring and controlling space',[32] made maps appear trustworthy, 'a seemingly indisputable representation of the world'.[33] The most striking and paradoxical evidence of the representative power of maps is in the way some routinely named the very parts of the world that, in reality, remained almost totally unknown. Declaring places to be unknown, however, was also a part of this process. In fact, as Suvendrini Perera has argued: 'To name its colonized periphery a blank is precisely the function of imperial discourse'.[34] The antipodean unknown – centring on the vast projected *Terra Australis* – was often marked as *Terra Australis Incognita*, that is, the 'unknown' southern land. European map-makers had marked the southern landmass as *Terra Incognita* from approximately the fourteenth century.[35]

Utopian Worlds

The depiction of the antipodean world as a place of opposites relied upon the projection of a new world, conceived of in relation to the old world of Europe. This made the setting of the antipodes uniquely suited to the utopian model, which postulated relational binary comparisons between one social model and another for the purposes of social critique. In one sense, all imaginative constructions of the antipodes can be thought of in utopian terms. The imagined region provided a position from which to view Europe objectively and so to compare the two worlds. The basic premise for envisaging utopian worlds is that societies can be improved by aspiring to better social models. Utopian fiction constructs its idealized visions of societies by drawing attention to negative social and political elements in familiar social orders. Writers typically achieve this by portraying places that are either miraculously free from vice or brought down by exaggerated forms of their vices. The vision of utopia is commonly a representation of an idealized metropolis or urban space. Whether in utopias (also known as 'positive utopias', where the imagined society represents a significant improvement upon the original society to which it is being compared), or in dystopias (also known as 'negative utopias', where a society in a worse social condition is put forward as a caricature of existing social problems), utopian writing provides a lens through which to view the contemporary world. Often, within one story, a travelling character visits a series of different societies, and so both narrative modes can be utilized.

Not surprisingly, the terms 'utopia' and 'imaginary voyage' have sometimes been used interchangeably.[36] Whether texts are called utopias, referring to the destination point of the story, or imaginary voyages, foregrounding the role of the voyage device, has been a matter for critical debate.[37] To envisage a utopian destination, it is almost always necessary to include a fictional journey. Even simply 'placing oneself "outside"...taking a "critical distance"' is, as Georges van den Abbeele argues, 'to invoke the metaphor of thought as travel'.[38] The voyage is the means by which a traveller is able to visit the utopia and return to tell the tale. While the archetypal utopia can be linked with Plato, utopian fiction has been recognized as popular in Europe in a variety of forms since the term was coined in the title of Thomas More's *Utopia*, first published in 1516. In More's story, Raphael Hythloday sails on Amerigo Vespucci's last voyage, eventually making his way to Taprobane. From More's time onwards, utopian thinking has been associated with rules of social control, including socialism and colonialism.[39] Indeed, *Utopia*, written in the Tudor period, can be read as possibly the first English attempt to formulate a theory of colonization relevant to new worlds such as the Americas and the antipodes. More 'appears to be the first Englishman to use the word *colonia* in a Roman (imperialistic) meaning'.[40] In his utopian colonial theory, the accusation that a land is 'idle and waste' is justification for colonizing it.[41] Incredibly, More's brother-in-law, John Rastell, actually attempted to begin a settlement in the Americas himself. More's imagined society may well have inspired Rastell to seek to create a real one.[42] Long before More's time, a prototypical utopian model had already been used to help imagine the southern continent. The first example of a utopia set in the southern hemisphere may have dated from the mid-fourth century BC, when the Greek author Theopompos of Chios described a land home to 'big and mighty beasts' and gigantic men who 'in the same climate exceed the stature of us twice', and live in 'many and divers cities' with 'laws and ordinances clean contrary to ours'.[43] This example suggests the strong hold that imaginative projection exerted, even as far back as two millennia before the antipodes were accessible to European explorers.[44]

The relationship between imaginary voyages and utopian fiction features in most critical discussions of the imaginary voyage genre. The majority of critics have read the idealized societies discovered in imaginary voyages in utopian terms as a return to the model of the Golden Age societies of ancient Greece and Rome. That is, they have understood them in terms of a return to lost values rather than as pre-texts for (or perhaps even critiques of) colonialism and cross-cultural contact. The traditional utopian reading directs attention away from the political contexts in which imaginary voyages were produced, making the texts seem as though they were removed in time as well as in place from contemporary colonial concerns. Some critics, however, see the eighteenth century as a pivotal time for the utopian form itself, when the discovery of the last places on earth effectively robbed writers of the space they needed to portray a remote utopian world or 'no-place'. The use of a realist rhetoric and increasingly real settings distinguishes imaginary voyages in this era from earlier, more traditional, examples of utopian fiction. David Fausett, citing three well-recognized writers of imaginary voyage literature – Henry Neville, Denis Vairasse and Gabriel de Foigny – argues that imaginary voyages of the seventeenth century 'departed from traditional utopian aims towards a documentary stance'.[45] He describes the convincing use of literary realism to render utopian societies as a kind of 'narrative doubling', with 'the insertion of an inner – usually utopian – story into an outer, authenticating (because purportedly authentic) one'.[46] This new orientation of an older literary form shows the influence of real voyages to the antipodes on the imaginations of writers in Europe. 'Writers of projective utopias in seventeenth-century England', Fausett argues, 'had used antipodean settings to invert their own referent-world, but the real discovery of Australasia rendered this device transparent and opened up new, more sophisticated uses of the theme'.[47]

It is instructive to observe that the very meaning of the word 'utopia' appears to have been going through a historical transformation that mirrored the general movement towards a more comprehensive European knowledge of the wider world, grounded in empirical facts rather than in mythical projections. A number of related definitions of the word 'utopia' are given in the *Oxford English Dictionary*. The first definition offered, 'an imaginary or hypothetical place or state of things considered to be perfect; a condition of ideal (especially social) perfection', which dates from the mid-sixteenth century (that is, around the time of More's archetypal *Utopia*), is qualified by the explanation 'now rare or obsolete'.[48] The emphasis had originally been on utopian societies as purely imaginary illustrations of theoretical social orders with no necessary physical connection to the real world. A later definition, 'an imaginary distant region or country', which dates from the early seventeenth century, omits any reference to social perfection and instead characterizes utopia simply in terms of a fictionalized distance from Europe.[49] While it is not possible to draw firm conclusions from these subtle shifts in meaning, it seems that the primary association of utopia with societal perfection in an abstract space, a 'no-place', was being augmented with an awareness of *distance* as a key to helping imagine social difference, and it was distance and difference that had driven visions of the antipodes since ancient times. In other words, the idea of utopia was drifting closer to the idea of the antipodes itself.[50]

Literary Criticism

There have been very few major studies of the imaginary voyage in English and only two that consider more than one European literary tradition. They include Geoffroy Atkinson's *The Extraordinary Voyage in French Literature before 1700* (1920)[51] and *The Extraordinary Voyage in French Literature 1700 to 1720* (1922),[52] Phillip Gove's *The Imaginary Voyage in Prose Fiction* (1941),[53] Paul Cornelius' *Languages in Seventeenth- and Early Eighteenth-Century Imaginary Voyages* (1965)[54] and David Fausett's *Writing the New World: Imaginary Voyages and Utopias of the Great Southern Land* (1993).[55] Shorter studies and unpublished works, in which imaginary voyages are discussed as a specific genre, include George Mackaness' *Some Fictitious Voyages to Australia* (1937),[56] John Dunmore's *Utopias and Imaginary Voyages to Australasia* (1988),[57] and Hi Kyung Moon's 'Fictitious Travellers in French and English Literature: A Study of Imaginary Voyages from Cyrano de Bergerac to Oliver Goldsmith 1657–1762' (1989).[58] Dunmore and Fausett are particularly well-versed in the French imaginary voyage tradition, each having translated examples into English from their original French versions. A useful reference source for earlier critical material is 'A Checklist of Secondary Studies on Imaginary Voyages', published in the *Bulletin of Bibliography* in 1974.[59] Other books that make reference to imaginary voyage literature include John Dunlop's *The History of Fiction* (1814),[60] Arthur Tieje's *The Theory of Characterization in Prose Fiction prior to 1740* (1916),[61] William Eddy's *Gulliver's Travels: A Critical Study* (1923),[62] Percy Adams' *Travelers and Travel Liars 1660–1800* (1962),[63] Werner Friederich's *Australia in Western Imaginative Prose Writings 1600–1900* (1967),[64] Ross Gibson's *The Diminishing Paradise* (1984),[65] David Fausett's *Images of the Antipodes in the Eighteenth Century* (1995),[66] Neil Rennie's *Far-Fetched Facts: The Literature of Travel and the Idea of the South Seas* (1995),[67] Jan Basset's edited collection *Great Southern Landings: An Anthology of Antipodean Travel* (1995),[68] John Dunmore's *Visions and Realities: France in the Pacific 1695–1995* (1997)[69] and Richard Phillips' *Mapping Men and Empire: A Geography of Adventure* (1997).[70] Imaginary voyages also have several pages devoted to them in a recent volume entitled *The World of the Book* (2007),[71] which draws upon the rare book collection of the State Library of Victoria, Australia.

One of the obvious difficulties of describing imaginary voyages in terms of a single genre is that many different sorts of literature across different times, languages and traditions have made use of the basic device of a fictional journey that transports one or more characters to a new physical location. Henry Weber named Cyrano de Bergerac's *The Comical History of the States and Empires of the Worlds of the Moon and Sun* (1687) as the prototypical imaginary voyage.[72] Like many later critics, Dunlop, in *The History of Fiction*, cited Lucian of Samosata's *True History* (c. AD 160).[73] Joseph Jacobs, in the *Book of Wonder Voyages* (1896), argued that Ulysses' voyage in the *Odyssey* was the 'grandest specimen' of the genre.[74] Fausett links the imaginary voyage with 'wonder books' that date from the eleventh century.[75] Justin Stagl makes connections with the specifically German literary form of *cosmographies*.[76] Rennie traces the form back a thousand years before the *Odyssey*, to the ancient Egyptian parable of 'The Shipwrecked Sailor'.[77] Many critics make connections with quest writing, including the fabulous tales of Alexander, chivalric romances from the Middle Ages, as well as pilgrimages to the Holy Land and the adventures of Marco Polo.[78] Some have focussed on literary hoaxes, such as the famous *The Travels of Sir John Mandeville* (c. 1357).[79] The historical sweep of these examples shows that the traveller's tale is perhaps as ancient and difficult to pin down as the idea of fiction itself.

Charles Garnier made the first known attempt to classify the imaginary voyage genre into various branches in his 36-volume compilation *Voyages imaginaires, songes, visions et romans cabalistiques* (1787).[80] He tried to sort examples into two categories on the grounds of the purported voyages being 'possible' or 'impossible', although at no point does he clearly state his criteria for making such distinctions. Dunlop tried to classify various branches of the genre by discussing the French *voyages imaginaires* and the English imaginary voyages in separate chapters and by making further distinctions within each of these traditions. He paid most attention to French literary works. Of four categories of French novels, *voyages imaginaires* are listed in the final category under the heading of 'fairy tales', along with 'the French imitations of the Oriental tales'. Although this brief inclusion of the *voyage imaginaire* as an example of a kind of fairy tale suggests that Dunlop was not impressed by their literary value, he nevertheless, somewhat grudgingly, noted that the genre 'would not be altogether proper to neglect'.[81] According to Gove, however, Dunlop may well have neglected it entirely if it had not been for the strong argument put forward by Garnier. Gove judged Garnier's work the first and most important single publication on the history of the genre in any language.[82] Despite its limitations and liberal borrowing from earlier critics, Dunlop's *The History of Fiction* was instrumental in providing belated recognition in England to a genre that had been recognized in France long before, if only in isolated literary studies and in passing editorial references. According to Gove, Dunlop's work was so well read that it became 'the probable source of nearly every subsequent employment of the term [imaginary voyage] in English'.[83]

In 1920, Atkinson published one of the very few comprehensive attempts at definition of the imaginary voyage genre, using the term 'extraordinary voyage', in his study *The Extraordinary Voyage in French Literature before 1700*. A number of later critical works refer to this definition:

> The term extraordinary voyage is used…to designate a novel of the following type: A fictitious narrative, purporting to be the veritable account of a real voyage made by one or more Europeans to an existent but little known country – or to several such countries – together with a description of the happy condition of society there found, and a supplementary account of the travelers' return to Europe.[84]

Atkinson foregrounds the capacity of imaginary voyage writers to feign truthfulness. Surprisingly, this appears to be the only definition that highlights the genre's close affinity with genuine voyage accounts. Atkinson describes the destination of imaginary voyages as 'an existent but little known country' or 'several such countries'. To be more accurate, few of the fictional lands in the imaginary voyages he discusses were known to have a corresponding existence in reality (although they were often described as being very near to known places) because fictional destinations in imaginary voyages are usually deliberately situated beyond the bounds of contemporary knowledge. This is especially the case in the seventeenth-century examples that are the focus of Atkinson's account, written as they were when there was very little empirical knowledge of the antipodes available in Europe. Atkinson also refers to the 'happy condition of society found there', that is, at the destination of the voyage. Again, this is too specific to be generally applicable. While many of the societies portrayed in imaginary voyage literature are indeed happy – in positive utopian fashion – many are miserable and belligerent, and it often takes the influence of the visitor to create a harmonious society based on a combination of European and antipodean values.

Proposing yet another framework for literary classification in his Gulliver's Travels: *A Critical Study* (1923), Eddy aimed to 'bring order out of the chaos in which imaginary voyages have been allowed to remain'.[85] While conscious that the boundaries between fact and fiction seemed to shift in the hands of writers, Eddy tried to separate fully the real from the imaginary by defining the imaginary voyage as 'a voyage that never had any existence outside… the writer's imagination'. He divided works into 'philosophic' and 'non-philosophic' or 'romantic' voyages (some voyages, he says, are 'purely romantic and fictional' but, again, without clearly stating his criteria for making these distinctions). Both varieties, confusingly, are then separated even further, into the 'fantastic' and the 'realistic' within each category.[86] Eddy's effort to define the parameters of the genre loses its original focus as he resorts to further distinctions between examples, emphasizing differences rather than similarities and continuities.

Gove's *The Imaginary Voyage in Prose Fiction* (1941) is a bibliographically dense survey of the imaginary voyage genre and remains the most comprehensive study of the evolving usage of the term. According to Gove, the roots of the genre lie 'in the first deviation from the truth in some prehistoric travelogue'.[87] Gove tracks the earliest critical recognition of the French term '*voyage imaginaire*' to a dissertation by François Augustin Paradis de Moncrif, entitled *Réflexions sur quelques ouvrages faussement appelés ouvrages d'imagination*, presented to the French Academy in 1741. The term '*voyage imaginaire*' had been used in France before this date, but not, according to Gove, as a literary classification.[88] In English, the term 'imaginary voyage' appeared much later. There was no recognition, discussion, or even passing usage of the term (not even in book titles, for example) before the nineteenth century.[89] Although Gove's study focusses on the eighteenth century (it includes an annotated checklist of 215 imaginary voyages published between 1700 and 1800), its aim is to provide a survey of the attempts made by critics from the eighteenth century to the early twentieth century to define the imaginary voyage as a distinct genre. Having consulted more than 150 dictionaries and encyclopedias up until 1940, Gove concludes that 'no completely satisfactory definition of the imaginary voyage as a type of literature has ever been devised'.[90]

Without being able to decide on a widely applicable definition, early critics instead tried to individually categorize various examples of imaginary voyages in the hope that this would provide a key to formulating a better general understanding of the genre. Rather than defining generic boundaries, these critics instead delineated subdivisions within the genre. Most of the critics Gove discusses also had a financial motive for trying to categorize the imaginary voyage genre. Many were editors themselves, or were assisting editors of travel book compilations. They needed to be able to explain clearly to readers why imaginary voyages were a compelling form of fiction that deserved separate attention. As it was, collecting examples to publish involved making difficult decisions because the imaginary voyage did not seem to be an 'exclusive' genre but a 'shifting division of fiction'.[91] Gove describes the early critical commentary as 'random, disparate, even...chaotic'.[92] The single broad conclusion Gove is able to reach in *The Imaginary Voyage in Prose Fiction* is that imaginary voyages should be thought of as a type of 'geographical fiction', a literary tradition 'comparable in scope to historical fiction'.[93]

Robinsonades and Gulliveriana

The term 'imaginary voyage' may have first been used in France, but England produced the two most popular and widely read examples of the genre: Daniel Defoe's *Robinson Crusoe* and Jonathan Swift's *Gulliver's Travels*. Throughout Europe, as Weber put it in 1812, these famous texts caused 'a great bustle among the literati to emulate their excellency'.[94] Making an even stronger case, Dunlop added a third text to these two landmark works and argued: 'no nation of Europe has produced three performances of equal merit with Robinson Crusoe, Gulliver's Travels, and Gaudentio di Lucca'.[95] As the first two were influential texts published within a decade of one another, their individual impact is impossible to gauge. *Gulliver's Travels* inspired the literary term 'Gulliveriana', coined to describe the literature modelled on its famous story.[96] However, the parallel form of the 'robinsonade', modelled on *Robinson Crusoe*, was even more successful. The story of a marooned sailor left to fend for himself on an isolated island became so popular that characters in later literary fiction were given the name of (or even re-named in subsequent editions as) Robinson, after Robinson Crusoe.[97] Earlier examples that used the same narrative format have been referred to as 'pre-robinsonades'.[98] *Robinson Crusoe* attracted a new readership following the publication of Rousseau's *Emile* in 1762, a work within which Defoe's story is set as an educational text on individualism.[99] The enduring influence of *Robinson Crusoe* has never been more evident than at the start of the twenty-first century, which saw the launch of a number of internationally popular television series set in remote island locations, with names such as *Castaway*, *Survivor* and *Shipwrecked*.

The 'robinsonade' indicates a formulaic literary structure and setting where, in Dunlop's words, readers 'are led to appreciate their own exertions by seeing what their species is capable of when in perfect solitude, and abandoned to its own resources'.[100] Many eighteenth-century works have been categorized both as robinsonades and as imaginary voyages, such as *The Life and Adventures of Peter Wilkins* (1750)[101] (see Chapter Three), *A Narrative of the Life and Astonishing Adventures of John Daniel* (1751),[102] *Voyages curieux d'un Philadelphe* [*The Curious Voyages of a Philadelphian*](1755),[103] *Histoire d'un peuple nouveau, ou découverte d'une isle...par David Tompson* [*Captain Tompson's Island*](1757)[104] and *Voyage de Robertson* [*Robertson's Voyage*](1767).[105] Robinsonades, because they always include a voyage and usually a shipwreck, can be thought of as a sub-genre of the imaginary voyage, conceived of in the broadest possible terms. Gove argues that the robinsonade is not an imitation of *Robinson Crusoe*, as some critics before him had suggested, but rather, that the robinsonade 'names a theme' (of island solitude) which is generic.[106] *Robinson Crusoe*, then, can be thought of as the archetypal example of a robinsonade, but the robinsonade, in turn, can be understood as a special kind of imaginary voyage, recognizable for its theme of island solitude.[107] I would argue, nevertheless, that the individual texts discussed in detail in the following chapters cannot generally be considered as robinsonades, since in each case the traveller arrives at a destination that is already populated, often very densely, setting up the conditions for cross-cultural encounters and negotiations.

With their related themes, *Robinson Crusoe* and *Gulliver's Travels* are representative examples of eighteenth-century imaginary voyages, and yet Defoe and Swift employed very different literary styles and strategies. As in the case of Foigny's *La Terre Australe connue* and Hall's *Mundus alter et idem* in the previous century, *Robinson Crusoe* and *Gulliver's Travels* arguably illustrate two alternative modes, one realistic and the other satiric. According to Dunlop, whereas Defoe 'confines himself to incidents within the sphere of possibility', Swift utilizes fictional worlds 'as the vehicle of the keenest satire' and as a means of conveying 'philosophical research'.[108] Weber described these texts as 'illustrious prototypes', indicative of the 'two classes' that 'productions of fancy naturally separate'.[109]

Despite their many divergences in opinion, interpretation, definition and analytical approach, most of the critics discussed here concur on one fundamental aspect of imaginary voyage literature that allows diverse examples to be understood generically. This single point of agreement is that imaginary voyages mentally transport the reader beyond the frontiers of knowledge into uncharted and unknown spaces – *terra incognita*. Tieje clearly spelled out this common ground and summarized the dilemmas that faced critics of the imaginary voyage up until the time of the early twentieth century when he was writing:

> ...its [the *voyage imaginaire*'s] history is usually that of a sub-variety in one or another school [of types of fictional literature] – with the result that the *voyage imaginaire* may have either coherent or incoherent structure, either nicely localized or wildly impossible setting, and either definitely realistic or hopelessly incredible characters. The aims, too, are naturally so diverse as almost to defy enumeration. For instance, the *voyage imaginaire* may outdo the nightmares of chivalric romance...; it may divulge scandal...; it may explain philosophic or scientific dogma...; it may satirize...fads...; or it may be...reformative and Utopian... If neither main aim nor structure nor characterization, then, made the pre-Richardsonians consider the *voyage imaginaire* a genre, what did? It was a subordinate purpose, that of carrying the reader into uncharted lands...[110]

The challenge confronting all of the early critics was that imaginary voyages seemed distinct enough to merit special attention as a literary form, and yet they also appeared to represent the continuation of other long-established traditions. Efforts made to distinguish between various kinds of imaginary voyages on the grounds of their plausibility usually resulted in interpretations that promoted arbitrary distinctions between individual texts. This analytical method, practiced by way of rigid categorization, nevertheless made it possible to begin conceiving of the genre in an intentionally theoretical way, even if it sometimes produced seemingly random results.

There is no doubt that the confusion between literary genres – between idealistic utopias, robinsonades and various other literary categories that can be thought of as sub-categories of the imaginary voyage – has deflected interest from a huge body of literature.[111] There has been further generic confusion in that the destination of imaginary voyages can be an inhospitable desert island or a populated, welcoming utopia. The prominence of utopian themes in imaginary voyages has also tended to draw attention away from their politicized imagery of colonialism in the antipodes. Since conventional wisdom has it that utopias are only truly effective when they are depicted as no-places, outside of time and space, an analysis on utopian terms makes it easy to forget that the antipodean setting was a growing reality for European readers, and that this had implications for how they would respond to these works. Looking back on these critical commentaries over the centuries, we can see that they offer not only an overview of opinion about imaginary voyage texts, but also a map of the shifting emphases and fashions in literary criticism itself. Caught up in debates about the dividing line between fact and fiction, or about stylistic and aesthetic effects, critics tended to gloss over, or not take an interest in, or perhaps not notice, connections between the rise of the genre and the rise of colonialism. What is most surprising is the fact that a literary form that maintained a readership and market for more than two centuries has disappeared almost without trace. There is no doubt that this can, in large measure, be attributed to its disappearance from critical consciousness, and that this, in turn, is related to its nebulous existence as a genre. With generic definition comes a sense of a body of literature that can be identified, conceptualized, discussed and so claim a place on the literary map.

Chapter 2

BLANK SPACES FOR THE IMAGINATION

SUNG IN HARMONY
...let us revel it while we are here,
And keep possession of this hemisphere.
— Richard Brome, *The Antipodes* (1640)[1]

Terrifying monsters and semi-human creatures had traditionally inhabited the imagined underworld of hell throughout centuries of artistic representation in painting, sculpture and scripture. Through long-established mythologies, the undiscovered worlds of the southern hemisphere came to be associated with that underworld. The first examples of imaginary voyages to the antipodes appearing from the start of the seventeenth century deliberately blurred distinctions between Christian beliefs, pure fantasy and tentative facts, reflecting fascination with the idea that there may actually be a hell on earth or, indeed, a heaven on earth, in the unexplored southern regions. Some considered such expressions to be heretical. They were trespassing into the moral and spiritual spaces that had long been claimed by religious iconography. These literary works were not merely whimsical extravaganzas of the imagination; they were arenas for critical comment on politics, the church, social systems and customs of the day and, perhaps initially by chance, they also began to construct a moral framework for colonial expansion into the antipodes. At the same time, these early imaginary voyages laid the foundations for the literary genre's development, closely linked to real exploration but fundamentally a form of fiction.

Over the course of the seventeenth century, geographical discoveries in the region of present-day Australia, New Zealand and the South Pacific added a new dimension to the myths and associations attached to the great southern continent of *Terra Australis* and its antipodean inhabitants. When explorers entered this southern realm, comparisons could be made that had never before been possible: between the geography of Europe and the geography of the antipodes; between the people of the antipodes and the Indigenous populations of other regions such as the Americas; and, most significantly from a historical viewpoint, between the antipodes as described by explorers and the myths that had made up for the absence of information over many centuries. The antipodes began to be transformed from a complex set of myths into an even more complex and contradictory set of realities for Europeans, with the two ways of seeing enmeshed. A symbiotic relationship was formed between the reality and the fiction of early discovery voyages that was to last for several centuries, with each animating and blending into the other. The fact that antipodean mythologies could not be dispelled easily by European discoveries in the seventeenth century indicates how deeply ingrained they were. Far from putting the myths to rest, travellers' tales often reinforced images of reversals, distortions and monstrosity, thus lending life to traditional myths with their own peculiar store of apparent evidence rather than significantly adding to the body of empirical knowledge. What explorers saw or discovered was always coloured by their expectations, received traditions and worldview, and over time imaginary voyages became part of that set of influences.

This chapter introduces two of the earliest examples of imaginary voyages set in the antipodes in the British and French traditions: Joseph Hall's *Mundus alter et idem*[2] (first published in Latin in 1605 and adapted into English by John Healey as *The Discovery of a New World* in 1609[3]); and Gabriel de Foigny's *La Terre Australe connue*[4] (first published in French in 1676 and translated as *A New Discovery of Terra Incognita Australis, or the Southern World* in 1693[5]). Here I will refer to David Fausett's 1993 English translation of Foigny's text, renamed as *The Southern Land, Known*.[6] Intriguingly, the earliest known use of the word 'Australian' is in the original English translation of Foigny's story.[7] In these works, the strangeness of the antipodes is portrayed through themes of behavioural oddities, role reversals, sexual aberration and hermaphroditism, adding new layers to the mythology of extreme bodily distortion that had long been connected with the antipodes, in both secular and Christian traditions.[8] Written more than 70 years apart, in different languages and in very different social contexts, the stylistic approaches of these two texts differ markedly. Hall's work is pointedly and humorously satirical whereas Foigny's highly developed verisimilitude was aimed at pursuading readers of the truth of his account. However, despite these fundamental differences, there are similarities that are important in the context of this study. Both works include fictionalized visions of European adventurers interacting with and exerting their influence over the inhabitants of vast southern lands. Written in an era when very little was known about the antipodes through European geographical discovery, both gesture thematically backwards to myths and traditions at the same time as looking forwards to the prospect of colonization.

Antipodean Inversions and Reversals

Arising out of both its pagan and Christian roots, fear of the antipodes was translated into a stock of often grotesque distortions, including people living in a world upside down and lacking in sunlight. Famous examples of such curious antipodean creatures appeared in the pages of Hartmann Schedel's *Nuremberg Chronicle* in 1493.[9] These include the 'Antipode' with feet facing the wrong way, the 'Sciapod' holding a giant foot head-high as a shield from the sun, and the 'Blemmyae' with no head at all, having a face positioned in the chest area (Figure 3).[10] At the other extreme, the region of the antipodes was depicted as an earthly paradise. Growing European knowledge of the East through trade suggested that paradise was not located there as was once thought. The region of the antipodes became a prime location for an imagined earthly paradise, and later, as large parts of the Americas, Africa and India were explored and colonized, the region became one of the last possible locations.[11] In the same way as traditional 'monstrous' antipodean imagery had been incorporated into their work by map-makers, illustrations of an imagined paradise were used to embellish world maps (the more optimistic ones), some of which also featured negative images, arguably for the sake of visually portraying a cautious or balanced outlook, echoing medieval Christian iconography with its balance of heaven and hell.[12] It is easy to dismiss such maps as inaccurate or as too fanciful or decorative to be relevant today. And yet, those very characteristics of inaccuracy and embellishment are important indicators of cartography's powerfully ambivalent role, integrating knowledge with imagination, in the process of its own evolution. That maps could incorporate factual information at the same time as lending support to myths, sometimes giving equal visual treatment to each, suggests the flexibility of knowledge before empirical methods of measuring the world were widely embraced. It was accepted – even expected – that maps would provide their own context and commentary on the current state of knowledge.

Figure 3. Images of 'Antipode', 'Sciapod' and 'Blemmyae', from Hartmann Schedel, *Nuremberg Chronicle* (1493).

In the thirteenth century, Marco Polo had indicated the location of a number of earthly paradises or kingdoms in the region of the antipodes by the names of 'Lucach', 'Beach', 'Reach' and 'Malateur', about which he claimed to have gained knowledge on his way to China.[13] As late as 1599, Theodor de Bry's map of the western hemisphere, 'Descriptio Hydrographica', displayed these names arrayed around the northernmost tip of a territory labelled as *Terra Australis Incognita* (Figure 4). Reinforcing an association between paradise and the discovery of gold in the antipodes that inspired Spanish explorers, Polo's account claimed: 'Gold is so plentiful that no-one who did not see it could believe it'.[14] On their maps, Abraham Ortelius and Gerardus Mercator, borrowing from Polo, included mythical elements such as 'provincia aurifera' ('gold-bearing land') and 'scatans aromatibus' ('overflowing with spices').[15] It is not clear when the search for an earthly paradise ceased, but there is no doubt that, in its fictionalized form, it continued and found new life in imaginary voyages.[16]

European explorers had begun to make discoveries in the southern hemisphere from around 1460 with the first Portuguese forays into the Gulf of Guinea. The belief that *Terra Australis* extended southwards from Africa and Asia was proven as incorrect in the late fifteenth and early sixteenth century by the reports of Portuguese explorers including Bartolomeu Diaz and Vasco da Gama. However, the voyages of Amerigo Vespucci in 1502, Binot Paulmier de Gonneville in 1503 and Ferdinand Magellan in 1519–22 continued to suggest the existence of a southern continent, leading to further attempts at its discovery in the course of the sixteenth century.[17] In 1570, Ortelius published his *Theatrum Orbis Terrarum* [*Theatre of the World*], regarded as the first modern atlas.[18] One of the maps of the Pacific has a southern landmass stretching northwest from the Straits of Magellan to the northern coast of New Guinea, a cartographical speculation that sparked substantial interest in England and Spain.[19] In a treatise arguing for the value of his atlas, Ortelius foresaw a global theatre in which geography is described as the 'Eye of History'.[20] Maps, he expounded, provide frameworks for seeing and for knowledge, 'these charts being placed, as it were, certaine glasses before our eyes, will the longer be kept in memory, and make the deeper impression in us'.[21]

By the turn of the seventeenth century, the region of the antipodes, ill-defined and barely known as it was, included the immense spaces of the Pacific, parts of South-East Asia and the area of Australia, and stretched further south into the Antarctic. It was an alluring space where as-yet meagre geographical knowledge merged with hearsay, fables, legends and wild speculation. Voyages were often undertaken with the aim of searching out the mythical places that punctuated largely formless maps. Rival European nations had different aims and agendas. There were also, however, strong arguments against travel, even well into the seventeenth century. Many

Figure 4. Theodor de Bry, detail of 'Descriptio Hydrographica' (1599).

thought that travel 'turned the mind away from God to irrelevant things; it loosened social and political ties and thus endangered the morals, manners and health of the traveller'.[22]

The first known European to set foot on Australian land was Dutchman Willem Jansz, who anchored the *Duyfken* off Cape York in the area of the Gulf of Carpentaria in 1606. Only months before, the Spanish Pedro Fernández de Quirós claimed to have discovered the southern continent while voyaging in the area of today's Melanesia, but in fact had discovered the island of Espiritu Santo in Vanuatu (New Hebrides). The idea of the antipodes as a potential paradise was supported in 1619 when Frederick de Houtman reported seeing Polo's paradisal 'Southland of Beach' between latitudes 32°S and 26°S. Following Dirck Hartog's visit to Shark Bay in 1616, the Dutch East India Company had advised its sailors to keep searching for the paradise Polo claimed to have found.[23] Contrasting images also fed into the perception of this southern realm, including the reports of Jan Carstensz, who explored the Gulf of Carpentaria and described an inhospitable natural environment and a hostile Indigenous population. In 1629, the *Batavia* was wrecked not far off Australia's western coast and the notorious mutiny and massacre followed.[24] In 1642 Anthony van Diemen, Governor-General of the Dutch East Indies, reintroduced a positive tone, asking Abel Tasman to seek out, once more, Polo's 'Southland of Beach'.[25] In 1656 another Dutch ship, the *Vergulde Draeck*, was wrecked, also in the vicinity of the *Batavia* disaster.[26] Because the region was so large, while each of these voyages may have generated valuable information about previously unknown places, they tended to offer only glimpses and so to highlight the overall lack of knowledge. By this time, however, much was already known about the Americas and so Europe's experience there provided a model to help conceptualize otherness and difference in the antipodes. Reports of discovery, trade, natural resources and cross-cultural interactions (including reports of savagery and cannibalism) in the Americas offered ample evidence of how great a variety could be accommodated in terms of geography, plants, animals, human societies and cultural practices.[27]

A spectacular set of French maps from the sixteenth century hints at a hidden history of the discovery of the Australian continent predating the Dutch. The controversial Dieppe maps, as they are referred to, are intricately drawn and artistically spectacular. The land of 'Java-La-Grande' – thought by Polo to be the largest landmass in the world – was indicated on the Dieppe maps from about 1540 to 1570 as if it were an extension of *Terra Australis*, and for this reason it is associated with one of the famous unsolved questions of Renaissance cartography.[28] The maps are obviously French but it has long been assumed that Portuguese navigators made an earlier discovery. The riddle facing historians is that there is no reference to that land on contemporary Portuguese charts. Pierre Desceliers' world map of 1550 is an example from the Dieppe school (Figure 5). The viewer must reorient this beautifully decorated map 180 degrees in order to read the text printed on the northern or the southern hemisphere. No matter from which direction the map is viewed, the text printed in the opposite hemisphere always appears upside down, reinforcing the notion of antipodal inversion.

Figure 5. Pierre Desceliers, detail of 'La Terre Australle' (1550).

Adding further weight to the belief that there had been visits to the southern continent predating the Dutch are two important maps that also date back to the sixteenth century. The 1571 map, 'Pars Orbis', prepared by Spanish theologian and philosopher Benito Arias Montanus, is regarded as the earliest cartographical evidence of a southern land that does not feature a vast *Terra Australis* (Figure 6).[29] The northern tip of an area of land that corresponds with present-day Australia is shown as though rising up through waves but it is almost completely submerged. This area is drawn three-dimensionally, whereas all the other land on the map is drawn

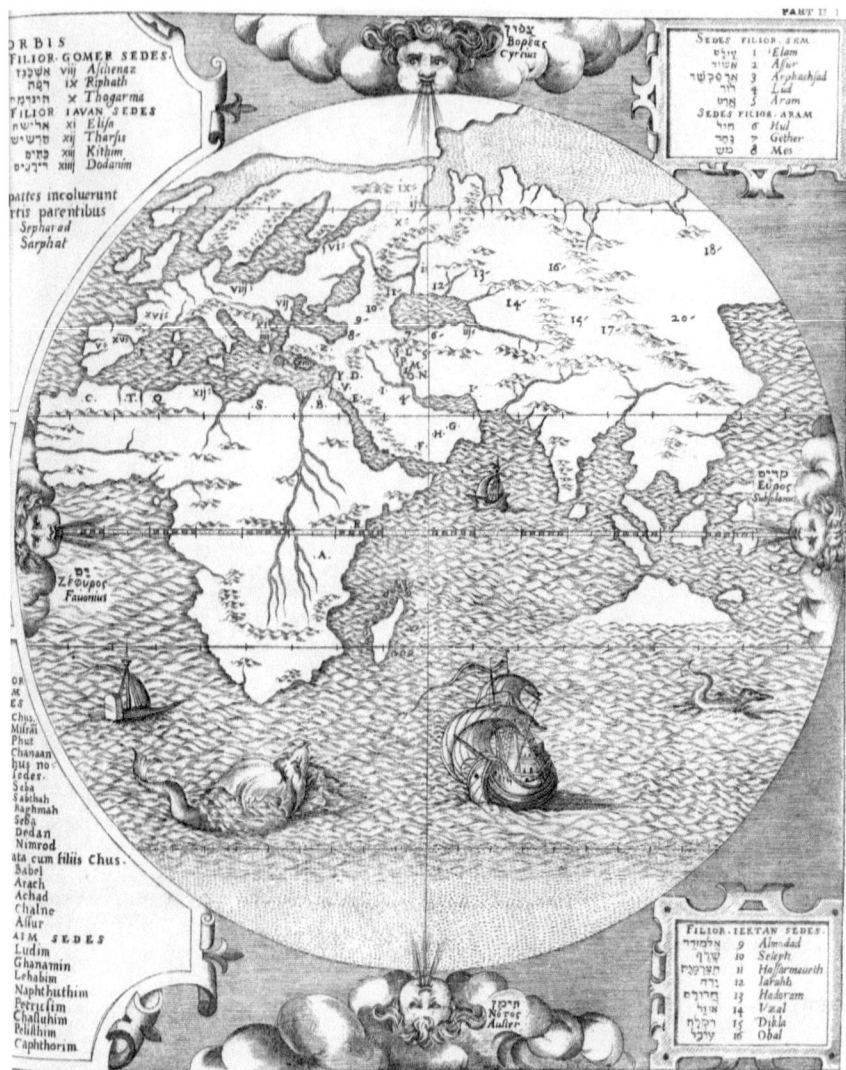

Figure 6. Benito Arias Montanus, detail of 'Pars Orbis' (1571).

two-dimensionally. Cornelis de Jode's 1593 map, 'Novae Guineae Forma, & Situs', which similarly provides detail that corresponds with the Australian northern shoreline, depicts mythical roaming beasts (Figure 7).[30]

It was against this backdrop of minimal and conflicting knowledge, and escalating investment in exploration in the seventeenth century, that the first, controversial, imaginary voyages set in the antipodes appeared.

Figure 7. Cornelis de Jode, 'Novae Guineae Forma, & Situs' (1593).

Joseph Hall's *Mundus alter et idem* (1605)

> It is as great a glory (thinke I) to bee called *The new worlds discoverer*, as her *conqueror*. And why may not wee have that success, and the like glory?
> – Joseph Hall, *The Discovery of a New World* (1609)[31]

Bishop Joseph Hall's *Mundus alter et idem* [*Another World and Yet the Same*] was published in Latin in 1605 under the pseudonym 'Mercurius Britannicus'. In this chapter I refer to the English adaptation by John Healey, published in 1609 with the title *The Discovery of a New World*.[32] In his time, Hall was a well-known satirist. His controversial work *Virgidemiarum* (1597) is recognized as one of the first successful attempts at Juvenalian satire in English.[33] *Mundus alter et idem* is regarded as a foundational text in the imaginary voyage tradition. Hall's satirical story tells of the adventures of a lone European voyager, Mercurius Britannicus, who travels on the appropriately named ship *Fancie* to *Terra Australis* and spends 30 years there. The southern world discovered is divided into four parts, with the names of: 'Crapulia' ('Tenterbelly' in the 1609 English adaptation), which borders the Indian Ocean and contains the provinces of 'Pamphagonia' ('Gluttonia') and 'Yvronia' ('Drinkallia'), a place where to be a leader one must be obese;[34] 'Viraginia' ('Sheelandt'), a lawless republic of only women; 'Moronia' ('Fooliana'), a land of fools and folly – including religious folly; and 'Lavernia' ('Theevingen'), home to criminals and crime.[35]

I

In an opening epistle, Hall's narrator refers to the blending of fact and fiction, and the sense of intriguing paradox, that characterized knowledge of lands distant from Europe in the early seventeenth century:

> A discoverie and no discoverie, of a world and no world, both knowne and unknowne, by a traveller that never travelled. Written first in Latine, and no Latine, and now translated, and yet not translated, by the same man, yet not the same man that first of all pend it.[36]

The preface that follows, entitled 'The Occasion for This Travell, and the Pre-Instruction for It', offers a fascinating satirical commentary on the ambiguous, fluid state of European knowledge of the antipodes.[37] The narrator discusses the issues of travel, discovery and the narrator's own 'unquenched thirst and desire of knowledge' at length, lamenting, '[w]ee (wretches) that like Tortoyses, are bound to our owne houses'. He admires the discoveries of pioneering sailors, especially those who put 'girdles about the whole world' and 'have first found out unknowne regions, or have brought them to order'.[38] Hall's narrator explains that he himself wanted to perform 'some noble enterprise of this kinde, such as the world might gaze at, and all posterity record with admiration'.[39] He reports frustration at the misleading speculations of inventive cartographers, with their illustrations of mythical places and fantastic creatures. The narrator complains:

> It hath ever offended mee to looke upon the Geographicall mapps, and finde this: *Terra Australis, nondum Cognita. The unknowne Southerne Continent.* What good spirit but would greeve at this? If they know it for a Continent, and for a Southerne Continent, why then doe they call it unknowne? But if it bee unknowne; why doe all the Geographers describe it after one form and site? Idle men that they are, that can say, this it is, and yet wee know it not: How long shall wee continue to bee ignorant in that which wee professe to have knowledge of?[40]

This limited degree of knowledge indicates a 'notorious idlenesse', a 'slouth of ours', a 'more than female feare', and a 'vaine carelessnesse', which 'robbes us of another world'.[41] 'What feare wee? Shadowes, or our selves?', the narrator asks. 'There is heaven, there is earth in that continent, and there is men, perhaps more civill then wee are'.[42] People of the antipodes, the narrator argues – in a parodic tone that opens the text to counter-colonialist readings – could well be laughing at Europeans, seeing themselves, the antipodeans, as 'two-ey'd', the Europeans 'one-eyd' and 'all the world else, starke blind'.[43] The solution is simple, however. He will attempt the exploration himself. 'I see the land lye unknowne', claims the narrator, so 'I will assay to discover it'.[44] This will take time, nevertheless, because 'great matters...require many premonitions, so doe they more premeditations'.[45] In this way, the narrator steps out of his role to that of voyager and explorer – or, at least, seems to do so.[46]

With its overtly satirical style, *The Discovery of a New World* was not intended to be easily mistaken for a genuine travel account, only designed to resemble one. The narrator poses the questions: 'What is there in all the knowne world, which mapps, and authors cannot instruct a man in, as perfectly as his owne eyes?', and '[w]hat part of *Europe* is there that affords more to a strangers eye then is related by one pen-man or other?'[47] Here, in suggesting a near equivalence between writing and experience, the narrator describes and also questions the foundation of what was to become a new approach to demonstrating truth in the developing methods of empiricism. The small-sized pages of the English adaptation have endless footnotes substantiating various claims and filling in particulars of unique and unusual cultural practices and beliefs, some containing more text than the main printed page (Figure 8). This strategy parodies the tendency of travel accounts at the time to incorporate exhaustive factual detail in order to establish a sense of authority and security for the reader. A brief footnote inserted in the margin (but without a corresponding number in the main text) offers a humorous metafictional signpost for the attentive readers who would have noticed it: 'for a lier must have a good memory'.[48]

II

In its Latin original, *Mundus alter et idem* featured five engraved folding maps, one showing the four regions of the southern continent as almost touching South America, Africa and Asia (Figure 9). Hall's introductory passage in English explains the projected physical relationship in these terms:

> The land of *Tenter-belly* is a region farre extending both in longitude and latitude, bounding on the North upon the *Ethiopian Ocean*, on the East upon *(a) Letcheritania* & *Shee-landt*: on the South, upon *(b) Fooliana the fatte*: and on the West upon *Filtching-fennes*. It lieth in that undiscovered Continent… In latitude it lieth full sixtie degrees, and in longitude seventy foure…and is situate almost directly opposite unto the Southerne frontiers of *Affrica*.[49]

The title page of the English adaptation has two small circular-framed maps of the four regions visited but with much less detail than the corresponding map included in the Latin version (Figure 10).

Hall does not stop at mapping the southern continent in relation to the known world. He also refers to respected cartographers and authorities on travel. The narrator claims, misleadingly, that Mercator's world map features the land purportedly visited, thus providing 'proof' of the existence of 'Fooliana'. The passage reads: 'Mercator in his *Atlas Geograph*, affirmes as much'.[50] Of course, there is no mention of this place on Mercator's actual map. In another example, the narrator describes the 'huge and monstrous Birde called…RUC' that 'snatcheth up (now and then) a whole Elephant at a stoope', as 'most of our Geographers in their moderne discoveries doe confirme'.[51] In the same spirit that he calls upon the evidence of geographers, Hall's narrator cites the recently published *Principal Navigations* (1598) of Richard Hakluyt,[52] including a note which reads 'Hackluits voyages affirme

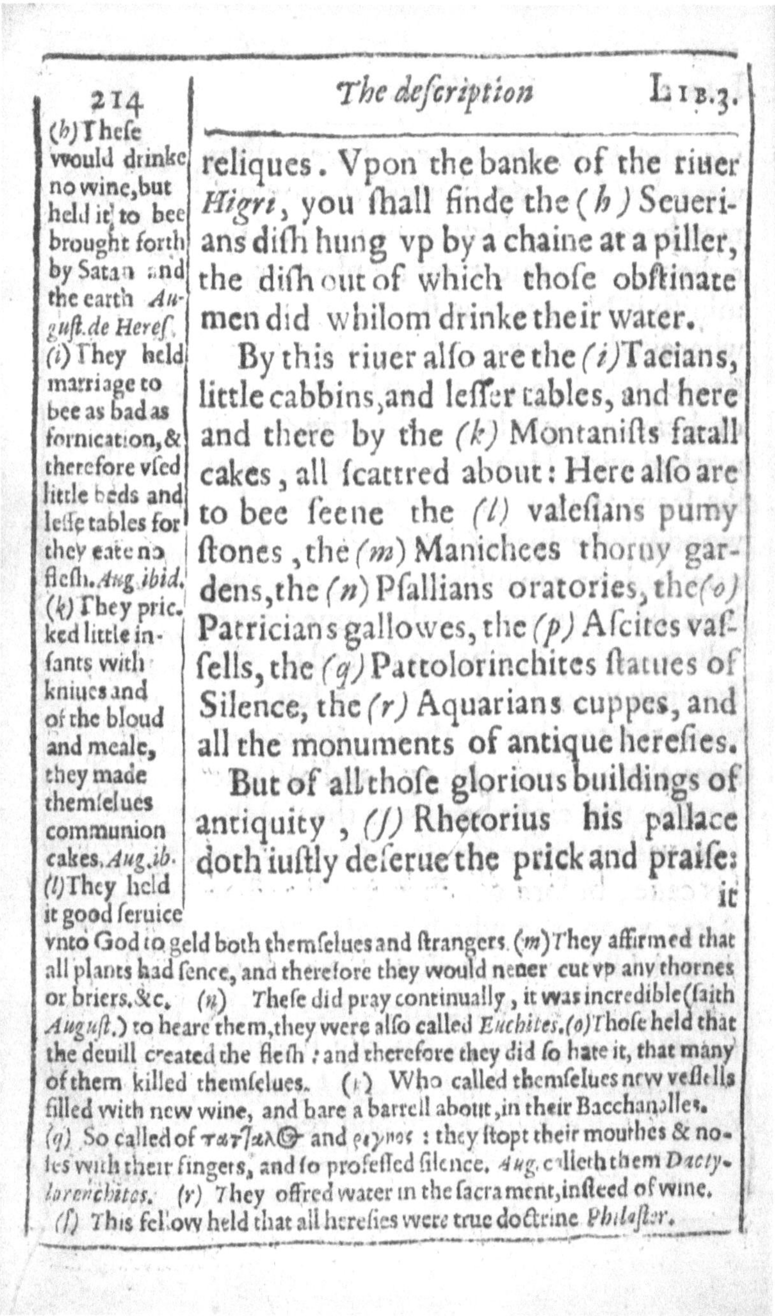

214

(h) These would drinke no wine, but held it to bee brought forth by Satan and the earth *August. de Heref.*

(i) They held marriage to bee as bad as fornication, & therefore vsed little beds and lesse tables for they eate no flesh. *Aug. ibid.*

(k) They pricked little infants with kniues and of the bloud and meale, they made themselues communion cakes, *Aug. ib.*

(l) They held it good seruice

The description LIB. 3.

reliques. Vpon the banke of the riuer *Higri*, you shall finde the (h) Seuerians dish hung vp by a chaine at a piller, the dish out of which those obstinate men did whilom drinke their water.

By this riuer also are the (i) Tacians, little cabbins, and lesser tables, and here and there by the (k) Montanists fatall cakes, all scattred about: Here also are to bee seene the (l) valesians pumy stones, the (m) Manichees thorny gardens, the (n) Psallians oratories, the (o) Patricians gallowes, the (p) Ascites vassells, the (q) Pattolorinchites statues of Silence, the (r) Aquarians cuppes, and all the monuments of antique heresies.

But of all those glorious buildings of antiquity, (s) Rhetorius his pallace doth iustly deserue the prick and praise: it

vnto God to geld both themselues and strangers. (m) They affirmed that all plants had sence, and therefore they would neuer cut vp any thornes or briers, &c. (n) These did pray continually, it was incredible (saith *August.*) to heare them, they were also called *Euchites*. (o) Those held that the deuill created the flesh: and therefore they did so hate it, that many of them killed themselues. (p) Who called themselues new vessells filled with new wine, and bare a barrell about, in their Bacchanalles. (q) So called of ταρ]αλ© and ριγνος: they stopt their mouthes & nostes with their fingers, and so professed silence. *Aug.* calleth them *Dactylorenchites*. (r) They offred water in the sacrament, insteed of wine. (s) This fellow held that all heresies were true doctrine. *Philaster.*

Figure 8. Page 214 from Joseph Hall, *The Discovery of a New World*, adapted into English by John Healey (1609).

Figure 9. Map of the fictional southern land, from Joseph Hall, *Mundus alter et idem* (1605).

as much'.[53] Using an opposite strategy that exposes the satirical trickery of Hall's account, the narrator refers to Thomas More's *Utopia* (a work of fiction) as evidence, claiming: 'Sir *Thomas Moore* in his *Eutopia* hath a river of the same name'.[54] This associative device creates a sense of narrative continuity between the setting of Hall's imagined world and other fictional settings. Later in the account Mercurius suggests further geographical links with the world known to Europe, visiting one town by the name of 'Lickingoa', a colony originally 'sent from Goa in the East Indies'.[55] Connecting to the real world of Spanish global commerce, this city is claimed to be home to exiled philosophers and former Spanish slaves.[56]

The traveller's arrival in the imagined world is uneventful when compared with the drama and heroism of arrival in many later imaginary voyages. When Mercurius sets foot on the southern continent, his first impressions are of a land of plenty: 'Touching the soyle, the fertilitie is most worthily admirable: the ayre most delicately temperate'.[57] However, this imagined world unfolds as a dystopia, a place where life is disagreeable and unappealing rather than a blueprint for a perfect society. The political satire is directed at European national traits, parodying contemporary English, French, German and Italian stereotypes, and the narrative includes antipodean towns that 'situate in the same longitude and latitude' as their equivalents in Europe.[58]

Figure 10. Title page, from Joseph Hall, *The Discovery of a New World*, adapted into English by John Healey (1609).

III

Taking full advantage of the imaginative potential opened up by such an extensive, and yet empirically unknown, geographical space, Hall populates his southern continent densely with all kinds of life forms, human and otherwise. Unlike later imaginary voyage writers, Hall had a blank canvas to work with. In each of the four regions Mercurius visits, the traveller encounters different belief systems, laws, customs and histories as well as dramatically different physical terrains. In fertile areas of 'Eat-allia', birds can only stay for a maximum of three months or else they become 'so ladened with the luggage of their owne fatned bodies, that they cannot possibly get wing so high as to over-toppe one of the meaner mountains', which results in the birds being forced to 'become sworne inhabitants of this fatte countrie all their lives after'.[59] In 'Starveling Iland, or Hungerland' people hunt anything they can find, including their own kind, 'otherwise...called cannibals'.[60] Elsewhere, in 'Shee-landt', there is a 'Double-sex Ile, or Hermophradite Iland'.[61] The narrative is filled with sensational descriptions of cultural difference and variety that compete at each turn for the reader's attention. To a modern reader, however, the intended resonances of many of these satirical depictions are no longer easily decipherable.

The Discovery of a New World comically invokes many of the myths that characterized the antipodes. Themes of monstrosity, duality and inversion are seen on various levels in the text, including in details of the southern world described. For example, Mercurius digs up from the ground a series of old coins decorated with designs such as Janus faces, a globe-like stone on a table and a many-footed fish.[62] The province of 'Still-more' 'is in the hands of a monstrous kinde of men, such as you see pictured in *Munster* and *Mandevill*, with heads like hogges... Their voice is a kinde of grunting, nor have they other speech'.[63] These creatures live the basest of lives, symbolically crawling on the ground like animals.[64] The people of 'Clawback-ourt' are 'the strangest monsters that ever man beheld: They beare every one... two faces, and speake with two tongues'.[65]

When Mercurius visits 'Solitaria the sad' he finds the 'most unsociable creatures' who spend their time 'in imagining & framing fictions to themselves of things never done, nor ever likely to bee done'.[66] So advanced is their imagining that some even imagine themselves dead. The way these creatures construct their own world seems to be much like Hall's narrative, making far-fetched and fanciful claims for new knowledge based purely on fictional projections. Evidence of the literary influence of Hall's tongue-in-cheek critique of the imaginative process to which he was also contributing can be found in Peter Heylyn's 1657 edition of his *Cosmography*.[67] Heylyn declared that he intended to 'make a search into this Terra Australis' to find 'such places as Fairy Land, the Lands of Chivalry and the ridiculous country described in Hall's *Mundus alter et idem*.[68]

Unlike many travellers in eighteenth-century imaginary voyages, Mercurius does relatively little to influence the societies he visits and does not take up a position of formal control in the imagined world. His role is primarily that of an attentive observer. What he finds is a southern continent filled with violence, mystery and irrational social systems based on ethics with which he disagrees. European culture, however, is foundational in the continent's social history. European colonizers have already achieved numerous modifications, not all of them admirable. Mercurius finds indications everywhere that it must have been originally the French who shaped the culture. The narrator speculates: 'the *Portugales* may brag of their travels and discoveries, let them do so, but I durst ventur a large wager, that if it could be tried, the ancient…*French-men* did first discover this country'.[69] The evidence is in the 'so many monuments remaining that shew it', 'the names of the townes', 'their most ancient lawes', and their 'chiefe coines'.[70] The Italian word for 'Butter flye' ('Farfellia') is also used as the name of one town, suggesting formative contact with an Italian traveller in the past. It is not a recent past, however, since this town is 'recorded to have altered the situation a hundred times since the foundation'.[71] There is also a long history of rivalry and war within the southern land. Monuments to the 'warres of the *Eat-allians*', for example, chronicle victories in a history of conflicts between the 'Hunger-landers' and 'Theeving-arians', which made 'many terrible invasions upon the *Eat-allians* borders'.[72] But the Eat-allians are not the original inhabitants, the 'Thrivingers' are. These 'ancient inhabitants of this land, have made many attempts to regaine their lost possession' but they 'have beene continually beaten backe by the *Eat-allians* good successe'.[73] In another case, the conqueror 'All-Paunch', a giant, took the country of the 'Thrivingois', 'drave them all out of the land, brought in a new people, and gave them new lawes'.[74] In a further example, the region of '*Cholerikoye*, the other Dutchie of *Fooliana* the craggie' is underpinned by a rule of '*Conquer and Possesse*'.[75] Here, '[i]f you have any minde to revenge a wrong, to regaine what was your owne, or take from another, you may call him to the field at any time, and he must come, or lose his estate'.[76] Visitors ignorant of the local customs are routinely hanged or beheaded.[77] However humorous and playful this text may be, its satire also points to some of the most negative aspects of early European colonialism – its Janus-faced double standards, its brutality and its unquestioning belief in its right to claim other people's lands.

In a last comic-satiric twist in the narrative, Mercurius sets up a school in which to 'read the lecture of spying marvels in the heavens…as methodically as any Star-gazer'.[78] It was here, in this school, that he penned 'an infallible prognostication of these present times'.[79] The footnote reads: 'Right, for this is but a discovery of *Mundus alter et idem*'.[80] When he finally leaves, Mercurius has an easy voyage home: 'growing weary of wandring, I returned into my native country'.[81]

Gabriel de Foigny's *La Terre Australe connue* (1676)

Gabriel de Foigny's *La Terre Australe connue*, first published in 1676, was translated to English as *A New Discovery of Terra Incognita Australis, or the Southern World* in 1693. The original English version is now rare, and yet, in its time, Foigny's work was well read, running into numerous later editions including in other European languages.[82] In a recent English translation, referred to here, Foigny's work is more correctly renamed as *The Southern Land, Known*.[83] The imaginary voyage follows the adventures of a fictional French traveller named Nicolas Sadeur. Orphaned as a child, he is, curiously, a hermaphrodite. Sadeur is shipwrecked on *Terre Australe* and stays 35 years on the continent. The 'Australians' he encounters there are strong and tall (standing approximately two and a half metres), red-skinned and they wear no clothes. Most unusually of all, the Australians too are hermaphrodites. In traditional utopian fashion, they live a well-regulated life, in an established society (they have records dating back approximately 8,000 years).[84] Although Sadeur admires the Australians' philosophy at the outset, his impressions change over time. As in Hall's text, this view of the southern world can be described as dystopian rather than utopian.

Fausett reads the book as a successor to More's *Utopia* and forerunner of Swift's *Gulliver's Travels*.[85] He also refers to the work's colonialist themes, noting: 'Foigny was clearly interested in a current of French thought…which favoured [the region's] exploration and colonization'.[86] In the French literary tradition, Geoffroy Atkinson labelled Foigny's work as the 'first complete novel of *Extraordinary Voyage* known'.[87] In other critical discussion of Foigny's text, George Seddon links the book with Robert Hughes' notion of Europe's 'geographic unconscious' as well as suggesting that it offers an uncanny reflection on late twentieth-century Australian society.[88] Richard Phillips reads the work as a 'radical adventure', its setting 'a space of transgression in which a heroic figure challenges all forms of boundaries', spatial and social.[89]

Foigny, like Hall, had a religious background. A Franciscan monk from the north of France, he was unfrocked for licentious behaviour. He then turned Protestant and moved to Geneva, where he is thought to have written *La Terre Australe connue*.[90] To disassociate himself from the radical views presented, Foigny claimed that the author was actually Sadeur. Foigny had already been persecuted by influential pastors for publishing earlier works without permission.[91] In *La Terre Australe connue* he is named only as an editor. Foigny told his publisher that a French bookseller named Bille had provided him with the manuscript and that a Jean Lullin, who had since died, initially approved the text for publication.[92] As Foigny would have anticipated, publication of the book elicited outraged and hostile responses. The hermaphroditic theme was seen as a vulgar attack against the church, and Pastor Amy Mestrezat deemed the work as 'unacceptable for its falsehoods, impertinences, fables, impieties and other stupidities'.[93] In 1679, Antoinette Bourignon, a French mystic, wrote a harsh review of the work, claiming:

> ...sin has disfigured in man the work of God... Instead of men being what they should be, they have become monsters in nature, divided into two imperfect sexes, unable to reproduce themselves alone – as do trees and plants, which in this respect are more perfect than men or women.[94]

Foigny was held to account for the scandalous work, but he defended his position, claiming that he had simply translated the text from the Latin original, without alteration.[95] Fausett's preface to the recent English translation of the work sets out further controversies.[96] The publisher apparently requested that Foigny provide the original manuscript, which of course he could not. But neither could the publisher produce any letter of approval for the work to be published in the first place, as no such letter had ever existed. The church demanded that Foigny confirm whether or not he shared the Australians' ideas. A legal case followed, but the charges were eventually dropped. Fausett argues that, despite the outrageous views in the text, Foigny had been treated unfairly, having been used as 'a pawn in a wider struggle between religious and secular forces in the Genevan government'.[97]

In the year Foigny died, 1692, an abridged version of *La Terre Australe connue* was published with the new title of *Les Avantures de Jacques Sadeur dans la découverte et le voiage de la Terre Australe*.[98] Some critics, such as Frédéric Lachèvre, have attributed the text to Foigny, keen to stir more controversy and gain further recognition. Others suggest it was Abbé François Raguenet, the presumed editor.[99] Various confusing changes were made, such as renaming Nicolas, the protagonist, Jacques Sadeur (who was Nicolas' father in the first edition). More significant than the origins of this modified edition is the fact that most critics up until the twentieth century drew upon this later version as the authoritative Foigny text. It was also the basis for the original English translation.[100] Further French editions of the 1692 abridged version were published in 1693 and 1705, and a 1732 edition was published in Amsterdam.[101] And yet, by the end of the eighteenth century, the work was more or less forgotten.[102]

I

The full title of the original English translation of Foigny's text promises exciting revelations:

> *A New Discovery of Terra Incognita Australis, or the Southern World, by James Sadeur, a French-Man Who, Being Cast There by a Shipwrack, Lived 35 Years in That Country, and Gives a Particular Description of the Manners, Customs, Religion, Laws, Studies, and Wars of Those Southern People, and of Some Animals Peculiar to That Place.*

In the preface, entitled 'Notice to the Reader', the narrator begins by explaining that '[m]an has no characteristic more natural than the desire to comprehend what he considers difficult and to penetrate what to many appears inaccessible'.[103] 'It is all the more astonishing', he claims (recalling the tone of Hall's narrator), 'that for four or five hundred years the existence of an unknown southern land has been suggested without anyone so far having had the courage and the inclination to make it known'.[104] Pondering the potted history of European contact with the mystical southern continent, the narrator notes: 'It is true that Magellan enjoyed for a while the glory of discovering it in 1520 in the name of "Terra del fuego," but the Dutch deprived him of that honor by proving that he only saw some islands to the south of America'.[105]

The means by which the narrator claims to have come into possession of Sadeur's original manuscript notes are then carefully outlined. The revelations these notes contain about the southern world are introduced as a resource for French national pride: 'Certainly, if I had not happened to be at Livorno in 1661 as [Sadeur] was disembarking, his memoirs would have fallen into foreign hands, which would, no doubt, have robbed him of this glory'.[106] The narrator goes on to describe the scene of their coincidental meeting:

> I was at the docks when the vessel that brought [Sadeur] from Madagascar anchored… our author…slipped off the gangplank and fell into the water with a small suitcase he was carrying. The fellow was tragically dying in port, without anyone lifting a finger to save him. I took pity…[107]

Sadeur, while grateful to be rescued from drowning, is also thankful to have the chance to reveal his knowledge of the southern continent: 'He repeated several times that he believed I was his angel and that God had sent me to bear witness to his story'.[108] Despite all efforts to keep him alive, Sadeur's health deteriorates and he dies the next day. The narrator explains that he was entrusted with

Sadeur's few possessions, including the manuscript notes of his adventures in the southern world from which he had only just returned.[109] Setting up another foil designed to draw the reader further into the illusion of textual authenticity, the narrator claims to have personally guarded the valuable documents for a period of 15 years, that is, long after it would have been possible for the claims made to be fully investigated. As the narrator explains: 'I have kept it for fifteen years as an inestimable treasure and have at last decided to publish it because, in revealing the workings of divine wisdom, it obliges us to admire the latter's influence'.[110] Anticipating the public response of disbelief to this radical vision of life in the southern world, the narrator asks that readers broaden the limits of their imagination: 'The merest tincture of reason suffices to persuade one that, because nothing in this story is impossible, one should at least suspend judgement as to what might be possible or real. In any case, I have reproduced our Author's text as closely as possible...'[111]

II

The account of Sadeur's adventures opens with a long and detailed explanation of the traveller's life and hardships. 'My father was Jaques Sadeur and my mother, Guillemette Ottin, both of them from Chatillon-sur-Bar in the district of Rethel in Champagne, a province of France'.[112] Sadeur's father was a skilled mathematician. Both parents were ultimately lost in a shipwreck but Sadeur survived.[113] 'I was just beginning a career of tragedy', Sadeur relates, 'that has already lasted fifty-five years and has been filled with so many and such strange catastrophes that I would scarcely be believed even if I were able to recount them all'.[114] Sadeur's journey is a longwinded adventure, with visits to a number of 'halfway' houses.[115] These are transitional in-between points from which to look forwards or backwards towards Europe or the antipodes and to view either world from a middle ground. The first of these visits is to the interior of Africa. Later, in a corresponding transition back to the familiar world, Sadeur returns to Europe via Madagascar.

Linking the adventures of a fictional traveller to a real voyage of discovery was to become one of the most common strategies used in eighteenth-century imaginary voyages to lend historical realism. Foigny's acknowledged source was Quirós,[116] but this imaginary voyage was likely to have been based on accounts of contemporary travels to the antipodes that followed a different course from that of Quirós, who crossed the Pacific from the Americas. The route taken by Foigny's traveller is via Africa and the Indian Ocean. In contemporaneous examples of imaginary voyage literature, Denis Vairasse made *The History of the Sevarites or Sevarambi* [*L'Histoire des Sevarambes*] (first published in 1675) convincing by linking the adventures of his fictional traveller, Captain Siden, to the 1656 shipwreck of the Dutch ship *Vergulde Draeck*, on the west coast of the Australian landmass.[117] In the following century, Swift claimed that Gulliver was William Dampier's cousin, travelling with Dampier on the *Roebuck*. Defoe based his character Robinson Crusoe on the real-life experience of Alexander Selkirk, marooned from August 1704 to February 1709 on Juan Fernández Island off South America.

The dangerous heroism of venturing into the southern world is more pronounced in Foigny's work than it is in Hall's. In Foigny's story, Sadeur undergoes a series of kidnappings and shipwrecks until, finally, he is cast away at sea in the vicinity of the southern continent:

> I floated for several hours on my plank, tossed about in a way I can only recall with a shudder: at times the violence of the waves dragged me under; at other times it rolled me over and over. I was unable to endure this treatment for long and passed out, after which I do not know what became of me nor what force preserved my life. All I remember is that on coming to and opening my eyes I found the sea calm and saw an island nearby.[118]

Sadeur's first encounter with inhabitants of the southern world is with the 'Urgs', flying creatures, which he later learns are a greatly feared enemy of the Australians.[119] He asks the reader 'not to be astonished that I call these birds "beasts"; their extraordinary size amazed me'.[120] 'I engaged one of them', Sadeur relates, 'and gave it such a clout that they were obliged to retreat, and then their joyful voices turned into rude shouts'.[121] Unable to defend himself for long, Sadeur is carried off by one of the Urgs, but eventually manages to attack it, dramatically, in midflight: 'in a fit of fury I went for its throat and then was able to tear out its eyes with my teeth'.[122]

III

The conflict with the Urgs is a ritual of entrance to the southern world. Luckily for Sadeur, who lost consciousness in the ordeal, the Australian 'coast guard' witnessed his brave display and fought off or killed the remaining attacking Urgs. Sadeur is then taken to the Australians who, as Sadeur explains, 'made a formal presentation of me, with the dead birds at my feet, calling the episode in their language the "Miraculous Victory of the Conqueror"'.[123] Nudity is customary for the Australians and Sadeur too is naked when he arrives. He is also bleeding from his injuries, suggesting a symbolic rebirth (common in classical utopias).[124] While his nakedness presents him as vulnerable and open to the influences of the antipodean world, Sadeur also represents a culturally transformative intervention from the outside. The Australians generally 'receive among themselves only those whose birthplace, nation, and ways are known to them'.[125] However, since Sadeur is a hermaphrodite like them, and also because they have 'admiration for [Sadeur's] valiant struggle', they admit him 'without question into the nearest community'.[126] He has an unexpectedly sensual welcome, 'where everyone came to kiss my hands and "parts"'.[127] Following this strange ritual, Sadeur is pleased to find that his 'board and lodging were provided for with a thoroughness and decency surpassing any in Europe'.[128] Sadeur reflects: 'I could scarcely believe what I was seeing was real. Sometimes I said to myself that I must be either dead or mad, even when I managed to convince myself that I was indeed alive and sane'.[129]

Foigny, like Hall, positions the southern continent using geographical coordinates, with the imagined world stretching southward from 40 degrees latitude.[130] At the polar end of the continent there are 'prodigious mountains far higher and more inaccessible than the Pyrenees between France and Spain'.[131] The southern continent is immense, with 15,000 'seizains', or provinces, home to a staggering 138 million Australians.[132] One could say that the density of human population is a measure of how much imaginative space there was on offer in the antipodes. Remarkably, 'the interior of the Southern Land is without a single mountain', and this is because 'the Australians had flattened them all'.[133] As a consequence, there is always even sunlight and there are no seasons, a fact, the narrator suggests, that 'will surprise the geographers'.[134] The result is 'a sort of perpetual summer…bringing everything to perfection at all times'.[135] This means that there are 'no flies, caterpillars, or any kind of insect, and they do not know spiders, snakes, or other venomous creatures'.[136] 'In a word', Sadeur explains, 'it is an earthly paradise that, while containing all the riches and curiosities imaginable, is exempt from the irritations of our world'.[137]

The Australians have a strict policy on reproductive purity: 'Each Australian has both sexes, and if a child happens to be born with only one, they kill it as a monster'.[138] Likely fictional sources for Foigny's version of the hermaphroditic theme include Hall's *Mundus alter et idem* and Thomas Artus' *Les Hermaphrodites*, which was also published in 1605.[139] The hermaphroditism is a symbolic manifestation of the desire to imagine the antipodes as an extreme, aberrant other. Eluding categorization, it can also be considered as a symbol of cultural hybridity that suggests a duality of perception, southern but northern, male but female, a state of doubleness and indeterminacy in terms of identity. Foigny's weird, hybrid images of the Australians have recently taken on new life in a series of remarkable paintings by Julia Ciccarone, inspired by Foigny's narrative. Shown in Melbourne in 1996 at her *Fictitious Voyages* exhibition, this series is a visual commentary on the book's themes of hermaphroditism and colonialism.[140] Reproduced here are: 'The Urgs' (Figure 11), 'Birth of the Australian' (Figure 12) and 'Birth of the Europeans' (Figure 13). Ciccarone also exhibited paintings inspired by *The Life and Adventures of Peter Wilkins*, four of which are reproduced in Chapter Three.

The imagined world of the southern continent is a place of miracles and wonders, with the Australians creating animals from crushed flowers and liquid. Sadeur lists 12 similarly amazing feats and observes many inventions during his time on the continent.[141] However, as in Hall's *Mundus alter et idem*, conflict and rivalry are a problem – both with the Urgs (Sadeur's own experience on arrival had demonstrated this) and also with the 'Fundians'. The area called 'Fund' is 'ruled by ten or twelve kings, who regularly engage in cruel wars against each other and seek to invade the austral lands'.[142] A satirical twist in the story that is striking from a postcolonial perspective is the mention of 'monsters', who cause further ongoing conflict and are said to arrive in ships from places unknown to the Australians. This is actually a confusing reference to an original Pre-Adamite race from which, according to the Australians, Europeans also evolved: 'when the island became overpopulated, they invented ways of migrating to neighbouring lands and spread their violent ways, with the resulting history of disorders that we know – this being our origin, according to the Australians'.[143] So, while the Europeans are the monsters who arrive from afar, they are also the original inhabitants. This literary device, which is likewise seen in Hall's text, is an early indication in the imaginary voyage tradition of what was to become a common theme: of past European presence in the antipodes. The world Sadeur describes is, in a basic sense, already claimed as European.

During his time in the southern world Sadeur has lengthy discussions with a 'venerable old man named Suains' who, he explains, 'defended my cause several times…having witnessed my combat with the birds'.[144] They compare the relative merits of European and Australian society but disagree on philosophical grounds. Sadeur is ultimately sentenced to death for his intimacy with a Fundian woman (amongst other related offences). Disillusioned, he eventually escapes the southern continent on the back of an Urg he caught and tamed.[145] Fausett summarizes well the nature of this society when he writes that the Australians are '[c]arried away by their rationalist powers, they live in a cocoon of abstractions, a kind of collective autism'.[146] The satire is double-edged, however, as Fausett also explains: 'A traditional (some would say reactionary) position is represented by his hero Nicolas Sadeur; a radical, or enlightened, position, by the society he visits. Either position could be seen as a positive ideal or as a cynical parody on the author's part'.[147] The figure of the hermaphrodite was ideal for carrying this kind of imaginative and moral ambiguity.

Figure 11. Julia Ciccarone, 'The Urgs' (1995).

Figure 12. Julia Ciccarone, 'Birth of the Australian' (1995).

Figure 13. Julia Ciccarone, 'Birth of the Europeans' (1995).

As in many of the imaginary voyages that would follow, in this story the text was able to straddle its contradictions and have it both ways in relation to the new antipodean space. If the Europeans were originators of the antipodean society, they had an ancestral right to return, and their entry, on whatever terms, was a re-entry and a homecoming; and yet, they were also perceived as strangers and monsters. If the antipodean place was paradise, then its inhabitants, whatever their social, sexual or physiological peculiarities, were part of an innocent world, where strangers could enjoy immunity from the moral and religious constraints of Europe; and yet, this innocence could also be viewed as ignorance inviting correction by the visitors. If the new land was a heaven on earth, then the inhabitants were welcoming angels, and it was right to enter, enjoy the fruits of that paradise and provide wise leadership; but if the new land was a hell on earth, the inhabitants were savages who were violent or morally lax and therefore needed to be thwarted, tamed and civilized. And, at the level of the narrative, to achieve these paradoxical effects, truth and fiction merged, mingled and changed places accordingly. However clearly readers may have understood that these stories could not be entirely true, their meticulously orchestrated connections with contemporary realities, their consolidation of old mythologies – coupled with the lack of knowledge of what the truth of the antipodes might be – made the imaginary voyage genre a particularly rich terrain for imaginative free play over the coming centuries.

Chapter 3

EXOTICISM AND ROMANTICISM

> The greatest liar has his believers, as well as the basest writer his readers; and it often happens that a lie only needs to be believed for an hour, in order to reach its purpose... Falseness flies, and truth limps behind; thus when men realize the deception, it is already too late: the hit has already gone home, and the lie has achieved its effect.
>
> – Jonathan Swift, in the *Examiner* (1710)[1]

Proposals for colonization, put forward by interested nations in the seventeenth century, laid the groundwork for exploration through voyages of discovery, and yet, in the first half of the eighteenth century, the fraction of the total area of the antipodes explored was relatively small. Maps featured blank spaces spreading from the western coast of the Americas right across the Pacific to the western coast of the Australian landmass, and the search was on to find the elusive Northwest Passage to the South Seas.[2] Major Pacific island groups such as the Hawaiian, Samoan and Society Islands, New Caledonia and New Zealand, remained unknown or practically unexplored, and the eastern coast of the Australian continent had not yet been discovered. The technical challenges of sea travel were an ongoing obstacle and there were also financial and political barriers to overcome. The extent of uncharted space understandably raised hopes of finding an abundance of natural resources for trade as well as room for colonies on a scale unheard of in the Portuguese, Dutch, British and French empires. However, most of the land surveyed by the Dutch, despite the promising possibilities that it raised, showed no significant signs of being able to provide useful natural resources. Together with internal political and economic difficulties in Europe, this deterred the Dutch from sending further voyages to the antipodes.[3] On the other hand, the continuing vacuum in knowledge had the opposite effect on rival nations Britain and France, which went on to explore and chart most of the region during the course of the eighteenth century.

Many of the discovery voyages of the late seventeenth century and the early eighteenth century were piratical or privateering expeditions rather than being government sponsored.[4] In 1688 and again in 1699, English buccaneer William Dampier explored the western coast of the Australian continent. He is remembered for his impression of the Aboriginal people, recorded in *A New Voyage Round the World* (1697), as the 'miserablest People in the World... they differ but little from Brutes', rating the people of New Holland at the lowest end of a spectrum of human types.[5] This view would stay in the minds of explorers throughout the eighteenth century. In 1770, for example, botanist Joseph Banks referred to Dampier's descriptions in his journal written aboard the *Endeavour*. Sighting occasional Aborigines along Australia's eastern coast, Banks admitted to not being able to control the effect of his preconceptions, writing:

> We stood in with the land near enough to discern 5 people who appeard through our glasses to be enormously black: so far did the prejudices which we had built on Dampiers account influence us that we fancied we could see their Colour when we could scarce distinguish whether or not they were men.[6]

Explorers often 'found' what they expected to find, based on received traditions and accounts.

Maps, too, could manipulate expectations and shape preconceptions. Jonathan Swift was well aware of the visual power of maps, which, like his own fiction, could fill in the gaps in knowledge with colourful imaginary landscapes. The following stanza, from his 'On Poetry: A Rhapsody', refers to cartographers' practice of including ornately drawn, stylized animals on African maps:

> So geographers in *Afric*-maps,
> With Savage-Pictures fill their gaps;
> And o'er uninhabitable downs
> Place Elephants for want of towns.[7]

Many maps of the region of the antipodes in the sixteenth and seventeenth centuries featured illustrations of elephants and other beasts, waterspouts and symbols of natural fertility as well as a set of standard images depicting trade and settlement (such as European ships, gold, other treasures and items for trade). Illustrations were usually set in the margins of maps, or in large uncharted spaces, including the centre of the projected southern continent. Justus Danckerts' map 'India quae Orientalis' (c. 1690) (Figure 14) and Vincenzo Coronelli's map 'Nuova Guinea' (1697) (Figure 15), for example, both have images of elephants placed in the continent's interior. Dutch maps, which had been exported in huge numbers to an international market throughout the seventeenth century, were well known for their elaborate detail and

Figure 14. Justus Danckerts, 'India quae Orientalis' (c. 1690).

embellishment.[8] The incidental illustrations were part of a repertoire of imagery associated with the unknown, wherever that unknown happened to be. In a similarly generalizing way, the desire to know the world fully, in geographical terms, was expressed in the conventional, but misleading, title given to world maps over the next century: 'A Complete Map of the World'. It must have been clear to viewers, by the numerous absent coastlines and the blank spaces on these maps, that the world map was by no means complete. What maps were doing was extrapolating in a manner that has similarities with stories of imaginary voyages. Starting from a basis of limited empirical information, they reached out, with a semblance of authority, into unknown spaces, even if only on the two-dimensional plane.

The tradition of imagining the antipodes by creatively speculating on the region's geographical and socio-cultural makeup was at odds with the aims of the systematically determined and scientifically detached logic of empirical observation and recording that was to become fashionable.[9] A gradual shift in emphasis towards valuing empirical methods had begun in the Middle Ages and was developed more fully towards the end of the seventeenth century, influenced by figures such as John Locke.[10] Ancient myths, including those which had promoted the belief in a torrid zone broaching the equator and a southern people characterized by bizarre physical abnormalities, were being

Figure 15. Vincenzo Coronelli, 'Nuova Guinea' (1697).

partially dispelled or at least diluted by the gradual influx of reported facts. As may be expected, early myths would be viewed as either too far-fetched or too simplistic in the face of accumulating evidence of the breadth of antipodean natural and cultural diversity. On the other hand, the same myths indisputably continued to inspire exploratory ventures.

By the end of the seventeenth century, as one critic puts it, 'the history of cartography had become a history of contractual abuse between map maker and map user'.[11] Whereas the earlier cartographers took pride in displaying mythical regions alongside known places with little inclination to differentiate one from the other, cartographers in the eighteenth century produced maps with fewer artistic embellishments. Maps gradually became more accurate and more consistent. Some early eighteenth-century maps make the absence of empirical knowledge a key feature, visually framing the antipodean region with boundary lines indicating the perimeters of knowledge but preserving a substantially blank centre as the point of focus. In 1714, for example, the respected French

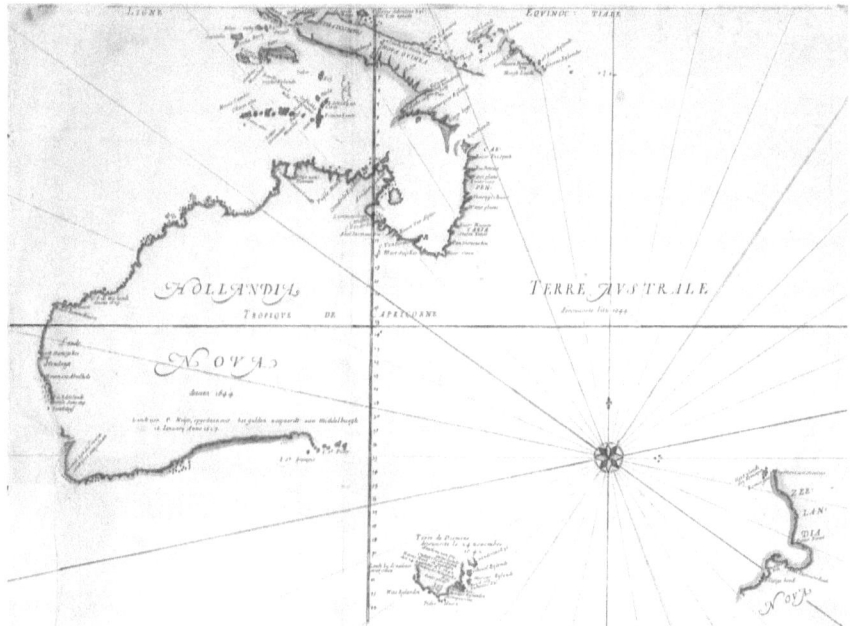

Figure 16. Melchisédech Thévenot, 'Hollandia Nova' (1663).

cartographer Guillaume de l'Isle published his map, 'Hémisphère Méridional', which shows the southern hemisphere based on an Antarctic polar projection with ocean at the southern pole.[12] This was the most famous of a number of maps that were based on Melchisédech Thévenot's map of 1663, 'Hollandia Nova' (Figure 16).[13] There is no mention of any *incognita* on these maps, but the Australian landmass, as was commonly the case, is labelled both as *Terre Australe* and *Nouvelle Hollande* (on de l'Isle's map) or *Hollandia Nova* (on Thévenot's map), indicating the various European national claims to knowledge of that space. The large, sketchy area of the southern continent seems to be filled with the potential for a vast new world to be drawn. In its own way the projected blankness helped to justify a continuing program of discovery voyages.[14]

In some especially revealing examples, blank spaces on maps were annotated with descriptions outlining their potential for colonization. Two later examples, John Senex' world map of 1725[15] and Emanuel Bowen's 'A Complete Map of the Southern Continent' of 1744 (Figure 17), fill in the blanks at the centre of the map with block paragraphs of text. The notes on Senex' map describe the soil of Hollandia Nova as 'barren and Desart', home to 'Rats as great as Cats', and 'vast numbers of troublesome Flies'. In the case of Bowen's map two decades later, the overlaid notes have a positively heroic

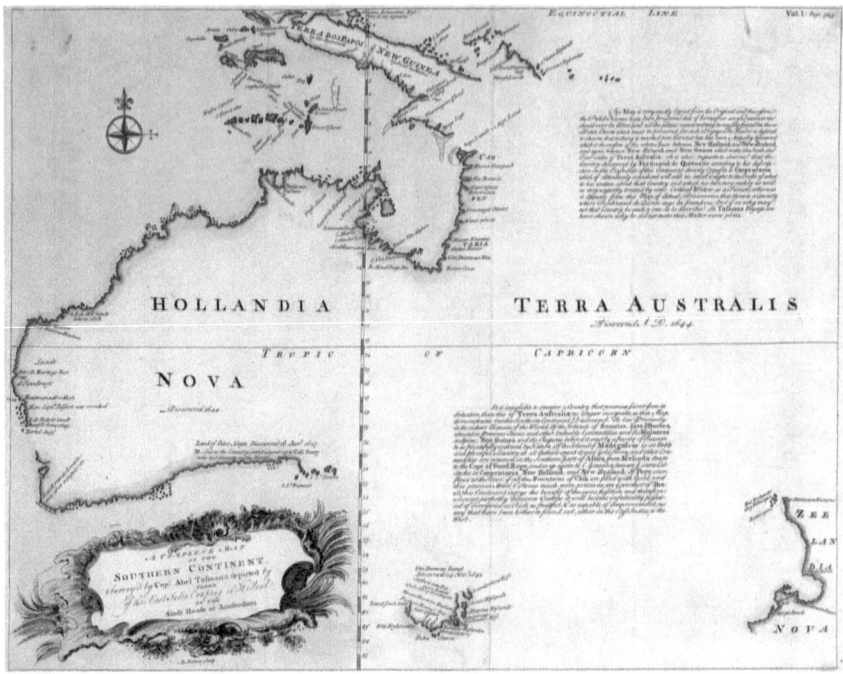

Figure 17. Emanuel Bowen, 'A Complete Map of the Southern Continent' (1744).

tone, putting forward Bowen's own argument for the value of further exploration of the southern continent with the optimistic prediction that:

> Whoever perfectly discovers and settles it will become infalliably possessed of Territories, as Rich, and fruitful, and as capable of Improvement, as any that have been hither to found out, either in the East Indies, or the West.

Bowen took the position that because the new continent lay at the same latitude as the 'rich lands' of Sumatra, Java, the Moluccas, Peru and Chile, it too must 'overflow with gems, ivory, precious metals and other valuable commodities'. This map also includes notes overlaying the area of Pieter Nuytsland (on the southern coast of today's Western Australia), which comment favourably on the climate there. One note reads: 'This is the country seated according to Pury in the best climate in the world'. Jean Pierre Pury was a Swiss trader who, in 1718, had put to Dutch authorities a plan to colonize the region around Pieter Nuytsland. Pury had earlier been employed by the Dutch East India Company, and he is remembered for his claim that the most suitable climates for human settlement are at latitudes 35 degrees north and south of the equator. In this example, a written narrative on the map spells out the benefits of colonization and gives the viewer an added framework for interpretation. The unknown is brought into reach in an act of speculation presented as an invitation.

The year 1720, famous for the controversial collapse of the South Sea Company, marked a hiatus in European attitudes to trade. Bernard Mandeville makes reference to what came to be known as the 'South Sea Bubble' in his satirical work *The Fable of the Bees* (1729).[16] An investigation later found that the Company had been illegally lobbied and had misrepresented its accounts. However, this stark warning – that speculation must be balanced by shrewd financial judgement – did little to deter writers of imaginary voyages. Daniel Defoe's *Robinson Crusoe* (1719) had been published the year before the failure of the South Sea Company. Defoe's *A New Voyage Round the World* (1724)[17] and Jonathan Swift's *Gulliver's Travels* (1726) appeared soon after. *Robinson Crusoe* and *Gulliver's Travels* very quickly became the models for adventure writers in all genres and retain their allure even now.

The Colour of Truth

> ...adventures, real or imaginary...may serve as pilot's charts, or maps of those parts of the world, which every one may chance to travel through; and in this light they are public benefits.
> – *Monthly Review* (1751)[18]

In this quotation, taken from a contemporary review of Tobias Smollet's satirical narrative *The Adventures of Peregrine Pickle* (1751), no distinction is made between real and imaginary adventures. Like maps, both kinds of travel writing act as guides for readers to imagine faraway regions. Whether factual or fictional, accounts of voyages to distant places had the liberating effect of transporting readers to new imaginative terrains. 'If we consider the true use of these writings', suggests the reviewer, 'it is more to be lamented that we have so few of them, than that there are too many. And where is the traveller who would complain of the number of maps, or journals, designed to point him out his way through the number of different roads that choice or chance may engage him in?'[19]

Real and imaginary voyages were, of course, different – at least, that is, when readers could tell them apart.[20] A contributor to the *Monthly Review* in 1750 wrote: 'Genuine voyage accounts are generally looked upon as truth' and because of this they have 'a much stronger claim to the reader's attention, than the most striking incidents in a novel or romance'.[21] No matter how exotic the scenes of a novel were, for the *Peregrine Pickle* reviewer the true account had an appeal that fiction could only begin to match by 'borrowing from truth its colour at least, in favour of fiction'.[22] Writers of imaginary voyages had routinely 'borrowed from truth', but some novelists were now leaning towards a more developed characterization of real life that would later be associated with romanticism and related aesthetic tendencies. This contemporary commentary is linked with debates hinting at stylistic tensions that would ultimately take the novel in new directions. Imaginary voyages, while recognized as a precursor to the modern realist novel, later fell out of favour because their very literal realism came to be seen as abrupt and unsophisticated in contrast to the more subtle characterization of nineteenth-century novels.

At the midpoint of the eighteenth century, it was a matter of achieving stylistic balance. At the same time as readers were interested in the detailed reporting of the facts of voyages, they also hoped for accounts that were written in an accessible manner and had a carefully considered balance between detail and interesting scenes. Narrative style came to be considered just as important as an exacting adherence to the truth, a point the editors of the *Monthly Review* reflected upon when they complained that 'sea journals usually afford matter for much entertainment…though little instruction'. This, they explained, is because sailors

> commonly stuff their journals full of bearings and distances, sea phrases and terms, with an eternal succession of the names of their ships' tackle and an endless series of such common events as always occur on that element, all of which are apt to exercise the reader's patience rather too much, especially if he be a meer land-man, as most readers are.[23]

'Instruction', in this context, suggests a conscious fashioning of ideas to serve the purpose of educating readers. The editors praise the young author of a *Journal of the Boscawen's Voyage to Bombay in the East Indies* for 'rationally employing the tedious hours of his passage' in making a thoughtfully constructed narrative rather than including the kinds of daily details that would bore readers. They conclude: 'We wish that such instances were more common'.[24] In his *Elements of Criticism* (1762), Scottish philosopher Henry Home described narrative as an evocative force equivalent to that of actual perception, claiming: 'a lively and accurate description…raises in me ideas no less distinct than if I had been originally an eye-witness'. Home described this positively as an 'ideal presence' and, drawing a correspondence with the writing of history, argued: 'Even genuine history has no command over our passions but by ideal presence only; and consequently...it stands upon the same footing with fable'. Fable, for Home, is 'generally more successful than history', while both depend 'on the vivacity of the ideas they raise'.[25]

Putting stylistic considerations foremost, some writers of genuine voyage accounts reportedly took the example of travel fiction as a guide to form and structure. Remarkably, for example, John Bell's *Travels from St. Petersburg in Russia to Various Parts of Asia* (1763) is said to have used *Gulliver's Travels* as a model. Bell is reported to have sought advice from the Scottish historian William Robertson, enquiring as to 'the style and the book of travels which he would recommend him to adopt for his guide', to which the historian replied: 'Take *Gulliver's Travels* for your model, and you cannot go wrong'.[26] Bell went on to produce what the *Quarterly Review* described as 'the best model perhaps for travel writing in the English language'.[27] In the eyes of some later critics, the early novel even became analogous to historical narrative. For example, in 1775, French author Baculard d'Arnaud, pronouncing the compelling power of realism to convey an intimate sense of the events of real life, wrote: 'our best history, leaving aside the sacred scriptures, is the least crude and most realistic novel'.[28]

Literary romance influenced important figures in the world of publishing in the second half of the eighteenth century, when the popularity of imaginary voyages rose to its peak. These included John Hawkesworth, editor of *An Account of the Voyages Undertaken by the Order of His Present Majesty, for Making Discoveries in the Southern Hemisphere* (1773), covering the voyages of John Byron, Samuel Wallis, Philip Carteret and James Cook.[29] Hawkesworth had earlier translated the famous French romance *Télémaque* (1699) by François Fenelon into English as *The Adventures of Telemachus, the Son of Ulysses* (1754).[30] Hawkesworth also edited and introduced various selections of the literature and letters of Jonathan Swift.[31] Although Hawkesworth had not travelled on any of the Pacific discovery voyages himself, he was steeped in the traditions of literary romance and the work of Swift in particular. Presumably it was for this very reason, that is, for his knowledge of the stylistic conventions of well-crafted literary fiction, that Hawkesworth was chosen to produce a voyage account that has since become a hallmark of eighteenth-century European travel literature. The many complex issues of textual authenticity in voyage accounts applied to Hawkesworth as much as to any writer. The *Monthly Review*, for one, took Hawkesworth to task over his alleged misrepresentation, in a professedly documentary work, of nautical detail in Cook's manuscript of his first voyage, writing: 'the *Captain* is not always to be blamed for what the *Doctor* has said'.[32]

It is important to remember that around this time the very concepts of fantasy and realism were not yet in use. Fantasy, as a term denoting genre, is often used anachronistically.³³ The word is used cautiously in this book, not in reference to literary genres but to the imaginative aspects of the European construction of the antipodes. When Kathryn Hume defines fantasy, it is as 'the deliberate departure from the limits of what is usually accepted as real and normal'. This definition, while it covers a range of literature from 'the trivial escapes of pastoral and adventure stories to the religious visions of Langland and Dante', notably excludes 'realistic novels and some satiric and picaresque works'.³⁴ Like fantasy, realism, according to standard dictionary definitions, had no usage as a literary term whatsoever prior to the early nineteenth century. The word 'realist', meaning 'a person whose occupation is with things rather than words', was in use from the early seventeenth century, but it had little relation to literary realism as it is understood today.³⁵

Robert Paltock's *The Life and Adventures of Peter Wilkins* (1750)

In 1750, the same year that Jean-Jacques Rousseau wrote *Discourse on the Arts and Sciences*,³⁶ *The Life and Adventures of Peter Wilkins* was published anonymously in London.³⁷ Classified by some critics as an imaginary voyage (it can also be described as a 'family robinsonade'³⁸) and by others as an early expression of romanticism, the work focusses on perhaps the most unorthodox of any cross-cultural relationship in the literature of imaginary voyages. It is the first example in which the cross-breeding of human with another species leaves genetic traces in the offspring.³⁹ The mechanical flying machine in *Peter Wilkins* is another notable feature. Both these themes in fiction were to become fashionable in the course of the nineteenth century.⁴⁰ Admired by the English romantics themselves, *Peter Wilkins* is a text that is important not only because it was popular and influential as a fictional work but because of the light that it casts on historical connections between the imaginary voyage genre, romanticism and colonialism.

A pseudonymous contributor to the *Monthly Magazine, or British Register* first identified Robert Paltock as the author of *Peter Wilkins* in 1802.⁴¹ He may have been the author of another contemporary imaginary voyage, *A Narrative of the Life and Astonishing Adventures of John Daniel* (1751),⁴² which also utilized the setting of a southern land and featured a flying machine.⁴³ *Peter Wilkins* was very widely read in Europe in the eighteenth and nineteenth centuries. Aside from *Robinson Crusoe* and *Gulliver's Travels*, it is the best-known example of an imaginary voyage discussed in this book. Recognized as a major source for later literary works,⁴⁴ it was published in French translation in 1763 and a German abridged version in 1767. In 1783 a second English edition was published. Thomas Stothard's commissioned illustrations 'heightened the gentle eroticism' and gave the work renewed appeal.⁴⁵ Through the nineteenth century it was published regularly in Britain and North America, sometimes in altered and abridged versions.

In the preface to the 1884 edition, A. H. Bullen deemed *Peter Wilkins* to be as important as the *Odyssey* and *Arabian Nights*, two archetypal accounts of imaginary travels. *Peter Wilkins*, to his mind, had earned its position among these famous texts as one of 'the world's benefactors'.⁴⁶ Bullen mentioned Swift, making the point that 'the author's obligations to Swift in the latter part of the book are considerable'. He argued, however, that 'in describing how Peter Wilkins ordered his life on the lonely island', Paltock 'was largely indebted to Defoe'.⁴⁷ In his introduction to the 1973 edition of *Peter Wilkins*, Christopher Bentley also identifies many of the thematic features of *Robinson Crusoe*, including 'the wayward youth determined to go to sea, capture by pirates, escape, encounters with savage beasts, storms, shipwreck, privations, moralizings and self-reproaches, and a solitary castaway with few resources developing a personal technology in order to master an unfamiliar environment'.⁴⁸ The characters in *Peter Wilkins* were praised for their carefully crafted complexity. In 1852, Leigh Hunt praised Paltock's female character of Youwarkee especially highly, claiming: 'a sweeter creature [than Youwarkee] is not to be found in books; and she does him immortal honour'.⁴⁹ More recently, Peter Fitting describes Paltock's adaptation of Defoe's Friday figure into a winged woman in terms of a shift from the realism of Defoe to a 'charming kind of fantasy'.⁵⁰ *Peter Wilkins* is mentioned in various histories of English literature as 'a minor classic', 'graceful' and 'homely yet sensitive and graphic in style'.⁵¹ The *Times Literary Supplement*, reviewing a new edition in 1925, regretted that *Peter Wilkins* had 'never taken its deserved place in the lists of popular literature'.⁵²

Not all critics, however, were impressed with *Peter Wilkins*. The *Monthly Review* was the first journal to respond to the book's publication. This was one of the two major critical journals of the second half of the eighteenth century (the other being the *Critical Review*), and may have been read by as much as 25 per cent of the literate population in Britain.⁵³ This reviewer disliked the way the author had tried to combine, as they saw it, elements of the different styles of Swift and Defoe, remarking:

> Here is a very strange performance indeed. It seems to be the illegitimate offspring of no very natural conjunction betwixt *Gulliver's Travels* and *Robinson Crusoe*; but much inferior to the meaner of these two performances, either as to entertainment or utility. It has all that is impossible in the one, or improbable in the other, without the wit and spirit of the first or the just strokes of nature and useful lessons of

morality in the second… [I]f the invention of wings for mankind to fly with, is a sufficient amends for all the dullness and unmeaning extravagancies of this author, we are willing to allow that his book has some merit; and that he deserves some encouragement at least as an able mechanic, if not as a good author.[54]

This critic's difficulty is with the mixing of genres and styles, and of utility with entertainment. Writing from a late nineteenth-century perspective, Walter Raleigh was also unimpressed with Paltock's work but for different reasons, assessing the book's stylistic qualities in disparaging terms with the words:

…his fancy, graceful though it is, is mechanical and mathematical in essence; there is nothing in it of the shaping spirit of imagination… All the realistic flummery that surrounds the flying people, their institutions and habits, is very easily conceived, and leaves the reader cold and unmoved.[55]

George Saintsbury summarized the mixed nineteenth-century reception of the book in 1913, when he reported:

It was once fashionable to dismiss Peter as a boy's book…it has more recently been fashionable to hint a sneer at it as "sentimental" because of its presentment of a sort of fantastic and unconventional Amelia… Persons who do not care for fashion will perhaps sometimes agree that, though not exactly a masterpiece, it is a rather charming book.[56]

The work's continuing popularity in the nineteenth century, however, is evidence that in spite of reports such as these, the public reception was overwhelmingly positive.

Peter Wilkins has been associated with romanticism due to its thematic treatment of a lone European traveller, and its celebration of naturalness, expressed through a phantasmagoric erotic dimension.[57] Many of the English romantics were familiar with *Peter Wilkins*, including Charles Lamb, Percy Shelley and Mary Shelley.[58] Robert Southey, noting Walter Scott's high opinion of it as 'a work of great genius', referred to the winged people as 'the most beautiful creatures of imagination that ever were devised'.[59] Samuel Taylor Coleridge, in *Table Talk*, is reported to have described *Peter Wilkins* as 'a work of uncommon beauty', claiming it 'would require a very peculiar genius to add another tale…to "Robinson Crusoe" and "Peter Wilkins"' and explaining that he himself 'once projected such a thing' but was stopped by 'the difficulty of the preoccupied ground'. For Coleridge, the literary quality that made *Peter Wilkins* special was 'the *desert island* feeling'.[60]

Over the centuries that have passed since *Peter Wilkins* was first published, later critics, in their appraisals, continued to associate the book with the kind of imaginative expression characteristic of romanticism. John Dunlop, for example, in *The History of Fiction*, commended Paltock for creating 'a new species of beings, which are amongst the most beautiful offsprings of imagination'.[61] Soon after, in 1823, an anonymous contributor to the *Retrospective Review* suggested that 'as a work of imagination, it appeared at a season...too early'.[62] In 1927, Rowland Prothero agreed with the 1823 reviewer. In his words, '*Peter Wilkins* appeared too soon', for it appealed 'to the sense of wonder and curiosity which characterised the romantic movement'.[63] Oliver Edwards claimed that Paltock 'had a poet's imagination' and that 'his descriptions of scenes and events have a sense of wonder and a delicacy allied to their matter-of-factness which weave an enchantment all his own'. Edwards pondered the question of whether Rousseau would have read *Peter Wilkins* and speculated that 'it must have delighted him if he did'.[64] Finally, in the introduction to the 1973 edition of *Peter Wilkins*, Bentley, offering an explanation for the book's lukewarm reception when it was first published, also claims that it had come before its time. A generation later, he explains, 'the Gothic novelists and the romantic poets had transformed literary values, and *Peter Wilkins* was discovered'.[65] *Peter Wilkins* is exceptional when compared with other imaginary voyages that have had less critical attention paid to them because it was read by the romantics and remained well-liked by readers in the nineteenth century when the genre had become less fashionable. Its romantic qualities, as they were perceived, secured it a tentative place in a mainstream literary tradition. Most importantly, in the context of this study, *Peter Wilkins* was a pivotal text in that it epitomized the allure of earlier imaginary voyages with their visions of new worlds while at the same time foreshadowing stylistic aspects of the nineteenth-century novel.[66] This helped to set the pattern for the fictional journey genres of the future – notably the science fiction of space exploration.[67]

I

The extended title of *Peter Wilkins*, reprinted in full below, gives an enticing glimpse into the imaginary world the book creates:

> *The Life and Adventures of Peter Wilkins, a Cornish Man: Relating particularly, his Shipwreck near the South Pole; his wonderful Passage thro' a subterraneous Cavern into a kind of new World; his there meeting with a Gawrey or flying Woman, whose Life he preserv'd, and afterwards married her; his extraordinary Conveyance to the country of Glumms and Gawreys, or Men and Women that fly. Likewise a Description of this*

strange Country, with the Laws, Customs, and Manners of its Inhabitants, and the Author's remarkable Transactions among them. Taken from his own Mouth, in his Passage to England, from off Cape Horn *in America, in the Ship* Hector. *With an Introduction, giving an Account of the surprising Manner of his coming on board that Vessel, and his Death on his landing at* Plymouth *in the Year 1739. Illustrated with several Cuts, clearly and distinctly representing the Structure and Mechanism of the Wings of the Glumms and Gawreys, and the Manner in which they use them either to swim or fly. By R. P. a Passenger in the* Hector.[68]

Like most imaginary voyages, *Peter Wilkins* is presented as though it were a genuine manuscript. In a note on the 1973 edition, editor Bentley explains that he has only made minor corrections to the text so as to preserve the style of the original, which includes inconsistent spelling and italicization.[69] Arguably, these inconsistencies act as planned literary effects that support the claim made that the text originated in a manuscript produced from dictation. The actual text I refer to here in detail was published in Dublin in 1751 and is held in the British Library.[70] Like Foigny's narrative (see Chapter Two), *Peter Wilkins* is a deathbed recounting. In an opening address dedicated 'To the Right Honourable Elizabeth, Countess of Northumberland', the fictional persona of Robert Paltock, 'R. P.', relates: 'it might be looked upon as impertinent in me to trouble the Reader with any of my own Concerns, or the Affairs that led me into the *South Seas*'.[71] In fact, since the intermediary role R. P. plays is crucial to the success of the presentation of the fictional text as a genuine manuscript, the descriptions that he goes on to give are vital to the construction of the imagined southern world. Although R. P. may be linked directly to Robert Paltock's name, R. P. is also a fictional presence, a character in the story who claims to have received the manuscript from a dying man.

The introduction explains the elaborate tale behind the story about to be related. It begins when R. P. is rounding Cape Horn as a passenger on the ship *Hector* on the way home to England.[72] Those on board hear the cry for help of a shipwrecked castaway. However, the appearance of the man scares the sailors, who, at first, are 'very fearful of assisting, or coming near him; crying to each other he must be a Monster'.[73] This person is Peter Wilkins, described as having 'an extravagant Beard, and also long blackish Hair upon his Head'.[74] The stranger, once rescued, has no way to pay for his passage on board the ship, explaining to the surprise of the crew that he 'had been from England no less than thirty-five Years'.[75] R. P. claims to have taken pity on the old man, telling him he would accept a written account of his adventures as recompense for being transported home. On the understanding that rights for sale of the account would go to R. P., Wilkins accepts, having already 'entertained a Thought of having his Adventures written'.[76] An argument ensues, however, between the captain and R. P. over payment for the voyage. This is more significant than it first seems because it introduces a debate over human morality, the first of a series of such debates that the reader encounters, each of them destabilizing conventional notions of being civilized or savage. In fact, it is the captain who is referred to as a savage on account of his inflexible approach to payment for Wilkins' passage, a needy survivor for whom the captain has no compassion. R. P. claims to have begged the ruthless captain to understand his need, relating how he 'expostulated with the cruel Wretch on the Inhumanity of the Action'.[77] R. P.'s efforts at deferring full payment to a later date are eventually successful, 'the Savage being resolved'.[78]

The writing of the account purportedly took place on the voyage home to England, with R. P.'s assistance. R. P. reports: 'we allotted two Hours every Morning for the Purpose of writing down his Life from his own Mouth'.[79] The persona of R. P. assures the reader that his voluntary part as writer was as an impartial intermediary, explaining: 'if I would answer for his Passage and write his Life, he would communicate to me a faithful Narrative thereof'.[80] Monetary payment was less of a priority, R. P. claims, than the immediate prospect of 'the Expectation I had of being fully satisfied in what I had so long desired to know', that is, Wilkins' story.[81] In the final paragraph of the book's introduction, R. P. explains that he had never intended to take the manuscript from Wilkins once they arrived in England. He felt that such a personal story should be his own to tell, but was not planning to reveal his generosity until they had finished writing it in full. Wilkins becomes increasingly ill on the trip home and dies soon after they land. Following this tragic event, R. P. is finally in the position where he claims to have felt obliged to publish the narrative, not for his own benefit but for the memory of his friend, that it 'may prove so very interesting, and perhaps useful'.[82] In this way the text exonerates R. P. and so, symbolically, legitimates the ownership of this remarkable account of adventures.

The first four chapters of the book build up a convincing portrait of Wilkins' life, including his childhood, academy schooling, marriage, parenting and other details of his personal history. Although Wilkins' adventure begins in the familiar setting of England, it soon takes the reader farther afield. As in the case of Robinson Crusoe, Wilkins leaves his family following a domestic dispute. He has many dangerous and life-threatening experiences at sea, in Africa, and later *en route* to the South Pole.

II

There is a long period of transition between the familiar world and the fictional one that Wilkins, in this story, soon plays a very active role in protecting and ultimately controlling. It begins when Wilkins and his ship are inexplicably attracted to what appears to be a large rock in open ocean. The ship moves towards it and is wrecked on a reef at the base of a rocky promontory. Wilkins salvages a small boat as well as some stores and equipment that stay accessible in the wreckage. He takes time to recover after the shipwreck and then he cautiously explores further. His remaining possessions, which symbolize many facets of the European identity he is about to bring into the newly discovered world, are listed in a passage that explains the process of carefully selecting supplies for an exploratory venture in these terms:

> I determined on having Provisions, Instruments of divers Kinds, and necessary Utensils in plenty, to guard against Accidents as well as I could. I therefore took another Sea Chest out of the Hold of the Ship, and letting it into my Boat, replenish'd it with a Stock of Wine, Brandy, Oil, Bread, and the like, sufficient for a considerable Voyage. I also filled a large Cask with Water, and took a good Quantity of Salt, to cure what Fish I could take by the Way. I carried two Guns, two Brace of Pistols, and other Arms, with Ammunition proportionable; also an Ax or two, a Saw to cut Wood, if I should see any, and a few other Tools, which might be highly serviceable if I could land. To all these I added an old Sail, to make a Covering for my Goods and Artillery against the Weather. Thus furnished and equipped, having secur'd my Hatches on board, and every Thing that might spoil by wet, I set out (with a God's Speed) on my Expedition.[83]

Whilst sailing alongside the rocky promontory, Wilkins is alerted to the sound of nearby falling water and at its source finds 'the Water roaring on all Sides, and dashing against the Rock with a most amazing Noise'.[84] Every moment, as he puts it, he expects his 'poor little Vessel would be staved against the Rock, and I overwhelm'd with Waters'.[85]

When he ventures in his small boat to explore the area around the rocky coast, Wilkins and his boat are sucked into a dark cavern. Wilkins survives, but 'after the Commotion had in some Measure ceased' he finds himself floating on a small stream in the dark, and frightened at 'the Horror which seiz'd me, on finding myself in the blackest of Darkness, unable to perceive the smallest Glimmer of Light'.[86] Without light, Wilkins imagines his own death by collision with 'such Craggs' as 'stood out from the Rock, by Reason of the Turnings and Windings'.[87] He follows a course for a full five weeks, as he guesses it, using up all of the oil he has packed on board to keep a lantern lit while he is awake. Desperate, and beginning to lapse into a mood of despair at the prospect of his own imminent death, Wilkins casts his dire situation in these terms, which give an indication of the special style of characterization that Paltock was praised for achieving:

> I had now cut a Piece of my Shirt, for a Wick to my last Drop of Oil, which I twisted and lighted… Sitting down, I had many black Thoughts, of what must follow the Loss of my Light, which I considered as near expiring, and that, I feared, for ever. I am here, thought I, like a poor condemned Criminal, who knows his Execution is fixed for such a Day, nay such an Hour, and dies over and over in Imagination, and by the Torture of his Mind, till that Hour comes: that hour, which he so much dreads! and yet that very Hour which releases him from all farther Dread! Thus do I – my last Wick is kindled – my last Drop of Fuel is consuming! – and I am every Moment apprehending the Shocks of the Rock, the Suffocation of the Water; and, in short, thinking over my dying Thoughts, till the Snuff of my Lamp throws up its last curling expiring Flame, and then my Quietus will be presently signed, and I released from my tormenting Anxiety! Happy Minute! Come then; I only wait for thee![88]

Soon after, Wilkins is relieved to come out of the underground watercourse into a beautiful lush land. He finds 'a prodigious Lake of Water', bordered 'with a grassy Down, about half a Mile wide, of the finest Verdure I had ever seen'.[89] At first, the new land seems to be uninhabited by any large living forms whatsoever, human or otherwise. This makes Wilkins rest easy. And yet, especially at night, he worries that there may be 'savages', and imagines himself surrounded by their voices.[90] While the point is not made explicit in the text, it is important to note that the image of arrival, cast here as a rebirth, gives a sense of utter naturalness and inevitability to the voyager's arrival in the alien antipodean space. This notion, coupled with the heroism, resourcefulness, and stamina required to make the journey and survive the transitional trauma, contributes to a sense of the rightness of his entry to the imagined world.

III

As is typical in longer imaginary voyages, the bulk of the *Peter Wilkins* story takes place before the European traveller exerts a significant influence on the society he visits. Wilkins begins by gradually transforming a protective cavern grotto he discovers into a comfortable living space, domesticating his surroundings as best he can. He then claims the cavern, calling it his 'kingdom', a symbolic early indication of the scale of his later influence in this southern realm.[91] His life is 'very easy, yea even comfortable' in the cavern, with plenty of food that he collects during warm weather.[92]

After some months, to his surprise, Wilkins observes a large group of human-like beings on a lake. 'I saw a Multitude of People', he explains, but ponders why there is no sign of boats as transportation.[93] He then notices that these creatures appear, remarkably, to be able to sail 'on the Water in no Boats' and fly 'in the Air on no Wings'.[94] Wilkins deduces that it is these flying people who have been responsible for the voices he has been hearing for so long, believing himself mad. One night, resolutely, Wilkins goes armed to the entrance. Without warning, there is a loud thumping noise.[95] This is when Wilkins first meets Youwarkee. As the result of an accident while playing with other young flying creatures she has been knocked out of the sky without any of her companions noticing until it is too late for them to find her. Confused, Wilkins thinks she is Patty, his English wife. While he quickly realizes that she is not Patty, he initially decides to continue believing in the illusion, since it gives him 'infinite pleasure' and relieves him of his sense of hopeless solitude.[96] Although Youwarkee is not able to understand Wilkins' attempts to communicate with her in English, he pretends at first, to himself, that she does, reporting: 'I then spoke to her and asked her divers Questions, as if she had really been *Patty*, and understood me; in return of which, she uttered a Language I had no Idea of, though in the most musical Tone, and with the sweetest Accent I ever heard'.[97]

When Wilkins carries the injured Youwarkee to his bed in the grotto, her body feels foreign to him. He sees that Youwarkee is far more attractive than Patty, who 'would no more come up to this fair Creature, than a coarse Alewife would to Venus herself'.[98] To begin with, Wilkins does not know for certain that Youwarkee can fly because her wings are concealed. The reader later learns that the reason Youwarkee fell out of the sky is that, while flying, as she explains: '[I] was brushed so stiffly against the upper part of my *Graundee*, that I lost my bearing'.[99] The term 'Graundee' refers to the flying wings of Youwarkee's people.[100] Wilkins finds out, using a basic system of communication they develop, that the males of her species are called 'Glumms' and the females 'Gawreys'. The story of the meeting of the traveller with this exotic creature and of the relationship they build is charged with undercurrents of eroticism. Symbolically, it explores the notion of mutual attraction and mutual benefits ('for their own good') that is at the heart of colonial thinking. As Peter Hulme puts it, the theme of transracial love offers 'the ideal of cultural harmony through romance', a mysterious blending and a suggestion of cultural reciprocity.[101]

Four of the series of six illustrations included with the first edition of *The Life and Adventures of Peter Wilkins* are reproduced here, showing 'A Glumm Swimming' (Figure 18), 'A Gawrey Extended for Flight' (Figure 19), 'The Use of ye Back flap when ye Glumm flyes' (Figure 20), and a battle administered by Wilkins later in the story, 'Nasgigs Engagement with Harlokins General' (Figure 21). These R. P. claims to have sketched. Wilkins,

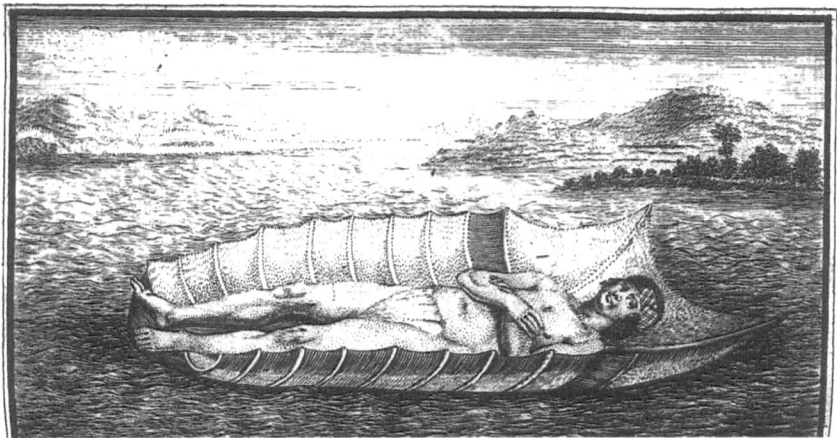

Figure 18. Louis-Philippe Boitard, 'A Glumm Swimming', from Robert Paltock, *The Life and Adventures of Peter Wilkins* (1751).

R. P. emphasizes, had personally inspected and approved them, remarking on their accuracy with the words 'such exact Delineations…perfect Resemblances'. Even 'the very Persons themselves could not have been more exact'.[102] These illustrations, with the verifying explanatory notes, demonstrate the extent to which the illusion of accuracy and faithful reporting was pursued. Also reproduced here are four of Julia Ciccarone's striking paintings, inspired by *Peter Wilkins*, that were featured in her 1996 *Fictitious Voyages* exhibition in Melbourne: 'Youwarkee: Flying Woman' (Figure 22), 'Half-Caste' (Figure 23), 'Peter Kills Harlokin' (Figure 24) and 'Hero' (Figure 25).[103]

Wilkins cares for Youwarkee and their loving relationship remains thematically central to the narrative, the two of them slowly discovering more about each other through a series of events that are lessons for both in cross-cultural communication and in their different social customs. Wilkins is able to learn adequately Youwarkee's language and she the English language. It is important to note that Wilkins arrives as a failed explorer in this imagined southern world, having given up hope of living when wrecked on the Rock. His survival of such a tragedy makes his later rise to power seem all the more heroic. His relationship with Youwarkee is significant in the context of Wilkins gaining an initial right of place in the new world, and she later helps him to win influence and respect amongst her own people.

As they begin to discuss the differences between their bodies, Youwarkee reveals to him her fear that Wilkins has likely had his Graundee wings 'Crashee', meaning slit or clipped, which is the punishment for serious crimes in her community.[104] The difficulty for Wilkins is that he does not properly

Figure 19. Louis-Philippe Boitard, 'A Gawrey Extended for Flight', from Robert Paltock, *The Life and Adventures of Peter Wilkins* (1751).

Figure 20. Louis-Philippe Boitard, 'The Use of ye Back flap when ye Glumm flyes', from Robert Paltock, *The Life and Adventures of Peter Wilkins* (1751).

Figure 21. Louis-Philippe Boitard, 'Nasgigs Engagement with Harlokins General', from Robert Paltock, *The Life and Adventures of Peter Wilkins* (1751).

understand the reference to wings because hers are kept completely hidden in their folded position, which makes them appear as though they are part of her clothing. Being injured, Youwarkee needs to keep her wings stowed away until she has fully recovered. Only then does she demonstrate her method of making them into the shape of a boat hull, which enables her species to glide effortlessly along the water's surface. Youwarkee, in fact, has never seen a conventional boat of the kind that Wilkins had salvaged, and cannot understand the need for oars. Youwarkee finally accepts his differences as natural, allowing: 'As you tell me you came from so many thousand Miles off, it is possible you may be made differently from me'.[105] Wilkins ceremonially marries Youwarkee by way of sharing 'Solemn Engagements' in the grotto. It is not a formal marriage, but the closest Wilkins can orchestrate.[106] He becomes her 'Barkatt', or husband.[107] On their wedding night, Wilkins is shocked to find her body 'being so wholly encased' in the Graundee wings, meaning, in his words, that there would be 'no conjugal Benefit from her, either to my own Gratification, or the Increase of our Species'.[108] Eventually, however, Youwarkee lets Wilkins into the soft folds of her Graundee: 'Putting

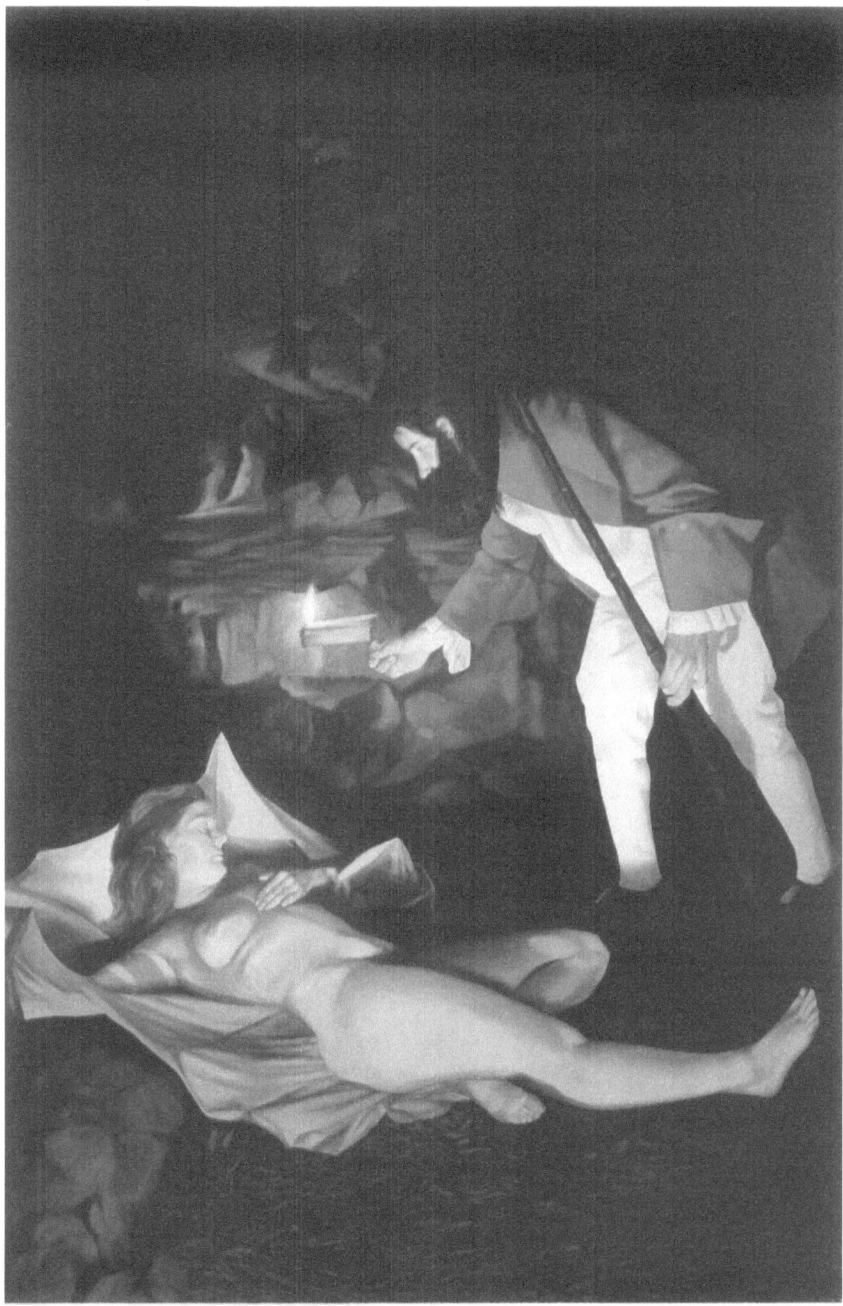

Figure 22. Julia Ciccarone, 'Youwarkee: Flying Woman' (1995).

Figure 23. Julia Ciccarone, 'Half-Caste' (1995).

Figure 24. Julia Ciccarone, 'Peter Kills Harlokin' (1995).

Figure 25. Julia Ciccarone, 'Hero' (1995).

forth my Hand again to her Bosom, the softest Skin and most delightful body, free from all Impediment, presented itself to my Wishes, and gave up itself to my Embraces'.[109] Wilkins is a courteous and gracious bridegroom, calling Youwarkee 'lady' and 'madam' until after their marriage ceremony. Even so, it takes some time before Youwarkee is willing to have her body seen in full view. Only after they are married does Youwarkee also explain that her original home is 'at a vast Distance' from the grotto.[110]

By the time of his marriage to Youwarkee, Wilkins barely remembers aspects of his life in England before going to sea. For the reader, this also makes it easy to lose the original bearings of the narrative. There has been a thematic movement deeper into the foreign territory of the new world, which is gradually made familiar to such an extent that Wilkins' European home now seems distant and strange (as with Gulliver in the land of the Houyhnhnms). When she is strong enough, Youwarkee flies to Wilkins' ship and collects more supplies, salvaging a second small boat from the shipwreck and again floating it through the cavern.[111] Wilkins is now equipped to build a home for them using salvaged tools. Wilkins and Youwarkee manage to produce children despite their obvious biological differences. The first, named Pedro, is part-human, part-Gawrey, and has the Graundee wings. Within three years two more boys are born.[112] More children follow, bringing the total to seven. Some have the Graundee and some do not. Half-human, half-animal creatures featured regularly in the mythology of the antipodes. However, creating a child with parents from entirely different worlds is perhaps the ultimate expression of cross-cultural engagement. In the real world, this was often as clear a sign of cultural violation as was murder. In this text, however, it is a harmonious and happy hybridization. As noted, *Peter Wilkins* is the first example up until 1750 of an imaginary voyage in which there is a mixing of human and other species that leaves genetic traces in the offspring.[113]

Youwarkee teaches Wilkins about her society's religious icon, 'the great *Collwar*'.[114] Traditionally, her people make 'Petitions to the Image' of Collwar. However, Wilkins moulds their family values based on his European beliefs. He reminisces: 'I would many a Time' have 'given all my interest in the Ship's Cargoe for a Bible'.[115] Youwarkee willingly follows Wilkins' Christian teachings from the beginning of their married relationship. '[Y]ou have convinced me it is better to pray to himself', she tells him, 'and I shall always do it hereafter'.[116] Thus Youwarkee fulfils the colonial desire to encounter willing acquiescence, in religious as well as sexual terms, in the new world.

In the next episode in the narrative, Youwarkee plans a flight back to her family in 'Arndrumnstake', a town in the 'Kingdom of Doorpt Swangeanti', where her father is a 'Colamb', or governor.[117] She flies a great distance there with some of the children while Wilkins stays at home with the others. He is apprehensive when she is gone, since they have not been able to find a way of communicating about distance and so he cannot picture exactly how far she is planning to fly. There are great celebrations on Youwarkee's arrival in her home town, as she was long thought dead, and 'nothing for seven Days was to be heard, through the whole district of *Arndrumnstake* but Joy and the Name of Youwarkee'.[118] While Youwarkee is gone, her brother Quangrollart returns to visit Wilkins and informs him that she is staying away longer than planned. When Wilkins gives a demonstration of his guns, Quangrollart is frightened, but Wilkins tries to persuade him not to have 'Apprehension for the Consequences of my Frolick'.[119] Wilkins' guns later become a recurring theme, 'everyone admiring my Gun, as we went'.[120] He explains: 'I had a great Inclination to gain the better of their Prejudices, and used abundance of Arguments to prove the Gun as innocent a thing as a Twig I took up'.[121] Wilkins argues for the gun's innocence at the same time as displaying its destructive power, a particularly pointed example of the strategy Mary Louise Pratt refers to as 'anti-conquest'.[122]

Wilkins ultimately learns that his arrival in the southern world is considered to be the fulfilment of an ancient prophecy amongst Youwarkee's people. This anticipates the famous case of James Cook later in the century, when Cook was greeted by thousands of Hawaiians in canoes. He was addressed as 'Lono' and ceremonial offerings were made.[123] In Youwarkee's home country, according to ancient legend, someone would arrive to protect the society against the constant threat of rebel factions, which are always rising in numbers. News of Wilkins' presence spreads fast and the flying creatures come to regard Wilkins as the prophetic figure they had been waiting for. The prophecy had been reiterated by all members of the population for 'about four times the Age of the oldest Man living'.[124] Wilkins is seen as the 'Person that can, according to our Prediction, destroy this Usurper, and restore Peace among us'.[125] An elaborate flying contraption is invented to enable Wilkins to be carried between eight Glumms on a chair with loops of rope attached. The weight of the weapons required for Wilkins to mount a confident attack against the rebels is so great that a second flying carriage needs to be constructed in order to transport them. 'If I can't use them all, I can teach others who may', he says.[126]

When Wilkins arrives in Youwarkee's homeland after a successful flight, it is as though the ancient prophecy has already come true. 'Most admirable Peter', says the king in welcome, 'you are the Glumm we depend upon to fulfil an ancient Prediction'.[127] Although at first Wilkins is reluctant to perform the role laid out in the prophecy, he expects that indeed he can, with his powerful arsenal, defeat any rival force. In Wilkins' words: 'I will go to the War in my flying Chair, and train up a Guard for my Person with Pistols and Cutlasses'.[128] From this moment onwards, Wilkins is given increasingly more power in the community, even though he resists at each stage, always modestly claiming that he is unworthy. When Wilkins ultimately agrees to the terms of the prophecy, there is a great ceremony staged, at which Wilkins announces: 'It is said, I shall destroy the Traitor of the West; I am ready to enter upon it, settle the ancient Limits of your Monarchy'.[129] In the course of Wilkins' rise to power, he is acutely aware that he is a cultural intruder. Before fully accepting his assigned role, he asks the congregation whether it is their unanimous decision that he should act in the way the prophecy dictates. To this question, 'every one answered yea'.[130] With the full support of the community, Wilkins is accorded status and authority, purely by invitation, without suggestion of any need for persuasion, let alone force. This degree of support is the key to the success of all of the subsequent reforming schemes he puts in place. In this way, through practical examples, *Peter Wilkins* makes plausible and attractive the idea of enlightened and benign colonization where the alien other is not a victim but, rather, a grateful dependant.

Chapter Fourteen chronicles, over the course of only a few pages, an astonishing series of events centring on the mass defeat of the rebels. With 'five Cannon, and three Swivel guns, and larger Quantity of Ammunition', Wilkins convincingly destroys the enemy forces.[131] Wilkins, with the assistance of 'Nasgig', personally engages 'Harlokin', the leader of the rebels. Wilkins returns, victorious, with the severed head of the enemy leader.[132] Later chapters detail further incidents in which Wilkins exerts his influence with the encouragement of the king and the people, who now support Wilkins' plans even more wholeheartedly than before because of his success in the battle to defend them. The subtitles listed for Chapter Fifteen give an idea of the range of Wilkins' reforming plans that are instituted in quick succession:

> *A Visitation of the revolted Provinces proposed by Peter; his new Name of the Country received; Religion settled in the West; Slavery abolished there;* Lasmeel *returns with* Peter; Peter *teaches him Letters; the King surprized at written Correspondence; Peter describes the Make of a Beast to the King.*[133]

The new name of the country referred to here is 'Sass Doorpt Swangeanti', which is affectionately derived from Wilkins' mispronunciation of the town's name of 'Normbdsgrsutt'.[134] When Wilkins unexpectedly retrieves a Bible from the wreckage of his ship, just as he had given up hope of ever finding one, he has the means to formally introduce Christianity. In a miraculous feat of bridging cultural divides, Wilkins translates the Bible into the local dialect, which he has now fully mastered.[135] In fact, he is even successful in influencing the beliefs of the wise 'Ragans' or elders, who have been prophesizing in their traditional way for 11,000 years.[136] The elders give him permission to install Christianity even as they continue to support the values of the prophecies that heralded Wilkins' arrival. Wilkins, therefore, now takes control in a more complex and foundational way than by the simple display of force that won him a place as a rightful and honourable leader. The contest between two radically different religious paradigms is one that Wilkins effectively wins. However, his modifications are at the invitation of the ruling representatives. It is as though Wilkins is a consultant for social reform, operating as a free agent outside of traditional social structures, but commanding great respect as a result of his perceived objectivity.[137]

Once most of his other plans are in place, Wilkins educates tradesmen in the techniques of metal forging so that weapons such as swords can be produced and so that the society will become more reliant on its own revamped resources. Already, by chance, there is a supply of the kind of metal needed to make musket balls.[138] Wilkins is cast as a war hero yet again in a second foray into resolving cross-cultural tensions between local rivals. This time he leads an armed force to 'Mount Alkoe' and overthrows a rival faction there, afterwards offering land to citizens in return for their loyalty.[139] A new colony is established in the name of the king, with Wilkins as its founder and benefactor. By this stage, Wilkins has risen to a status rivalling the king's. He now makes decisions without consultation, at which the king seems pleased as long as his own leadership is not contested directly. In this way, the notion that Indigenous cultures can thrive undisturbed, in harmony with a controlling colonial presence, is convincingly demonstrated by Peter Wilkins' story.

Wilkins rarely stops to consider that he might be irreparably changing a unique culture and that this could be seen as a loss. His impulse is always to mould the society to European standards. When his wife Youwarkee dies of a sudden illness, he leaves with little sense of attachment to the place. Perhaps this is because, as Bentley suggests, Wilkins ran out of reforming ideas.[140] Only at one point does he notice that his actions may not have benefited the flying people in the way in which he intended. This is a startling moment for the reader because it is an isolated example of European colonial influence being cast explicitly as negative. Wilkins reflects, briefly: 'I am afraid, I have put them upon another way of thinking, tho' I aimed at what we call civilizing of them'.[141] The bulk of the narrative, with its heroic portrayal of Wilkins assuming control in the antipodes, endorses the precept of European superiority. However, Wilkins' passing but illuminating moment of self-reflection on the profound influence he has had on this culture and its relationship with neighbouring societies serves to underline how rarely European literary fiction explicitly offered other voices in the debate over the relative value of colonial ventures. It is a short statement, but a sharp reminder to readers that social transformations brought about by colonial intervention, even those apparently endorsed by all parties involved, *can* also be culturally destructive. This revelation, while it is now the defining concern of postcolonial studies, was less open to theorization in the mid eighteenth century, and if it disturbed the unquestioning assurance of this unusual imaginary voyage it did so only for a moment.

Chapter 4

FINDING PARADISE AND UTOPIA IN THE PACIFIC

The second half of the eighteenth century is the most significant in the history of British and French exploration and colonization in the Pacific. An abundance of travel literature, about real and imaginary voyages, formed a creative palette for synthesizing information from more than a century of European discovery in the antipodes. Imaginary voyages continued to draw upon well-known antipodean imagery and to offer utopian critiques of European society, and they weaved in the increasing material evidence of new geographies and new cultures. More imaginary voyages were published in this period than at any other time. Many examples engage with or comment directly upon the political and philosophical issues raised by the growing European presence and cross-cultural encounters taking place in the antipodes. Out of this environment emerged the two anonymously published texts, *Fragmens du dernier voyage de La Pérouse* [*Fragments from the Last Voyage of La Pérouse*] (1797)[1] and *The Life of La Perouse, the Celebrated and Unfortunate French Navigator* (1801).[2] They offer a fascinating glimpse of how writers of fiction were able to capture and exploit the appeal of contemporary exploratory voyages. In these marvellously realistic stories, distinctions between fact and fantasy are carefully masked. Both examples are framed around the mystifying disappearance of the famous French navigator, Jean-François de Galaup de La Pérouse, a tragedy that was a magnet for public speculation.

References to the 'great south land' and 'South Seas', respectively alluding to an immense area of land and of ocean, emphasized a broad-brush perspective and drew attention to the extent of uncharted spaces, awaiting discovery, that kept driving exploration. Jacques Bellin's 1753 map of Australasia[3] features a hypothetical coastline drawn between Van Diemen's Land (today's Tasmania) and the Australian mainland, and Robert de Vaugondy's 1756 map, 'De l'Australasie' (Figure 26), repeats the same imaginative connection. Maps remained inaccurate until the chronometer was invented, allowing longitude to be measured by way of astronomical observation.[4] While, by the mid eighteenth century, most European commentators had accepted that no great southern

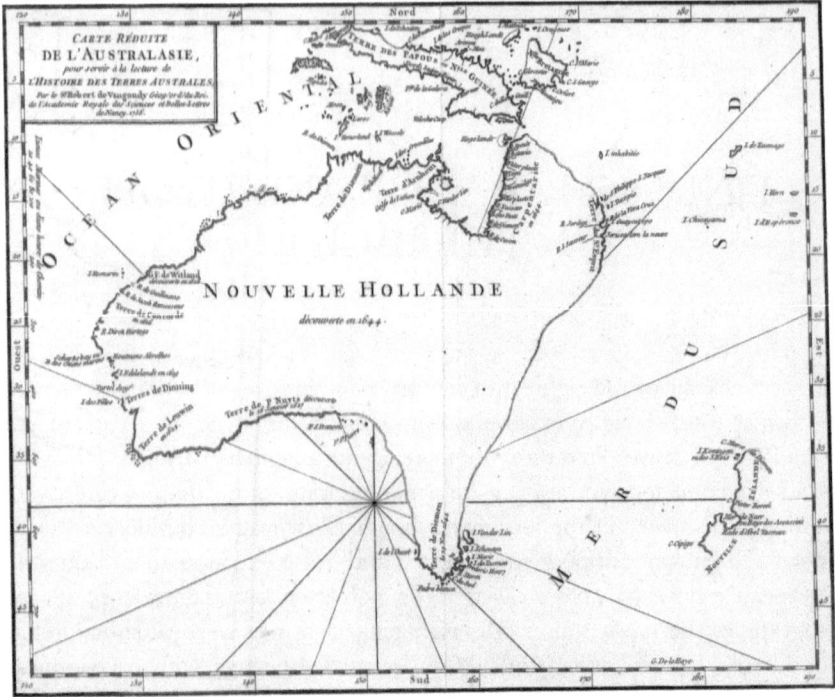

Figure 26. Robert de Vaugondy, 'De l'Australasie' (1756).

continent existed to correspond in size with the mammoth land of myths, the theory still had some strong advocates.[5] The South Pacific remained largely unknown until the closing decades of the century. Even by the late eighteenth century, maps continued to draw attention to the gaps in geographical knowledge of the antipodes as much as to the lands and seas they plotted.

Major discovery voyages of this period include those of George Anson in 1740, John Byron in 1764, Philip Carteret and Samuel Wallis in 1766, Louis-Antoine de Bougainville in 1767, James Cook between 1768 and 1779,[6] and La Pérouse in 1785. These expeditions were driven by the desire to expand knowledge as well as empires, and for Europeans to define themselves and their world in relation to others. It was a 'season for observing', as Dening puts it, when 'the nations of Europe and the Americas saw themselves acting out their scientific, humanistic selves'. It was also 'a time of intensive theatre of the civilised to the native, but of even more intensive theatre of the civilised to one another'.[7] This stage of exploration in the Pacific expanded significantly the existing conceptions of Indigenous 'types'. Although the distant southern world could no longer be thought of exclusively in mythical terms, the desire to discover the qualities of natural fertility and human happiness characterizing projections of paradise there competed with the spectre of barren lands and of hostility and cannibalism. Reports from explorers seemed to confirm both extremes. Christopher Columbus had brought home equally diverse reports on the Americas, an illuminating example of how interpretation of newly discovered places tended to educe a full range of competing first responses, from delighted wonder to terror. James Cook's death in Hawaii in 1779 underscored the need to be cautious of the dangers of cross-cultural contact in the Pacific and dramatized the complexity of European/Indigenous relations.[8]

The Indigenous peoples of the antipodes, when encountered, were often believed to have no culture of any kind. Regardless of whether they were depicted as compliant friends or as hostile savages, they were typically seen as ready to benefit from Europe's influence. Both stereotypes helped to justify colonial intervention by seeming to offer evidence that there was an obligation on Europe to instil its cultural values. On the one hand, the myth of savagery validated colonial control in the form of missionary work; on the other hand, the image of welcoming and receptive natives promoted a widespread belief that the antipodes was a space awaiting, and even inviting, the indisputable benefits of European civilization. In 1756, Charles de Brosses argued for a fair-handed approach to 'the natives'. His instructions, expounding the value of the civilizing mission of colonialism in spite of the practical complexity of imposing educational schemes, read:

> Every possible effort should be made to gain the goodwill of the natives. It is, of course, to be expected that difficulties will occur, and that the greatest possible discretion will have to be used. One cannot wonder at finding them scared at the sight of so many objects, strange, unknown, and so extraordinary to them.[9]

Later, in 1771, Alexander Dalrymple, the last serious proponent of the great south land theory, put forward a plan to bring British civilization to New Zealand. Dalrymple was equally optimistic about the positive impact European social conditioning would have on the Maori population, spelling it out as a responsibility on humanitarian grounds. He challenged readers to contemplate the lot of 'our Fellow-Men', who 'have canoes only; not knowing Iron, they cannot build ships', asking, 'does not Providence, by these distinguishing favours, seem to call on us, to do something ourselves for the common interests of humanity?'[10] A voyage to the 'other side of the Globe' is intended, Dalrymple explains, 'not to rob them, not to seize their lands, or enslave their persons; but merely to do them good, and enable them as far as in our power lies, to live as comfortably as ourselves'.[11] Despite the professedly benevolent intentions of these supporters of colonial ventures, cross-cultural contact in the antipodes in the second half of the eighteenth century followed a familiar pattern, with colonialism frequently resulting in violent conflict and relations of radical power inequality.

Tahiti first entered European consciousness when it was discovered in 1767 by Samuel Wallis. In 1766, the French government had commissioned Bougainville to circumnavigate the globe on an exploratory voyage. Bougainville stopped at Tahiti for several months in 1768, bringing the first major French influence and giving the island the name of *Nouvelle Cythère*, after the birthplace of the Greek goddess of love.[12] Subsequent visits by the French and British to Tahiti, including Cook in 1769 (there to observe the transit of Venus across the sun) and William Bligh in 1788, consolidated its status as an island of friendly, sexually available, women.[13] Bougainville's book *Voyage autour du monde* (1771) was read widely in France and translated into English in 1772 as *A Voyage Round the World*.[14] Bougainville had completed the first French circumnavigation of the globe and also instigated French colonial claims in the Pacific. He confirmed that Espiritu Santo was an island and not a continent, as had been Pedro Fernández de Quirós' belief. He also tried, without success, to find an entrance to the Great Barrier Reef, and so only just missed out on finding Australia's eastern coast.

Following the lead of thinkers such as Jean-Jacques Rousseau, Bougainville, through his voyage account, helped to popularize further the idea of the natural man or noble savage in Europe.[15] Denis Diderot, inspired by Bougainville, drew upon Rousseau's ideal of a natural state of humanity in his *Supplément au voyage de Bougainville* [*Supplement to the Voyage of Bougainville*], a work that can also be understood as a critical commentary on colonialism.[16] The text was first circulated as a manuscript in 1772, but like most of Diderot's writings, was only published after his death in 1796.[17] The description Bougainville had given of Tahiti resonated with Rousseau's ideas about humankind at a perfect stage of development.[18] While this view questioned the naturalness of the notion that Europe was bringing a benefit to the antipodes through its concept of civilization, it also romanticized the noble savage into a position of powerlessness as well as innocence. Rousseau's philosophy did nothing to retard colonial ventures. It simply provided another fascinating template for viewing cultural others from the high ground of European knowledge.

It is difficult to overstate the importance of the discovery of Tahiti on the European imagination in the context of utopian projections seemingly becoming real.[19] Tahiti rapidly permeated European mythology. In November 1769, six months after Bougainville had returned to France, the *Mercure de France* published an article by the expedition's naturalist, Philibert Commerson, lending life to myths by describing Tahiti as a utopia, 'the only corner of the earth where men live without vices, without prejudices, without needs, without strife'.[20] Through the discovery of Tahiti, the celebrated ideal of life on an idyllic antipodean island could be attached to an exemplary real place. Associated as it was with ideals beyond its immediate reality, the case of Tahiti illustrates the extent to which discoveries were capable of producing new and equally enduring myths in place of, but in tune with, the ones they superseded. One island group set a new standard by which to measure other parts of the antipodes – and the world – as seen from Europe. In contrast to the mainland of the Australian continent (a massive, uncontained and still largely unknown space) and New Zealand (with its aggressive Maori population), Tahiti came to represent the paradise that Europeans had searched so long to find in the antipodes.[21] Subsequent European discoveries, measured against the benchmark of Tahiti, helped to reinforce two contrasting images of native types, 'in which the South Sea island is symbolized either by the nubile, welcoming island girl, or by the threatening, cannibal male'.[22] This set of imagery was consolidated by the end of the eighteenth century. Much scholarly attention has been paid to these antithetical gendered constructions. Citing Nicholas Thomas, Rod Edmond argues that there had, in fact, been a general '"vacancy of otherness", a lack of singular character or physique accorded to the other' prior to the eighteenth century.[23] Comparisons made following the discovery of Tahiti led to the formalization of ideas of noble and ignoble, or soft and hard, primitivism, in the course of the eighteenth and nineteenth centuries. In an era when a great deal of cultural diversity was being discovered in the antipodes, interpretation was being directed by a binary model for understanding cultural difference, demonstrating surprising similarities between the workings of ancient mythology and developing evolutionary theories.[24]

While new myths were evolving in response to Europe's experience in the antipodes, the earlier paradigms remained remarkably tenacious. In the interpenetration of fact and fiction in the travel literature of the later period of antipodean exploration, we can see, vividly dramatized, the power of the imagination to influence all acts of observation and interpretation. The apparently simple, causal correspondence, whereby scientific knowledge gradually supplanted mythology, was clearly far more complex. Imagining and mythologizing continued, in literary fiction and cartography – as it did in many related modes – even alongside a growing store of authenticated knowledge. Empirical methodologies, for all the surety they may have provided, also limited the scope of interpretation. As with a telescope at its limits, only imagination could go further, helping to fill the gaps and resolve contradictions in empirical knowledge.

The Disappearance of La Pérouse

Jean-François de Galaup de La Pérouse, France's most respected late eighteenth-century explorer of the Pacific, was also Cook's rival in the final stage of major European discoveries. The two French frigates, *Boussole* and *Astrolabe*, departed from Brest on 1 August 1785. This was a famously well-equipped expedition – especially in relation to those of Cook – supported financially by the French king Louis XVI and totalling 225 men, including scientists, artists and other specialists.[25] The scale of investment reflected competing national interests, with the planned voyage of discovery intended to complete what Cook had left unfinished when he was killed at Hawaii.[26] 'Little will be wanting to complete the geography of this part of the world', wrote an unnamed crew member anticipating the findings of La Pérouse's expedition of which he was part, in a letter sent to Paris from Russia and published in *Scots Magazine* in 1788.[27] The same language of imminent completion was featured in 1798 in the *Monthly Review* in response to the publication of the official edited version of La Pérouse's journal extracts, which had been sent back to France in instalments. 'The voyage', a reviewer explained, 'assists, in some degrees, towards completing the geography of the South Seas'.[28] In the words of a journalist at the time, Cook had really 'extended the world'.[29] And while Cook's explorations over the course of his three long voyages were difficult to match, names such as 'La Pérouse Strait' and 'Boussole Strait' testify to La Pérouse's subsequent success in contributing significant new information about the physical layout of the Pacific.

La Pérouse arrived at Botany Bay only days after the British First Fleet in 1788, having been redirected there to report on rumoured colonial activities. Members of the infant British colony were in the midst of moving from Botany Bay to Port Jackson. In an unlikely meeting of colonial sea powers far from home, the British and French crews visited one another's ships.[30] So friendly was the interaction that La Pérouse made arrangements for the latest instalment of his invaluable journal to be delivered to France on board the next British ship returning to Europe. Once La Pérouse's expedition had left the Australian mainland, however, his two ships vanished at sea without a trace. According to his last letter, dated 7 February 1788 and written from Botany Bay, La Pérouse expected to reach the French colony of *Île de France* (today's Mauritius) at the end of that year. The French public, awaiting news of a national icon, were anxious to know the fate of La Pérouse and his two ships. He should have arrived by mid 1789 at the latest, and by 1790 there were calls for the French government to send a proven navigator such as Bougainville on a search mission. In 1791, Bougainville helped to plan an expedition eventually undertaken by Bruny d'Entrecasteaux with the ships

Recherche and *Espérance*. The choice of d'Entrecasteaux, the most senior leader of French voyages to the Pacific, to command the expedition, was evidence of its importance.[31] In 1800, French captain Nicolas Baudin visited the Pacific, also actively searching for La Pérouse.[32] Neither d'Entrecasteaux nor Baudin, however, had any success. While exploring the Gulf of Carpentaria in 1801, Matthew Flinders, conscious of La Pérouse's disappearance, recorded in his journal, 'the unfortunate situation…was always present to my mind'.[33]

Fragmens du dernier voyage de La Pérouse (1797)

> …these two points should finally settle doubts of the geographers who will then only need to let their imagination travel along the outline.
> – La Pérouse, in *The Journal of Jean-François de Galaup de La Pérouse 1785–1788*[34]

The publication of a series of books on La Pérouse's life and career at sea was one response to his disappearance. There was also contemporary drama, poetry, and two French imaginary voyages.[35] *Fragmens du dernier voyage de La Pérouse* [*Fragments from the Last Voyage of La Pérouse*] (1797), discussed here, provides a striking example of the imaginary voyage genre's tenuous existence at the borderline of fact and fiction. For the curious public in France, the disappointment at the long-delayed closure of the story of their acclaimed navigator was compounded by the fact that the government was not willing to publish parts of La Pérouse's journal, returned to France in instalments, until it was sure that he was lost beyond hope.[36] An official account was finally published in 1797 as *Voyage de La Pérouse autour du monde*, compiled and edited by General Milet-Mureau, who was provided with La Pérouse's journal extracts and letters.[37] Three translations of La Pérouse's official journal were quickly issued.[38] In print nearly ten years following the unexplained loss, the account did not sell well, partly because revolutionary conflicts in France had subdued the book market,[39] but perhaps also because readers had become more interested in the unsolved riddle of his disappearance than in his achievements. The lure of the unknown may have been stronger than the attraction of recorded facts. Remains from La Pérouse's expedition were eventually found in 1827, almost 40 years after his ships were last seen. On his travels in the Pacific, Jules Sebastian Cesar Dumont d'Urville heard news of unexplained French artefacts and reports of two wrecked ships through Englishman Captain Peter Dillon.[40] The reports were correct and d'Urville erected a simple memorial on the island of Vanikoro (in the Solomon Islands) where the items had been found.[41] When an expedition was sent to collect objects for identification, a decorated plank was recognized as a part of the taffrail of one of La Pérouse's ships. The people of Vanikoro had used it for a door panel.[42]

The French pamphlet *Fragmens du dernier voyage de La Pérouse* [*Fragments from the Last Voyage of La Pérouse*] was published anonymously in 1797, in the same year as the official account of La Pérouse's expedition.[43] In this short imaginary voyage, the suggestion is that La Pérouse had survived but may have retreated to a Pacific island paradise. This, indeed, had been considered as a possibility and was still being discussed by the *Quarterly Review* as late as 1810, that is, 22 years following his disappearance, when the frustrated editors wrote that 'no state of mind can be more agonising than that of doubt and uncertainty'. They speculated:

> The multitude of unfrequented islands, scattered over the wide surfaces of the Pacific Oceans, the steady breezes, the mild weather and smooth water that generally prevail in those seas, were circumstances which rendered the expectation not unreasonable, that the whole or a part of the officers and seamen might have survived the wreck of the ships, and escaped in their boats to some of those islands.[44]

Fragmens du dernier voyage de La Pérouse is utopian, pro-colonial and antirevolutionary, depicting the roots of French colonialism in the Pacific at the same time as attacking the social systems that caused revolutionary conflict in France during the previous decade. In this utopian world, aspects of antipodean and French life are blended. The edition drawn upon here is the first in English, translated by John Dunmore, published by the National Library of Australia nearly 200 years after the original French text as a commemorative gesture linking the bicentenaries of the French and English meeting in Botany Bay.

In introducing the text, Dunmore explains that the sources of *Fragmens du dernier voyage de La Pérouse* are difficult to identify. Because the Milet-Mureau edition of La Pérouse's journal was published around the same time, it is very unlikely that the author could have seen the genuine account.[45] When the two are compared, it is clear that *Fragmens du dernier voyage de La Pérouse* has errors that could have been avoided by an author with access to the official publication. One discrepancy concerns a purported visit by La Pérouse to Tahiti. '[T]he islands of *Sandovick* [Hawaii] and *Otayti* [Tahiti] had offered us only a cold imitation', the narrator reports.[46] In real life, La Pérouse had decided not to visit Tahiti because the area had already been substantially charted and so offered little opportunity for new discoveries.[47] Another example is a reference made to 'our sailors who had suffered so much through the labours they had had to endure in Rock Cove'.[48] There is no corresponding Rock Cove known to have existed. Samoa was the only place at which the expedition had stopped for a notable length of time after departing from Kamchatka.[49] There is a further misleading reference to the '*Noota* expedition', which can be assumed to be a misspelling of Nootka Sound, on Vancouver Island.[50] It was Cook, in fact, who had visited Nootka Sound, not La Pérouse.[51] There are also examples of inconsistencies involving crewmembers. Montarnal, for example, who in this fictitious narrative is said to have gone ashore on the island described, had in fact tragically drowned in Alaska early in the journey. Others who had been sent home or since died are also mentioned. These include Lamanon, who was killed in Samoa, and St Céran, who had left the expedition in Manila.[52]

I

Despite the historical inconsistencies between the fictional *Fragmens du dernier voyage de La Pérouse* and the official account of La Pérouse's expedition, this imaginary voyage is written so as to appear truthful. The sense of veracity is achieved, in part, through providing extensive narrative detail. A high degree of detail continued to be desired in all kinds of travel literature, as the *Monthly Review* had reported in 1791, when a contributor wrote: 'it is true of all narrative works, and particularly of relations of adventures, and descriptions of countries and their inhabitants, that the pleasure and information to be derived from reading them, depends, in a great measure, on the continuity, and on the minuteness, of the detail'.[53] The simple fact that this fictional account was published long after La Pérouse's disappearance (almost a decade) must have helped to obscure its fraudulence because the historical detail was effectively closed to immediate scrutiny. In addition, the public was still searching for an adequate explanation for the loss and therefore would likely have wanted to believe in such a narrative. More than any other imaginary voyage discussed in this study, this text sold itself – and was even mistaken by a noted historian – as an authentic article, a genuine historical account linked with a real discovery voyage.[54]

The account opens with a foreword that provides a note on the text's purported origins. An introductory statement lays much of the groundwork needed to form and sustain the illusion of authenticity. The narratorial voice is of a fictional crewman on the British ship *Charlotte*, an actual convict transport in the British First Fleet.[55] The unusual sense of amity between the British and French at Botany Bay provides an imaginative opening for the story. Using a device that has the paradoxical effect of encouraging the reader to regard the story as truthful, however, the narrator does not reveal his own identity. He explains that he must remain unnamed because of the nature of a crime he confesses to having committed. The sailor admits to stealing a notebook from aboard La Pérouse's ship *Astrolabe*, claiming to have accompanied British Captain Watkin Tench there on a friendly visit. The narrator relays the following series of events, which serve to explain the peculiar means by which he obtained the narrative:

> Intercourse based on esteem and friendship was soon established between our [British] leaders and the French officers. An ordinary seaman, I one day accompanied Captain Watkin-Tenck on board the *Astrolabe*, a few days before the death of Mr. Receveur, a professor of Natural History, and – I admit it – I could not resist the temptation of removing a handwritten notebook which I saw in a French officer's cabin.
>
> For as long as I could still believe that La Peyrouse might reappear, I was prevented by a very natural feeling of reluctance and shame from publishing the notes I had stolen; but since unhappily he cannot see his homeland again, having been sought in vain throughout the South Seas, it is fortunate that I did commit a theft which can provide us with some information about one of his most agreeable calls.[56]

The abnormal spelling of 'La Peyrouse' with a 'y' in *Fragmens du dernier voyage de La Pérouse* may have been a repetition of the spelling used by Watkin Tench in his accounts of the colony at Port Jackson in 1788.[57] Here the spelling 'La Peyrouse' is used when referring to the character in *Fragmens du dernier voyage de La Pérouse*, and 'La Pérouse' when referring to the real-life figure. By utilizing the actual meeting of the British and French crews to fictional ends, the reader is 'led along…leg astutely pulled', writes Dunmore.[58]

Explaining the circumstances of the final publication of this purportedly stolen text, the unnamed sailor, as narrator, claims to have been, by a 'series of misfortunes', wrecked on the French coast 'following a prolonged battle between the *Amazon* and the *Droits de l'Homme* during the night of 13–14 January 1797'.[59] He tells the story of how he was then taken 'a prisoner in Quimper' with an obligation to repay a 'Citizen H***', having given away the rights to his stolen manuscript on agreed terms. The sailor claims to have put 'Citizen H***' 'under the strict condition that he will never reveal my identity to anyone. He is the only being to whom I have mentioned this text'.[60] In an editorial note at the back of the pamphlet, an unidentified editor speculates on the implications of the revelatory secret diary. Only then is the suggestion spelt out that La Pérouse is still alive, settled contentedly in isolation in the Pacific. The narrator asks:

> Would it be surprising if, in such a mood, having learned of the revolutions in France, La Peyrouse and his companions had retired to this

island? D'Entre-Casteaux cannot have any knowledge of it. It would redound to the honour of France if a second expedition were organised to seek, under their disguise of bark cloth, those lost navigators.[61]

An anti-revolutionary, utopian argument lends weight to the view that La Peyrouse had found a better place to live than contemporary France. The narrator poses the question: 'But were they to be recalled to their country, would La Peyrouse and his good friends gain anything from the change?' The passage continues:

> While this delicate question is being decided, I like to think that these famous navigators are living happily among bowers of flowers, in the midst of the luxury and the wealth Nature provides, under the patriarchal rule of the worthy elders, in the arms of beautiful Indian women, and far from the furies of Roberspiere, from our financial disorder and our fears of the future.[62]

As Dunmore writes, *Fragmens du dernier voyage de La Pérouse* is an 'allegory for the ideal Revolution, a might-have-been, with the French philosophers liberating their people from their age-old servitude and establishing the new and perfect society which moderation then preserves for all time'.[63]

In an appendix that concludes the work, fictional descriptions of ten plant species make up a botanical compendium. The convincingly scientific names include the new genus of *Peyrousia*, with the varieties of '*Peyrousia Microcarpos*' ('Small-seed Peyrouse') and '*Peyrousia Leucanthema*' ('Peyrouse with white flowers').[64] Like the maps that included fictional elements in the same grid as factual information, this list of newly named plant species within a botanical discourse enhances the textual realism because it connects these discoveries directly with an authenticated body of scientific information. In the history of European discovery in the antipodes, plants were often named after explorers. In Australia, Banks had the *Banksia* named after him, for example, and Flinders the *Flindersia australis*.[65]

II

Even though La Pérouse's disappearance is the vehicle used to transport the reader vicariously beyond the boundaries of the familiar world, the figure of La Peyrouse features only occasionally in the diary purportedly written by a French officer under his command. La Pérouse's genuine voyage to the Pacific fades away in significance once the device has allowed imaginative access.

Of the six works that are the focus of this study, *Fragmens du dernier voyage de La Pérouse* includes the most abundant scenes of fertility, happiness, pleasure and health in the antipodes. The diary begins with the words: 'We finally reached the land from which storms had kept us so long' – reported by the narrator after being 12 days at sea in rough conditions with 'contrary winds'.[66] The landscape is not visible immediately because it is dark and foggy. A sample from the early part of the narrative describes the unexpectedly welcoming scene on arrival, in highly figurative, exuberant language that celebrates the landscape:

> The closer we got to the land, the more riches the country spread before us; the shrubs that grew along the shore, their light leaves brushed by the waves, seemed covered with red fruit, the size of a hen's egg; the great trees which dominated these two hills were laden with pyramid-shaped flowers, similar to those of the horse-chestnut tree, with wide lacy leaves. As we came closer we were deafened by the twittering of a million birds which our appearance frightened off and who, in a thousand different shapes, rose up in a cloud; nothing was so varied as their flight or the colours of their plumage; between the trees we could see vast lawns of a grass as thick but of a finer green than that of English parks.[67]

In this luxuriant display of natural abundance and beauty, La Peyrouse's expedition is a passive presence. The most powerful descriptions are given in negative terms, to convey the incomprehensibility of the wonder unfolding before their eyes: 'There never was a calmer basin, never a more transparent sea... never has Nature presented a more beautiful adornment'.[68] On this island, known as Blue Island, there are black swans.[69] Tracks of a large animal are noted, but there seems to be no imminent threat of attack.

The fertile island is a place for recuperation, an 'opulent land' that 'held a promise of resources for our sick who were once again attacked by scurvy, and for the crew who were enduring hardships'.[70] A temporary hospital is set up next to a stream 'that cascaded over a bed of smooth stones and ran in rivulets towards the sea across a green and flowery sward, kept fresh and healthy'.[71] There were recent precedents for the health-promoting benefits of the climate of the South Pacific islands. It is feasible that the author of *Fragmens du dernier voyage de La Pérouse* was inspired by exaggerated accounts such as the one given below of Norfolk Island, the British colonial outpost established in 1790 on the grounds that it was more promising for agriculture than the Australian mainland, as it had so far been explored in the first years of settlement.

In 1793, John Hunter published *An Historical Journal of the Transactions at Port Jackson and Norfolk Island*, in which he wrote of the miraculous health and fertility of Norfolk Island in these terms:

> Norfolk Island is…remarkably healthy. I do not think I can give a stronger proof of the salubrity of the climate, than by observing, that I never saw the constitutions either of the human race or any other animal, more prolific in any part of the world; two children at a birth is no uncommon thing, and elderly women, who have believed themselves long past the period of child-bearing, have repeatedly had as fine healthy strong children as ever were seen.[72]

In *Fragmens du dernier voyage de La Pérouse*, members of La Peyrouse's crew are transformed by the replenishing serenity of the island they have discovered, enjoying a 'unity, friendship and brotherhood' and making up 'a kind of academy' of learning and philosophy.[73]

Blue Island is mysterious because there appear to be no signs of human habitation. The narrator ponders the question of why such a naturally beautiful place should be uninhabited when 'so many small islands in a bitter and wild climate and the rocks of Tierra del Fuego could be so populated'.[74] The narrator reports: 'the beautiful country we just discovered…was inhabited only by buffaloes and birds'.[75] La Peyrouse nevertheless chooses a cautious approach. He is non-confrontational, having 'prohibited the use of guns and muskets in this peaceful haven'.[76] His aims are 'to husband the resources offered by these birds and not to frighten off the natives if there was a group of them in the neighbourhood'.[77] This initially sets the scene for a friendly encounter with whomever or whatever may live on the island.

Halfway through the narrative, a group of French sailors comes across an unanticipated scene of human civilization. The narrator articulates his bewildered response at the first sighting of human life on the island, reporting:

> I reached a hillock where I saw – what a spectacle! – a crowd of men and women in rows along a grass amphitheatre, dressed in white, their hair untied. The multitude was seated; twenty active groups were exercising in a circle where the earth, bare of grass, seemed to be beaten like a threshing floor. I saw no weapons. On a kind of rise I noticed twenty-four white-bearded elderly men each holding a white stick.[78]

92   VIRTUAL VOYAGES

Although it is unlikely that the author could have seen La Pérouse's official journal, there are striking similarities between the tone of extracts from *Fragmens du dernier voyage de La Pérouse* and the tone of the extracts compiled below, taken from La Pérouse's account of real-life encounters, in English translation:

> ...the dullest imagination can conjure up an image of happiness in this charming simplicity; [t]he freshest French springtime has never produced such a range of vivid greens; [j]ust as we were about to return to the ship we saw a canoe draw up to the shore with seven men who in no way seemed frightened of our number...among them were two venerable elders with long white beards, dressed in a cloth made of the tree bark; [n]owhere in the world could one meet better people. The chief or elder came to welcome us on the beach; What imagination could conjure up the happiness one would find in such an enchanting site... we commented that these islanders were the happiest inhabitants of the earth.[79]

This language further demonstrates how the themes of real and imaginary voyages were now intersecting in a way that promoted visions of cross-cultural encounters in strikingly similar, highly figurative, terms. In other words, the effective intermingling of the real and imaginary to produce a convincing historical document was as much a triumph of language and style as of content. Indeed, this demonstrates the unavoidable interdependence of fact and fiction, objectivity and subjectivity, in any historical narrative.

At the first sighting of the island inhabitants in *Fragmens du dernier voyage de La Pérouse*, they are clothed in Graeco-Roman style. The neo-classical depictions, a reflection of European taste at the time, also featured in illustrations included in the Milet-Mureau edition of La Pérouse's journal. A parallel example in a cartographical context is Giovanni Cassini's map of 1798, 'La Nuova Zelanda' (Figure 27). The cartouche in the top left-hand corner has Indigenous New Zealanders prostrating themselves at the feet of Captain Cook as he gestures with his arm outstretched towards the coast, to where his ship is anchored nearby. Cassini's accompanying map, 'La Nuova Olanda' (Figure 28), shows natives striking classical poses and holding cupid-like bows and arrows, again with the obligatory European ship at anchor in the distance. As in the case of Bellin and de Vaugondy's maps, this example includes a hypothetical coastline joining Van Diemen's Land to the Australian mainland. What is most notable about these fanciful images is not their peculiar neo-classical flavour, but the fact that they accompany real maps and real travel accounts and therefore offer themselves as extensions of that reality.

Figure 27. Giovanni Maria Cassini, 'La Nuova Zelanda' (1798).

Figure 28. Giovanni Maria Cassini, 'La Nuova Olanda' (1798).

III

La Peyrouse's arriving party is greeted with the utmost respect during the initial cross-cultural encounter. This baffles the French sailors as they, instinctively, prepare to be threatened. Against their expectations, what follows is an extraordinary scene of joy and celebration on the part of the islanders, described by the narrator who is surprised at the cultured demeanour of the elders, referred to here as 'senators':

> No sooner were we noticed hastening down the hillside, with our waving greenery, our weapons and our uniforms, than the dance stopped; the music ceased; they ran towards us with shouts and demonstrations of joy, of a friendliness we will perhaps not encounter on reaching the bosom of our family in France. The commotion was general. The twenty-four elders had got up, they were advancing majestically towards us: we joined them in the middle of the arena. I was impressed by the appearance of these elderly senators; there was no sign of harshness, roughness, or wildness about them.[80]

To their astonishment, the chief elder welcomes the travellers by speaking a few barely recognizable words in French, confusingly indicating that their peoples shared a cultural heritage. The narrator relates the initial cautious attempts at communication, describing the unanimous support for the French visitors as well as a genuine warmth and apparent familiarity:

> The one who seemed to be their chief, having looked at me for a few moments, included clearly in a few unintelligible phrases the word *French* which ten thousand voices repeated immediately with extraordinary joy. I cannot describe the extent of my surprise. It increased when, shaking my hand, pressing me in his venerable arms and against his bosom, he uttered some disconnected words which showed me he had had some connection with people from my homeland; I tried out a few words which he understood.[81]

Dunmore's reading of *Fragmens du dernier voyage de La Pérouse* brings out the patriarchal nature of this fictional society in which a learned council of male elders directs decisions. Younger members of the community unquestioningly follow the values of the elders, and the girls are regarded only for their beauty.[82] From one perspective, it is a static society. As Dunmore writes: 'Traditions are already enshrined, there is no feeling of challenge from anywhere and, somewhat conveniently, since that is where real challenges originate, the middle-aged are not in evidence'.[83] Outlining his reading of the text as utopian, Dunmore argues that the island is protected from the influence of colonial profiteering in the sense that the inhabitants 'respond by living in amity in an almost classless society with a minimum of artefacts. Isolation has protected them from the cupidity of European entrepreneurs who would seize upon the island's fertility for mere profit'.[84] And yet, from a postcolonial perspective, it seems that a great many social transformations have already taken place. As the narrative progresses it becomes clear that European models profoundly influence every visible element of the society. Describing the effects of colonialism as they are presented, Dunmore explains, uncritically: 'Civilisation has not corrupted a happy primitive society; rather, it has brought its benefits, pacified the fierce savages it encountered on the shore, taught them simple and adequate crafts and instilled moderation and brotherly love'.[85] From today's vantage point, this can be read as the fulfilment of the colonizer's dream: potentially noble savages embracing eagerly the opportunity to take on the knowledge and values of the benign colonizer.

Next in the story there is a gradual learning process that takes place, whereby the French visitors slowly discover, through witnessing various rituals and ceremonies, why the people of the island now accept and worship them so wholeheartedly. As in other examples of imaginary voyages, displays of firepower become a prominent theme as a kind of communication in the absence of shared language. And yet, reminiscent of *The Life and Adventures of Peter Wilkins* (see Chapter Three), the narrator claims that these displays are not intended to be violent or threatening.[86] While La Peyrouse has a policy of not intervening in the traditional life of the inhabitants, by the close of the narrative he is hailed as a god-like figure. This vision of the righteous European invader invites counter-colonialist readings, and yet any direct critique is obscured – at least to the modern reader – by the highly realistic rhetoric used. The visitors do not realize their own role in the drama until the very end of the narrative when the puzzle of these people's unexplained European-like customs is solved in a ceremony restaging the moment the islanders first came into contact with a party of French explorers some time in the past. At this grand event, famous French composer Rameau's 'March of the Natives' is performed, which enhances the scene of French heroism re-enacted. Rameau himself had been honoured and rewarded for his contribution to French culture by Louis XV with a court appointment and a pension.[87] Here French romantic music becomes another symbol of cultural power. The ceremony is summarized in a long passage, selectively reprinted below:

> Scattered groups of natives were walking about, armed with clubs, their hair unkempt, and wearing fierce expressions of such realism that we were momentarily struck by fear and were reassured only by our numbers and our weapons.
>
> They performed dances on the shores as wild as those of the natives of New Zealand; they crouched in a circle and mimed some strange gluttony; they devoured raw meat and uncooked herbs; they split into two groups and acted a bloody battle, and the women whose manners had been so gentle, covered in mosses and leaves, indulged in every kind of disorder.
>
> Suddenly all this agitation ceased. A longboat in the European style appeared in the distance; curiosity broke up the groups of savages; the object grew larger. Imagine our surprise: we saw four individuals in European clothes... Shouts of rage resounded; stones and arrows were flung towards the boat. The illusion was so complete that we were about to march to the rescue of the people in the boat when the good elders stopped us with a laugh; we soon realised that a play was being enacted.
>
> ...a few chiefs stepped forward onto the shoreline and forbade any hostile action: silence reigned throughout the assembly and the sound of an oboe was heard from the boat. Although it was absurdly distorted we could nevertheless make out a certain passage which resembled our old music, Rameau's march of the natives.

The actors on the shore pretended to be moved; they threw down their arms and welcomed with expressions of admiration and joy the strangers who were now landing.

...[the] Europeans taught them the...art of building solid and attractive houses and of clothing oneself, dancing, music, and a more polished, more civilised way of life...

The pageant came to an end...with all the skills of gardening and agriculture, and with some kind of deification in which they prostrated themselves at the feet of the Europeans... The tools of the past, the heaps of weapons and clubs, the containers of times of ignorance, their rough and dirty clothing, everything was torn, broken up and burned on a pyre.[88]

Through this astonishing display – one of the most striking demonstrations of the projected superiority of European culture to be found in an imaginary voyage – the islanders joyfully obliterate the works of their Indigenous past. The French sailors come to understand and also celebrate the civilizing influence they represent in the minds of the Indigenous people of Blue Island.

The anonymous author of *Fragmens du dernier voyage de La Pérouse* was skilful in combining actual events and people with the fantasy of a Pacific island setting, filled with antipodean abundance, fertility and colonial potential, in the language of an eyewitness account. The text's only hint at the fictional nature of the ideal condition described in the antipodean setting can be found in a rare moment of self-reflexive irony at the end of the narrative, when the narrator claims: 'This is the condition that is best for us, if we give up all of our works of fiction, our follies, our pomp, our systems, our dreaming'.[89]

The Life of La Perouse, the Celebrated and Unfortunate French Navigator (1801)

One of the most intriguing examples of imaginary voyage literature discussed in this study is the anonymously published *The Life of La Perouse, the Celebrated and Unfortunate French Navigator* (1801), which deals with the same topic as *Fragmens du dernier voyage de La Pérouse*.[90] To the best of my knowledge there is no available critical commentary on the text. The third edition (copies dated 1801 and 1802) was bound together with a summary of scenes from a popular pantomime by John Fawcett, *La Perouse, or The Desolate Island*, which was inspired by the story of *The Life of La Perouse, the Celebrated and Unfortunate French Navigator*. Here I refer to a copy dated 1802 held in the State Library of New South Wales, Australia. The work also appeared in various abridged and altered forms in 1807 and 1829. The National Library of Australia has two copies dated 1807, one entitled *Life of Perouse and His Surprising Adventures in a Voyage to the South-Seas* and the other entitled *The Life of the Celebrated Navigator La Perouse and Surprising Adventures in His Voyage to the South Seas*. The 1829 edition, published in a compilation of travel stories for children as *Bysh's Edition of The Voyages and Adventures of La Perouse*,[91] is illustrated with a series of eight simple, cartoon-like engravings that offer a visual summary of key scenes in the narrative, highlighting moments of cross-cultural conflict and resolution (Figure 29). The National Library of Australia has a faded typed note affixed to one of the 1807 versions that summarizes the main plot as:

> A rare and interesting fictitious narrative, according to which La Perouse was captured by the inhabitants of a South Sea island, but was saved from death by a chief's daughter, though his companions were slaughtered. He eventually married her and she bore him a son. In the meantime Madame La Perouse and her son were on a search ship and, visiting the island where La Perouse was living, were reunited with him.

As in the case of *Fragmens du dernier voyage de La Pérouse*, the reader eventually learns of a past European benefactor, but this time he is an Englishman. This revelation explains the paradox of why a French navigator is chosen as the hero of a story published in Britain at the time of the French Revolution. There are many similarities between this account and *Fragmens du dernier voyage de La Pérouse*. It may have been an inspiration for the later work but the author would need to have read it in French. Even if there is no direct correlation, the similarities are significant in that they suggest how prevalent literary themes reinforced contemporary stereotypes of the heroism of exploration and discovery, and of colonial encounters in the antipodes.

I

The narrative of *The Life of La Perouse, the Celebrated and Unfortunate French Navigator* is pitched at a broad audience, covering 'every feeling mind'.[92] The small size of the book and the melodramatic tone used indicates that it was aimed at a popular readership. Although the book is not very long, a great deal of action is packed into the narrative. The narrator begins by praising La Perouse as 'an individual, of superior genius and enterprize'.[93] Cook also features in this fictional account, in references designed to lend credibility to the text, such as 'which tended to confirm Captain Cook's...' and 'so accurately described by Cook'.[94] This associative device, claiming

Figure 29. Compilation of eight illustrations, from *Bysh's Edition of The Voyages and Adventures of La Perouse* (1829).

connections with the voyages of famous navigators, is a key element in the repertoire of literary tactics used by imaginary voyage writers. The first half of the narrative faithfully reports on La Pérouse's actual voyage. Making use of a very similar imaginative opening as in *Fragmens du dernier voyage de La Pérouse*, the fictional portion of the account that follows is presented as being from La Pérouse's own journal, with an episode again describing the historic meeting of the French and British ships in Botany Bay.[95] As in *Fragmens du dernier voyage de La Pérouse*, it is not until the closing passages that the mystery of the circumstances of the account being published is revealed. The narrative is said to be based on documents included in La Pérouse's last mail dispatch. There is also the suggestion of official involvement of the French government, to whom the documents were purportedly delivered 'on the arrival of the *Nymphe* at Bourdeaux'.[96] Adding further realism to the portrayal of the French visit to Botany Bay, *The Life of La Perouse, the Celebrated and Unfortunate French Navigator* reports on the genuine exchanges that took place between La Pérouse and groups of Australian Aborigines, with whom La Pérouse traded toys, hatchets and other small items for supplies.[97] In this fictional account, the expedition leaves Botany Bay and visits the Isle of France (Mauritius). The voyage then continues, 'to make discoveries on the northern coast of Japan'.[98] In reality, La Pérouse sailed from Botany Bay and was never seen again.

II

Arrival in the imagined world takes place by stages in *The Life of La Perouse, the Celebrated and Unfortunate French Navigator*. The plot structure features the device of a voyage within a voyage – a second fictional journey that is narrated within the first – setting up a number of obstacles to be negotiated and barriers to be crossed by traveller and reader. As in *Fragmens du dernier voyage de La Pérouse*, the transition begins when the narrator reports a 'very severe storm', which subsides to 'a perfect calm'.[99] Fog lingers, 'impenetrably thick', so as 'to preclude the possibility of seeing the shore, even at the distance of only half a mile'.[100] Just as La Perouse's party is casting anchor, both ships hit a submerged reef, the vessels 'expected to go to pieces every moment'.[101] A tragic scene at daybreak shows that only La Perouse's longboat has survived the night, now protecting La Perouse, his First Lieutenant and just ten other men; 'all the other boats had either been dashed to pieces upon the rocks by the breakers, or overwhelmed in whirlpools'.[102] La Perouse 'looked around in vain for his comrades; – they were gone forever! – He called through a speaking-trumpet, but no friendly voice answered'.[103] The few survivors go ashore, taking as many provisions and weapons as they can carry.

The first encounter with 'the Indians' is at sunrise.[104] The figure of an Indian is seen near the entrance of the cavern shelter in which the French party has taken refuge. Outside there is a group of approximately 'two hundred Indians, armed with bows and arrows, marching rapidly to the attack'.[105] La Perouse makes gestures of peace and friendship, 'similar to those he had formerly seen used by the Japanese', which are effective in halting their advance.[106] The chief now signals that the group of Frenchmen should give up their weapons.[107] When they refuse, a violent conflict is sparked, leaving only La Perouse and one sailor alive.[108] The rest of the French party is shot by arrows. 'Thus perished the unfortunate but brave companions of La Perouse'.[109] The two survivors are taken as prisoners to a neighbouring island, 'with yells of triumph' from the Indians.[110] 'Our hero was wounded in several parts of the body; his clothes were sprinkled with blood; and in this state he was dragged to a large village, and exhibited to the barbarous inhabitants'.[111] Both prisoners are then tied to trees in preparation for their imminent execution.[112] Luckily, the daughter of the Chief, named Aura, begs for La Perouse's life at the very last moment, entreating her father to let him go free – a scene reminiscent of the famous account given by Captain John Smith of Pocahontas saving his life in 1607.[113] She 'rushed forward, threw herself on her knees before her father, and interceded in favour of La Perouse'.[114] La Perouse is saved, but his 'less fortunate countryman was shot before his eyes'.[115] With La Perouse left alive and the rest of his crew dead, there are now the ingredients in this imaginary voyage for a robinsonade, as well as the beginnings of an element of romantic emotional interest that runs through the narrative and later becomes a means of exploring the theme of interracial marriage and procreation.

La Perouse is accepted by Aura's father and is received into the family. Using another tactic customary in imaginary voyages, information relating to the first moments of cross-cultural encounter and to the ready acceptance of the French traveller is omitted. In *The Life of La Perouse, the Celebrated and Unfortunate French Navigator* the only reference to this process is made in a single sentence describing La Perouse's ceremonial welcome, which reads: 'The Indians now considered the stranger as one of their own tribe; he was formally adopted, and entertained with rice-bread and fish'.[116] The island of 'Miona', to which he has been taken, 'formed a remarkable contrast with the rocky and desolate isle where La Perouse had landed after the shipwreck'.[117] The island has a population of 'about five thousand, including women and children'.[118] The explanation of their social system is also completed in one sentence: 'Their form of government was a kind of aristocracy, with one supreme head'.[119] This brevity is in contrast with the typically long-winded descriptions of social systems common in seventeenth- and eighteenth-century utopian fiction.

At the time of the initial meeting between La Perouse and Aura, she 'was in the flower of youth… Her demeanour was majestic'.[120] Regarded as the most beautiful woman on the island, Aura is also the best channel for influencing her father, the Chief. La Perouse, however, has a competitor for Aura's attentions. His name is Verado, '[a] young warrior who had often distinguished himself against the tribes of other islands'.[121] When Aura directs her attention to La Perouse, Verado is jealous and angry. Unwittingly, La Perouse becomes a rival, 'doomed to destruction'.[122] Aura tends to La Perouse and nurses him back to health after the shipwreck. Being in Aura's favour means being protected from Verado. But despite her care, La Perouse is emotionally shattered by his experiences and is not able to respond to Aura's romantic advances. She misunderstands his confused emotional state as a lack of affection for her and promptly decides to stop protecting him. 'Chagrined at his neglect', the narrator explains, 'Aura resolved to withdraw that protection, which had preserved him from the ferocity of the Indians since his arrival among them'.[123] The rivalry between La Perouse and Verado culminates in Verado shooting La Perouse. In a dramatic scene, La Perouse is '[d]isconsolate, forsaken and alone' after 'the savage pierced him with an arrow, and left him weltering in his blood'.[124] This has the unintended effect, however, of rekindling Aura's sympathies for La Perouse, and she tends him back to health for a second time. When she pleads with La Perouse for marriage, he 'yielded to necessity'.[125]

Wanting to secure the utmost protection from Verado, Aura arranges, with her father's support, for her and La Perouse to return to the adjacent barren island where La Perouse first landed. Here they domesticate a cavern dwelling (a familiar element from the story of Peter Wilkins and Youwarkee). The couple is visited regularly with supplies, and the chief commands Verado, 'on pain of death', not to visit the barren island.[126] Marking a halfway hiatus in the narrative, there is a pause to 'contemplate the hopeless situation of our hero', described as: 'Detached from civilized society, with all his prospects of advancement and fame obscured – and confined to an intercourse with barbarians'.[127] '[W]hat must have been his feelings!', the narrator asks.[128] After a period of marriage, Aura gives birth to their son, whom they name Orion. Despite having a child with Aura, which strengthens their relationship, La Perouse still regrets being separated from his former wife, the memory of their separation 'exciting the most unpleasant emotions' in him.[129] Aura is physically comforting, however, and he responds to 'the rich cordial of female tenderness', which 'served as an anodyne to alleviate his sorrows'.[130] Although there is formal acceptance of La Perouse's role as her husband, conflict is brewing because of Verado's continuing interest in Aura.

III

Although *The Life of La Perouse, the Celebrated and Unfortunate French Navigator* is a relatively short text, its anonymous author created a sense of historical depth by combining two different fictional journeys in a single narrative. So far I have only discussed one of these. The second comprises a rescue attempt mounted by a fictionalized Madame La Perouse, the French wife of La Perouse, 'whose tenderness for her long-lost husband continued undiminished'.[131] The setting is 1799, when 'a stout vessel is fitted out, by order of the French Government, and sent on a voyage of discovery'.[132] This courageous search becomes a story of powerful love and devotion. Accompanying Madame La Perouse is Henry, La Perouse's son by her whom La Perouse has not yet met. Assisted by a Captain Montaigne and a servant, Madame La Perouse embarks on the ship *Intrepid*. Travelling in a roundabout route via the coast of China and stopping to observe the movements of a Chinese fleet, she is able to pick up rumours about the fate of her husband. The general consensus, she learns, is that La Perouse 'had either been cast away, or destroyed in a contest with the people of some of the islands which lie scattered along the northern coast of Japan'.[133] A second French ship, commanded by a trader, joins Madame La Perouse and her crew in their search. Together the two ships are confident in their numbers against the perceived 'treachery of the Indians'.[134]

At the time the author was penning this piece of popular literature, there was more than a figurative association between the images of barren and fertile islands. Linked with developing ideas about soft and hard primitivism, fertility symbolized natural success and prosperity. In a pattern made fashionable in the eighteenth century by *Gulliver's Travels*, Madame La Perouse visits a number of different lands. From the ships, her party sights an island that is remarkably beautiful and has signs of cultivation. 'They were in hopes that the manners of the inhabitants were humane'.[135] This is not the island where La Perouse is now living with his new wife Aura, but it is the one traditionally utopian stop in this imaginary voyage's quest. The crew lands briefly at this island nation of 'Asperia', where the Indigenous inhabitants are tall, muscular, well-proportioned and have features related to those of the Chinese.[136] In the first moments of cross-cultural encounter, the arrows of 500 Indians are aimed at the approaching visitors, but this is only a momentary act of defence. The population of approximately 12,000 is described as having 'a gentleness of look and demeanour', with 'soft, harmonious voices'.[137] Madame La Perouse is treated as though 'the queen of the European visitors'.[138] The reader learns that these normally gentle people, who live in a sort of earthly paradise where the abundant land supports relatively few people very well, have been forced to fight against invaders from barren islands.[139] Before Madame La Perouse leaves with her ships, they are loaded with supplies provided by the islanders. The island of Asperia is an example of the literary feature of the 'halfway house', to use David Fausett's expression.[140] Whereas in *Peter Wilkins* the halfway houses he visits are real locations (the interior of Africa and Madagascar), in *The Life of La Perouse, the Celebrated and Unfortunate French Navigator* Asperia is a purely fictional location.

There is a brief gale that marks yet another transition in the meandering course of the narrative. Then, in the evening of 21 June 1788, the search party finally comes 'in sight of the very island that contained our hero!'[141] Madame La Perouse is drawn to this 'bleak and barren spot, notwithstanding its forbidding appearance'.[142] However, the Mionan natives (Aura's people) land on the island at the same time as the French. The visitors 'beheld these fierce islanders, who immediately advanced with bows bent, as if to attack'.[143] The French party, 'consisting of only twenty men' is 'surrounded by three hundred hostile savages'.[144] The French are shown as making gestures of peace to no avail, at which point one Frenchman is killed and two others wounded by flying arrows.[145] There is a conflict involving three parties: La Perouse and Aura, the Mionan natives, and Madam La Perouse and crew. The Mionan natives start the violence and also suffer the worse losses. The fighting ultimately 'did terrible execution among the savages, killing or wounding upwards of forty men'.[146] However, when La Perouse and Aura come out together from their cavern they are able to stop the conflict immediately since each side acknowledges either his or her authority.

Madame La Perouse and her crew 'find the object of their search in the person of their deliverer!'[147] Madame La Perouse then has a series of fits and falls unconscious. La Perouse and Aura nurse her, but La Perouse does not recognize his first wife until she is fully recovered. He is then in the extremely difficult position of confessing to Aura that his affection for her is secondary to his affection for his French wife. Aura is shattered by this revelation. The reader is asked to imagine the scene as La Perouse – 'dressed in the Indian habit, and his features much changed by the lapse of years, and the variety of hardships he had suffered' – is reunited with his French wife and meets their son Henry for the first time.[148] 'The venerable name of father had never been before addressed by him to any other being'.[149] At this point, the devastated Aura finds that she 'must relinquish the object of her fondest regard to a stranger!'[150] She leaves for the neighbouring fertile island along with the Mionan natives and son Orion.[151]

The formalized European marriage is valued, with the other commitment less significant and less binding. Further, because this second 'marriage' was imposed upon La Perouse rather than sought by him, the story exonerates him from blame at the same time as casting Aura into the unnatural role, in European terms, of a female predator. The naturalness of conquest and the lower value placed on the conquered are aspects of the sexual as well as the cultural politics that this text, like other imaginary voyages, promotes – using fantasy settings that are given credence through their carefully integrated connections with stories of actual colonial exploration.

More high drama soon follows, with Verado mustering a 200-strong army of supporters to fight against La Perouse. 'The fierce and jealous Aura herself accompanied them on this expedition; and with arms in her hands, and vows of revenge on her tongue, she led…in the largest canoe, accompanied by Verado'.[152] Verado decides to initiate a spontaneous attack on the French camp and gives the orders 'to take the cavern by surprise, and put La Perouse, his wife, and child, to death, without delay'.[153] However, Verado's party is seen advancing in time for the French to resist an attack. Their sophisticated weapons give them a tactical edge, and 'the superiority of fire-arms over bows and arrows, soon rendered the defeat of the Indians inevitable'.[154] When Aura bursts boldly through the barrier at the entrance to the cavern with the aim of killing La Perouse, she comes towards him, dagger in hand, but at the moment of attack, 'the dagger dropped from her nerveless hand, and she fainted away!'[155] Meanwhile, the remaining natives are taken as prisoners by the French. In the twists and turns of this narrative, the islanders (beautiful Aura included) have finally been cast as the enemy and have been successfully defeated. 'The victory was now complete, and the Indians were pursued to their canoes by the conquering Europeans'.[156] The French are the moral as well as the military victors in this antipodean world. Aura 'cast a reproachful look on her conductors, and turned away'.[157]

The last four pages of the book hold the key to an implied question that has not yet been answered: Why, in a work published in Britain, is there is such a glorification of the French historical figure of La Pérouse? The answer is that in this story a heroic English character is about to feature even more prominently as a ruler in the antipodes. While on a scouting mission without La Perouse or his wife, the remaining European travellers discover an island nearby that 'on account of the appearance of its verdant fields and woods, was particularly inviting'.[158] The finding of a new fertile island is by now a standard theme in this story, but it is the comprehensive agriculture and sophisticated planting techniques that sets this one apart and impresses the visitors. The inhabitants had 'several herds of cattle, and flocks of sheep', which, in true antipodean fashion, are 'remarkably large' in comparison with normal animals.[159] Already something seems unusual about this place. The sailors' instincts are correct and the party soon meets a community of very civilized natives, living in a large village, 'whose neatness of dress, and cleanliness of person, was equal to that of the most polished nation'.[160] The visitors' 'astonishment was inconceivable' at seeing familiar European instruments including a sundial, a spire and a clock.[161]

The party meets Thomas Windham, ruler of the island, an Englishman who can speak to them in French and is able to relay his own story of having been shipwrecked on the island in the year 1778, that is, over a decade before. The natives 'had given him a hospitable reception', and in turn Windham had helped them to mould their society on the model he offered to them with himself as leader.[162] This example then had a spreading effect, with other islands following the example of the first. Windham had 'directed them in the construction of their houses and other buildings, the culture of their fields, and those improvements in their dress and manners, which rendered them so much superior to the people of the other islands, who were gradually imitating them in those refinements'.[163] In this setting, Windham lives in a 'large and cleanly cottage', tended by local servants. He is married to the queen of the native people, described as though she were a prize he won, 'a reward for instructing her people in the useful arts'.[164] Windham is in control of a devoted population who respect his 'genius'. As the narrator explains: 'The alacrity and zeal with which they obeyed the commands of their benefactor, and the reverential awe with which they seemed to attend all his motions, sufficiently demonstrated the ascendancy of his superior genius over their grateful minds'.[165] Windham, in charge of his own island, has no wish to return home to England, even though he now has a means of getting back there.[166] As an expression of gratitude for his hospitality, and ultimately as support for his maintenance of control over the island, the French sailors give him presents, including 'two muskets, a quantity of ammunition, several spades, hoes, and other implements of husbandry'.[167] The narrative closes with the crew returning to the barren island, where they find La Perouse and his French wife waiting in safety but now anxious to depart on their voyage home. The narrator concludes by speculating that: 'La Perouse, we believe, has not yet reached Europe; but whether his delay has been occasioned by the continued indisposition of his wife, or whether some new misfortune has befallen him, time alone can discover'.[168]

The dramatic story of *The Life of La Perouse, the Celebrated and Unfortunate French Navigator* makes for a sometimes erratic reading experience because of the sudden changes in plot direction and pace. While its emphasis is not on political satire, the work combines many other elements that are common in imaginary voyages of the second half of the eighteenth century, all packed into one short text. This practically forgotten example goes to great lengths to generate a vision of cross-cultural encounter that acknowledges the seductiveness of antipodean paradisal life at the same time as the need to tame it and bring it into line with Europe's values. The beginnings of actual colonial settlement in the antipodes made these stories, in their contemporary context, more politically charged and more relevant than ever.

Chapter 5

AUSTRALIA'S MYTHIC INLAND

Whether Botany Bay was made in a merry mood of Nature, or whether it was her first essay in making continents, we shall never know; but we may be quite sure, that every thing found there will be diametrically opposite to the ordinary productions and inventions of the Old World.
— *Monthly Review* (1794)[1]

There is something so strangely different in the physical constitution of Australia, from that of every other part of the world; – we meet with so many whimsical deviations, on the two islands of New Holland and Van Diemen's Land, from the ordinary rules and operations of nature in the animal and vegetable parts of the creation…
— *Quarterly Review* (1835)[2]

Known colloquially the world over as the land 'down under', Australia has a reputation as a place 'so strangely different', where the rules of nature are turned upside down. The stretching horizons, the flatness and the particular quality of light mean that, even now, many claim Australian spaces are somehow different. Apparent contradictions show themselves in contrasting stereotypes of Australia as the land of the lucky, of opportunity, of the endless summer, at the same time as being an underdog culture with roots in a penal colony past.[3] In the nineteenth century, the term 'antipodes' came to be associated specifically with the settler colonies of Australia and New Zealand. In *Alice's Adventures in Wonderland* (1865), Alice ponders, 'I wonder if I shall fall right *through* the earth!' Invoking the 'down under' myth, she imagines:

> "How funny it'll seem to come out among the people that walk with their heads downwards! The antipathies, I think –" (she was rather glad there *was* no one listening, this time, as it didn't sound at all the right word) "– but I shall have to ask them what the name of the country is, you know. Please, Ma'am, is this New Zealand? Or Australia?"[4]

Australia was seen as an 'unhistoried nakedness', as the poet Judith Wright famously put it.[5] The Australian continent was the largest geographical remnant of the great south land, and, for a time, Australia's interior – which resisted European exploration for decades – invited the kind of wild speculation that was once associated with the whole of the southern hemisphere. So strong was the impulse to discover worlds that were new and confronting deep within the Australian continent that it has continued to generate myths of the last undiscovered places and peoples.[6] In the period 1800 to 1840 the immense inland spaces of the continent were explored. But the fact that it remained impenetrable and unmapped for so long and the final disappointment of its 'dead' centre have made a dramatic and lasting impact on Australia's national identity, politics, literature and sense of itself in relation to Europe as well as to other nations of Australasia and the world.

This chapter considers the unique place of Australia and the Australian interior within the antipodes – geographically and mythologically – in the early part of the nineteenth century. Extracts from Australian explorers' accounts and British periodicals set the scene for a detailed reading of one of the last antipodean imaginary voyages, entitled *Account of an Expedition to the Interior of New Holland*[7] (published anonymously in London in 1837), in which Australia's interior is a fertile paradise home to a harmonious European/Aboriginal society.[8] The book's themes are as much a testament to the tenacity of utopian visions of the antipodes as they are a social commentary on possibilities for colonial Australia's future. This example, written long past the literary form's peak of popularity in the late eighteenth century, describes a land expedition rather than a sea voyage. It shows, once more, how closely the genre of the imaginary voyage shadowed the course of actual discovery, capitalizing on the lingering fascination with rapidly diminishing unknown regions. In this case it is a fictional journey to one of the antipodes' last remote locations.

Australia in the Antipodes

> We were now exactly in Captain Cook's first track, and arrived the next morning in Botany Bay. This place I would by no means recommend to the English government as a receptacle for felons, or a place of punishment; it should rather be the reward of merit, nature having most bountifully bestowed her best gifts upon it.
> – Rudolph Raspe, *The Surprising Adventures of Baron Munchausen* (1785)[9]

Geographical knowledge of the Australian continent acquired from the beginning of the eighteenth century to the time of settlement in 1788 was scarce in comparison with knowledge of the major Pacific island groups. The first reports of the Dutch, and those later given by William Dampier – with his damning assessment in the final years of the seventeenth century of the Australian Aborigines as the 'miserablest People in the World'[10] – remained largely unchallenged. Rudolph Raspe drew upon Cook's initial, misleadingly positive, images of Botany Bay in the quotation above, taken from his well-known imaginary voyage which goes there, *The Surprising Adventures of Baron Munchausen* (1785), published just before British settlement in 1788. New South Wales had been chosen by Britain as a place to send convicts, and this was a new ingredient that fundamentally altered the way Australia would come to be seen within the shifting framework of the antipodes. With British settlement, alternative, colonial myths needed to be built up to justify permanent settler presence and provide frameworks for gauging the colony's success from a European perspective, and increasingly also from the Australian perspective.

As a colony, New South Wales quickly began to gain its own identity. In 1828, Sydney Smith, one of the founders of the *Edinburgh Review*, wrote that in true antipodean style the colony's settlers, 'instead of treading in the steps of their progenitors, almost invariably render themselves conspicuous by a course of life directly opposite'.[11] In a similar vein, Archbishop Richard Whately told the House of Lords in 1840 that in New South Wales moral laws were reversed: 'a new standard of opinion had been set up which makes vice virtue and virtue vice'.[12] The ancient model of difference and distortion in relation to Europe was being used to characterize the very people whose ancestors had generated far-fetched myths of the antipodes in centuries past. British settlers were *becoming* antipodean by embracing what they saw as the oddities of this new world – its much mythologized otherness – as a key to forging a unique Australian identity. Despite the ease of travel in today's globalized world, Australian identity continues to be defined partially by a physical distance from centres of world population and power. The Sydney 2000 Olympic Games, 'on top of the world down under',[13] showcased a particular version of that identity, centred on larrikinism and fun. Purpose-built technology infrastructure contributed to a public view of Australia as distant and relaxed, but also as a world leader, an image that worked against the backward stigma once associated with Australia and New Zealand as distant outposts of the former British Empire. These are outward projections, however. They suppress or gloss over the ongoing and ever-present sense of internal conflict over Indigenous rights and sovereignty within Australia. Brian Castro has referred to this as the latest manifestation of the 'cultural cringe', describing it as 'a blindspot: the denial of cultural differences inside the nation by means of an assumed, homogenised reaction to the outside – Australia against the world'.[14]

On 6 September 1800, explorer Matthew Flinders, having just returned to London, wrote to Joseph Banks outlining his plans for navigating the perimeter of the Australian continent, explaining that 'the interests of geography require that this only remaining considerable part of the globe should be thoroughly explored'.[15] When Flinders charted the coast of Van Diemen's Land in 1801, he reported that the island 'appears to be superior in fertility to the same space of ground in any known part of New South Wales'.[16] In 1802–3 he completed the first circumnavigation of Australia, charting a passage between the Australian mainland and New Guinea and exploring the area of the Gulf of Carpentaria before returning to Sydney along the west coast.[17] In 1803, with his ship *Investigator* deemed unseaworthy, Flinders set sail to return to England as a passenger on HMS *Porpoise*. However, this ship was wrecked on a coral reef approximately 1100km north of Port Jackson. Flinders navigated the ship's cutter back to Sydney and arranged for the marooned crew to be rescued.[18] The tragic event inspired an imaginary voyage entitled 'Account of the Loss of His Majesty's Armed Vessel *Porpoise*, and the *Cato*, upon Wreck Reef', published anonymously in the *Sydney Gazette*.[19] I am not aware of any other writings that could be categorized as imaginary voyages published in the colony of New South Wales in the first 50 years – perhaps a symptom of declining interest in the literary form, but also suggesting the special vicarious appeal of imaginary voyages to readers at a distance. Flinders and his crew did not initially receive the acclaim that would be expected for such significant discoveries because Flinders spent six and a half years detained in prison at Mauritius *en route* to Britain.[20]

At the turn of the nineteenth century, British readers were being offered a variety of representations of the Australian Aborigines, drawn from contemporary first-hand accounts and included in summaries being published of the first 20 years of Australian settlement. In *An Account of the English Colony in New South Wales, from Its First Settlement, in January 1788, to August 1801* (1802), Lieutenant-Colonel David Collins argued that 'the savage inhabitants of the country' continued to reinforce their reputation as savages, 'instead of losing any part of their native ferocity of manners'.[21] He wrote that the natives, 'by an intercourse with the Europeans among whom they dwelt…seemed rather to delight in exhibiting themselves as monsters of the greatest cruelty, devoid of reason, and guided solely by the impulse of the worst passions'.[22] In 1805, John Turnbull also described Australia's Indigenous peoples in deprecatory terms, writing: 'These aboriginal inhabitants of this distant region are indeed beyond comparison the most barbarous on the surface of the globe'.[23] Collins had described the people of Van Diemen's Land as 'inferior even to the despised natives of the continent'.[24] Such impressions helped to justify the large-scale eradication of Tasmania's Indigenous population.

Responding to the publication of the second volume of Collins' *Account*, the *Monthly Review* attacked the nature of convict society as the reason for the reported lack of success in civilizing the Aborigines around Sydney Cove, firmly associating the criminal element in the new society with the convicts rather than with the settler colonists.[25] Here is an illustration of a circular pattern of blame for the 'state of the natives' that began very early in the history of British settlement. It is a pattern that has been perpetuated for over two centuries with the result that formal recognition of the abhorrent past treatment of the Australian Aborigines has been sidestepped until very recently.[26]

In the context of ongoing British contact with more immediately appealing places like Tahiti, the question of 'whether colonial possessions are eventually advantageous to the parent state' was debated. Was it worth 'maintaining at an enormous expense the refuse of society' on 'such distant and unpromising shores'?[27] This question was asked in relation to the New South Wales colony around the turn of the nineteenth century. Widely held was the verdict that 'the final success of the experiment is more than doubtful'.[28] In contrast to Tahiti, Australia at the time was rarely cast as an exotic antipodean paradise. And yet, in the eyes of some, Tahiti itself was losing its appeal in the nineteenth century as a result of intense European interest and influence. In 1807, Henry Brougham, another founder of the *Edinburgh Review*, reminisced: 'Our readers will recollect, that in the good old times of Cook and King, a few red feathers would open all the treasures, nay, buy all the crowns of these little realms'.[29] This quotation is taken from a contemporary review of John Turnbull's *A Voyage Round the World* (1805), in which Turnbull described being attacked by warring Tahitians. Turnbull estimated that the island's population had dropped from around 100,000 to about 5,000 when he arrived on the *Duff*.[30] Now revoking its status as a living utopia, he wrote: 'Otaheite so mingled her bitters with her sweets, that the lot of the Otaheitans is not superior to the rest of the world'.[31] Brougham, nevertheless, continued to marvel at the natural beauty of Tahiti and the attractions of island life, writing: 'We are forcibly struck, in reading all these South Sea voyages, with the difficulty of preventing desertion'. He lists 'the women, climate, and above all, the indolence in which the natives live' as 'seductions which our seamen can scarcely be forced, by any discipline, to resist'.[32] By 1812, the *Quarterly Review* was calling on readers to envisage the potential glory of the British settlements in spite of the discouraging tone of recent reports, inviting them to 'imagine these wide regions in the yet uncultivated parts of the earth flourishing like our own, and possessed by people enjoying our institutions and speaking our language'. In this vision, 'Britain should become the hive of nations, and cast her swarms'.[33]

The full account of Flinders' discoveries was only made available to the public once he had been released from jail in Mauritius. Published finally in 1814 as *A Voyage to Terra Australis*, it told in detail of his voyages around the Australian coastline as well as of his experiences in Mauritius before returning to England. Reviewing his account, the *Quarterly Review* noted that Flinders' voyage exposed a historical enigma related to the European mapping of the area of the Gulf of Carpentaria that is linked with the riddle of the Dieppe maps. Prior to Flinders' voyage, the region, sketched on maps at the northern extreme of the Australian landmass, was only an 'imaginary tracing of an undulating line intended to denote the limits between land and water'. It was a 'blank line', the reviewer reported, 'copied by one chart-maker from another, without the least authority, and without the least reason to believe that any European had ever visited this wide and deeply indented gulph'. When Flinders had charted the area, however, 'this imaginary line' was found to be 'so nearly to its true form as ascertained by survey' as 'to leave little doubt that some European navigator must, at one time or other, have examined it'.[34] 'Henceforth', Flinders claimed, 'the gulph of Carpentaria will take its station amongst the conspicuous parts of the globe in a decided character'.[35] Franz Swoboda and Martin Hartl's 1815 map of Australia displays Flinders' and Nicolas Baudin's latest discoveries, and features a coastal perimeter reinforced with orange ink on a neutral light-brown background (Figure 30). The cartographers could not help but add their own guesswork, dividing the Australian mainland in two with an imaginary strait separating the east and west portions of the continent. Today the area of the Gulf of Carpentaria, which includes the coast of northern Arnhem Land, is a symbolic area of traditional Aboriginal culture. In a historic political gesture in 1963, the people of Arnhem Land presented the Yirrkala bark petition to the Federal House of Representatives. Although it was unsuccessful as a land rights claim, it paved the way for general recognition of Indigenous rights in Commonwealth law.[36]

The numbers of Australian Aborigines had been reduced significantly from the time of settlement, partly by the unintended effects of contact, such as introduced diseases, but also through a colonial program that arguably included sanctioned genocide.[37] The Aborigines, the convicts and the land were all thought of as degraded, and this underscored continuing pessimistic images of Australia in the early decades of the nineteenth century. In 1814, the *Quarterly Review*'s response to Flinders' reports of the Aborigines was to write that 'in this rank of beings, even the Hottentot is superior to the original native of New South Wales', reinforcing earlier assessments by remarking that the Australian Aborigine 'may perhaps be justly placed in the lowest division

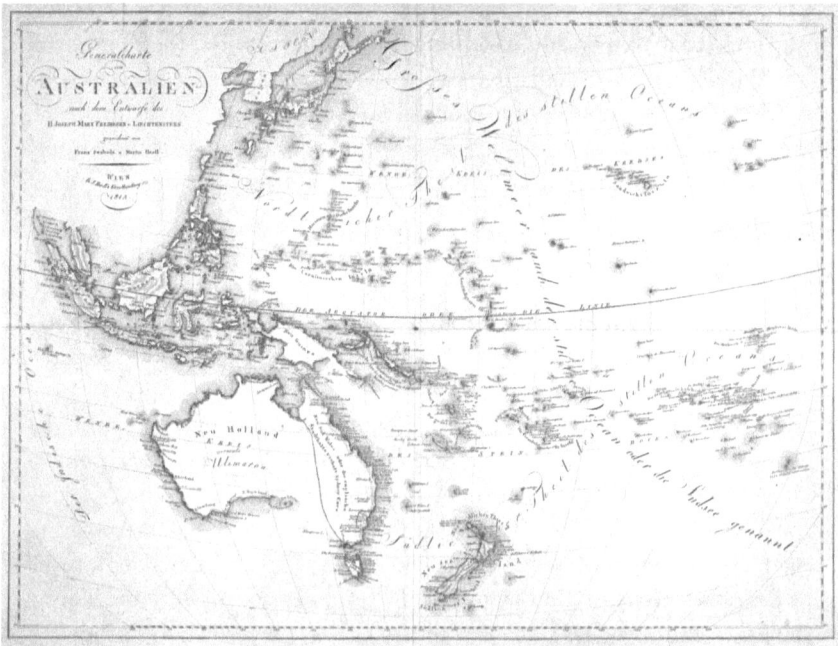

Figure 30. Franz Swoboda and Martin Hartl, 'Generalcharte von Australien' (1815).

of the scale of human kind'.[38] Views of the land around the colony of New South Wales in the following year were similarly disparaging. The *Monthly Review* cast it as of 'so unpromising a nature as to discourage the cultivation of farther acquaintance with it'.[39]

The British periodical press featured regular articles on convict uprisings and punishments. Remarkably, there was a belief among Irish convicts at the turn of the nineteenth century that there was another settlement in the hills just beyond the settler colony. Some even believed that this place was in fact China.[40] In 1814, the *Quarterly Review* observed that in the early years of settlement, 'scarcely a week elapsed without a party setting off to walk to China', relaying the claims of one man who discovered 'upwards of fifty skeletons lying in the woods, of those unhappy beings who had perished by famine on their way to China'.[41]

The assumed rights of Europeans as colonists in the antipodes were laid out plainly by the *Monthly Review* in 1815, in relation to recognition of the 'First Discoverer'. Within this framework, the colonization of New Holland was a morally appropriate act. The case is argued in this way:

> It is the nature of human existence in this world that knowledge is power, and power will have dominion; and with respect to the New Hollanders,

> Europeans have few, if any, sins to expiate. It is true that New Holland was found inhabited: but, excepting the northern parts, the number of inhabitants was so small that the land occupied by them cannot be supposed to amount to one thousandth part; and the state in which they were found was so wretched, that benefit, not injury, may reasonably be expected to accrue to them from the settlement of Europeans in their country.[42]

Even though the same writer argues in general terms that land cannot be 'first discovered' if it is already occupied, it is clear that this rule refers only to the first discovery by a European, and disregards claims to Indigenous ownership:

> According to moral intelligence, a land found with inhabitants cannot be said to be then first discovered; and all claims, which involve a right of possession advanced on such a pretension, are usurpations. Strictly speaking, only uninhabited lands, and such as were not before known to man, can be first discoveries: but, according to the political maxims as well as the phraseology of Europeans, by the term *First Discoverer* is understood the European who finds a land which before was unknown to Europeans. We do not say this fanatically, or in any spirit of cant; nor do we mean to advance that Europeans are of a more usurping disposition than the rest of mankind: but we would see the matter in its proper light.[43]

By this logic, the land was available to any European power. There had been prior claims made by the Dutch, for example. The *Monthly Review* acknowledges the first right of the Dutch but explains that rights expire if not used in a 'reasonable' time period (which is not finally specified). The reviewer puts the case:

> The Hollanders were the first European discoverers of a great part of the coasts of three sides of this land; and it is consonant both to reason and to custom that an exclusive right of occupancy shall be vested in the first discoverers: but not indefinitely. If neither occupancy nor intention of occupying follows the discovery within a reasonable time, the exclusive right gradually abates, and at length expires; because, otherwise, a large territory might be in perpetuity locked up from the use of mankind. Nearly two centuries had elapsed from the first discovery of the *Terra Australis* by the Hollanders, and a century and a half from their discovery of *Van Diemen's Land*, without any settlement or indication of intention to form a settlement being made by them when Captain Cook discovered the eastern coast; and, subsequently, several years passed,

during which the *Terra Australis* was wholly unnoticed as to any scheme or intention of colonization, by the nations of Europe: consequently it lay open to all.[44]

When the reviewer discusses the issue of competing European national interests, the Aboriginal claim to the land is totally absent from these calculations:

> In considering a land as unoccupied, and open to the first comer, it might seem that, when possession is taken of a part, the right to the remainder would continue the same as before: but entries into possession are cases of too complex a character for this to be admitted as a general rule. In small territories, and in some of considerable extent, *the actual possession of a small part is respected as comprehending a right of possession to the remainder* [emphasis added]. This extension of right beyond the portion which it may be convenient to occupy is often essential to security, and chiefly on that principle it ought to be regulated: but, when the taking possession of unoccupied land by one people does not affect the security of another, it would be unjust, because unreasonable, to obstruct the entry. On the other hand, it must be held that, when the formation of new settlements would be productive of insecurity to settlements already established, the party threatened with such injury is required to seek and to use means of prevention.[45]

Australia, so envisaged, was open to colonization on the grounds that only a small part was occupied and the land to be claimed by the colonizers could therefore be thought of as unoccupied. There is a paradox in this conception of the first discoverer in the context of this study. In imaginary voyage literature, the southern land was imagined as awaiting European discovery, but it was almost always occupied by some kind of inhabitants, never vacant. When British settlers arrived in Australia, they found a way of seeing the land that could simultaneously contain two competing realities – they could regard it as empty at the same time as reporting that it was inhabited.

In 1788 about 700 people formed the settlement in New South Wales. In 1821 there were nearly 40,000 spread over 200 square miles.[46] Forty years after British settlement, the Aboriginal population continued to be referred to in contemporary journals as the most degraded of native races. Sydney Smith reiterated: 'these poor creatures are among the lowest, if not the very lowest, in the scale of human beings'.[47] Systematically comparing the different native types to be found in various parts of world, the *Quarterly Review* isolated the Australian Aborigines, separating them out from 'The Hottentot and the Kaffer', 'The New Zealander', 'The Eskimaux' and 'The Negro' on the grounds that they make 'no provision for a future day' and by 'their having no habitation, no domestic animal of any description for food, and of their never having planted a tree or put a seed into the ground'.[48] And yet, asserting the need for further European intervention, this reviewer added: 'it is also agreed on all hands' that the 'aborigines are a shrewd, intelligent race'.[49] This is a counter-image upheld as reasoning for future missionary work. Such images existed side by side, justifying colonial occupation in terms of often contradictory myths of the savage. When missionaries first came to the antipodes, they saw a primitive world awaiting their civilizing influence. In nineteenth-century missionary work, there was a notable change from seeing the antipodes as a paradise – spiritually intact, pure, and waiting to be discovered – to thinking of it as a place of ignorance, in need of spiritual education imposed from the outside. Whereas early explorers had searched for paradise itself, missionary organizations were seeking appropriate bases from which to spread their word.

John Alexander Ferguson's *Bibliography of Australia* (published between 1941 and 1986) takes five volumes to cover the period 1784 to 1850, listing over 2000 early Australian texts to the year 1830 alone.[50] Most of the 'Australian' literature was printed and published outside of Australia and produced for a non-Australian readership. This body of literature is usually overlooked in the kind of nationalistic accounts that focus on colonial literary traditions as they evolved in Australia itself, a history with a late start because literature and arts were secondary priorities in new colonies, especially in convict settlements. In a letter to Earl Bathurst in the *Edinburgh Review* in 1823, Sydney Smith explained it plainly, writing: 'A man who thinks of pillars and pilasters, when half the colony are wet through for want of any covering at all, cannot be a wise or prudent person'.[51] Although the colony of New South Wales did not have an established literary tradition, Sydney was a fast-growing town that was now living up to exactly this kind of imagery of elegance in the eyes of some. Take the example of Jacques Arago, draughtsman to French captain Louis de Freycinet, arriving in New South Wales for the first time in 1823. Arago seemed overwhelmed by what he saw in Sydney. His rapturous response, given here in English translation, reads:

> I will not give you a description of the town, which I have just gone through: I am enchanted, and I had rather give my admiration some respite. Magnificent hotels, majestic mansions, houses of extraordinary taste and elegance, fountains ornamented with sculptures worthy of the chisel of our best artists, spacious and airy apartments, rich furniture, horses, carriages, and one-horse chaises of the greatest elegance,

immense storehouses – would you expect to find all these, four thousand leagues from Europe?[52]

While Sydney may have boasted architectural grandeur, there was very little art or literature. A significant number of official books and pamphlets were produced in Australia in the early years of the colonies, and yet Ferguson's *Bibliography* notes that the 'first work of general literature' was not printed in Australia until 1818.[53] European writers had the ongoing role of creatively constructing the antipodes for European readers. Colonial Australian literature had little recognition in Britain until the time of the nationalistic movement associated with writers such as Henry Lawson later in the nineteenth century. By then, novelists in Britain 'imagined that the colonies were peripheral to their domestic concerns, and rarely felt that the colonial world impinged on the metropolis'.[54] Distant colonies had lost some of the magic of their mystery, but they provided convenient locations for 'beginnings, turning points and endings' in fiction.[55]

The Dead Heart

> Mr. Oxley has shown, that Nature will have her caprices in spite of hydrographers and map-makers – that she does not consult Mr. Arrowsmith – and flows where she pleases, without asking permission of Mr. Barrow, or inquiring what direction will best suit the hypotheses of Mr. Maxwell or Mr. Reichard. We have no doubt that some of our geographical people will be very angry with these rivers; but they must learn, in this age of discovery, to hold their theories at single anchor – often to acknowledge their supposed land to be fog-banks – and to turn flexibly and obsequiously, as they are impelled by the breath of science.
> – Sydney Smith, in the *Edinburgh Review* (1820)[56]

Seeking fertile land for crops and livestock and a better quality of life, early British settlers turned their hopes towards Australia's interior, often comparing it with the fertile centres of other continents. Joseph Banks, making a comparison between the Australian landmass and that of continental Europe, wrote to Under-Secretary John King on 15 May 1798:

> We have now possessed the country of New South Wales more than ten years, and so much has the discovery of the interior been neglected… It is impossible to conceive that such a body of land, as large as all Europe,

does not produce vast rivers, capable of being navigated into the heart of the interior; or, if properly investigated, that such a country, situate in a most fruitful climate, should not produce some native raw material of importance to a manufacturing country as England is.[57]

Comparisons were also being made with Africa. Flinders, for example, cited the inland explorations of Mungo Park in Africa as a model for future Australian expeditions, advertising that the explorer had offered himself 'as a volunteer to be employed in exploring the interior of New Holland, by its rivers or otherwise'.[58]

Pondering the question of the lack of rivers discovered flowing to the eastern coast of the Australian continent, and also referring to Africa, the *Quarterly Review* in 1814 reported on two widely held beliefs about the interior, explaining that 'the supposition of an internal sea affords the only solution', unless, that is,

> ...we suppose that the country is principally composed of sandy deserts which, as in some parts of Africa, absorb the waters that fall from the clouds, and that the streams which descend from the mountains, creep unperceived under the sandy surface of the sea.[59]

It was a perplexing issue for this reviewer (as it was for most commentators), who goes on to explain that by and large, after 25 years of settlement, Europeans 'yet know very little more of the nature of the country...than what was known in the first three years of the settlement', regretting that 'the Blue Mountains are an impenetrable barrier, beyond which all is nearly terra incognita'.[60] This reviewer, however, was not aware that Gregory Blaxland, William Lawson and William Charles Wentworth had already successfully crossed the Blue Mountains, in May 1813.[61]

In 1820 the Lachlan and Macquarie Rivers were charted by John Oxley, who had set out to answer the question, as Sydney Smith put it, of whether these 'immense supplies of water' end in an inland sea, 'and whether this inland sea, if it exists, has any communication with the ocean'.[62] Writing in 1820 from Bathurst (200km inland from Sydney), Oxley foresaw a glorious rural future just on the doorstep of the new colony, reflecting: 'The mind dwelt with pleasure on the idea that at no very distant period these secluded plains would be covered with flocks bearing the richest fleeces'.[63] Oxley, who made famous his expectation that he would find an inland sea, discovered that the Lachlan and Macquarie Rivers petered out into marshes, with 'the channel of the river, which lay through reeds, from one to three feet deep'.[64] For Smith, the behaviour of these rivers, failing to become grand watercourses, provided a demonstration of the peculiarly antipodean, opposite nature of New South

Wales. His reaction can also be seen as disappointment at the rivers' refusal to fulfil the myth of the inland sea. Smith wrote:

> Here are, for instance, two rivers, the Lachlan and the Macquarie, which Mr. John Oxley, arguing upon analogy, supposes to flow on and increase till they empty themselves into the sea. But in three or four weeks he rides them fairly down into the bogs, where they are lost among millions of barren and unhealthy acres, impervious, unfit for human life, abandoned to reeds, ducks and frogs.[65]

In 1821, the *Quarterly Review* joked that the Dutch had a great deal of foresight without being aware of it when they chose the name of New Holland after their own marshy country, 'little dreaming, perhaps, that at some future period the similarity of it to the old country would be found to sanction the name... That such is the case, the recent discoveries of Mr. Oxley seem to leave very little doubt'.[66] The reviewer summarized the contemporary divide between the various hypotheses on the nature of Australia's interior, writing:

> It may be concluded that the surface of this vast country somewhat resembles that of a shallow basin whose margin surrounds the sea coasts, from which the waters, descending towards the interior, form a succession of swamps and morasses, or perhaps a vast Mediterranean sea.[67]

Mindful of potential French colonial claims, the reviewer also sounded a note of relief, claiming that Oxley's lack of discoveries demonstrated that there should be no fear of the French trying to colonize part of the western coast because it seemed unlikely that there was anything in the centre of value to contest. However, by this time the French were not regarded as a genuine threat, since their discovery voyages to Australia's western coast in the late eighteenth and early nineteenth century had been as unrewarding as Dampier's.[68]

The unfulfilled journeys of Oxley and others before and after him became lines on maps that ended abruptly, often tracing the recorded courses of rivers and stopping when the terrain became impassable or the water ran out. And yet, these journey lines gave to the otherwise plotless map of Australia a sense of sequence and narrative potential, always pointing further towards the centre. A speculative map dated 1827 and entitled 'Sketches of the Coasts of Australia and of the Supposed Entrance of the Great River' was included in Thomas Maslen's *The Friend of Australia* (1830) (Figure 31).[69] In contrast to contemporary maps that only sketched a limited degree of trusted information, this map pictures a huge network of waterways originating in the centre of the continent and flowing out from the 'Great

Figure 31. 'Sketches of the Coasts of Australia and of the Supposed Entrance of the Great River', from Thomas J. Maslen, *The Friend of Australia* (1830).

River, or the Desired Blessing' towards the eastern coast. Maslen wrote: 'if there are desert tracts of large extent, there are also doubtless many highly fertile, beautiful, and, perhaps, curious portions of country, possessing novelties which the imaginations of the geographer and traveller would never have anticipated'.[70]

By 1828, the *Quarterly Review* was continuing to lament the lack of discoveries made in the large unknown spaces of the interior, expressing surprise that 'so little progress has been made in discovery, where so extensive a field of *terra incognita* surrounds the settlers'.[71] In the same year, Sydney Smith, in the *Edinburgh Review*, stated: 'so far as relates to the interior of the continent, we are sorry to say that this amounts really to nothing'.[72] Conceptualizing the perimeter of the continent as a surface to be broken through, Smith wrote: 'it is but too evident that the coasts of New Holland present one unvaried face of the most dreary barrenness', which has been 'nowhere penetrated farther than forty or fifty miles, and at a very few points only, so far'.[73] Reviewers were continually repeating their own frustrations.

Even so, for Smith the potential seemed to lie there waiting to be realized in 'as great an extent of unknown land, marked by at least as striking features, as in any other portion of the globe'.[74] He reminded readers that a fulfilled expectation of the inland space would guarantee the future of the British Empire there. Oxley's discovery of marshes, in Smith's mind, kept alive the dreams of a great body of water flowing from the centre, where no explorers had yet been able to venture. Smith wrote:

> By these discoveries, the reproach of barrenness, which rested for some time upon New Holland, has been thoroughly removed... with the vast unknown interior there is here space to locate successive bodies of emigrants for another half century, and in fact to form an empire greater and more populous than that from which it sprung.[75]

The *Quarterly Review* was less positive. Making a comparison between North America and Australia, a reviewer reflected:

> In New South Wales we should look in vain for those noble rivers, those expansive lakes, and wide-spreading meadows, chequered with magnificent forests of the finest timber, which form the most remarkable features in the North American landscape.[76]

This reviewer, nevertheless, also held out some hope for future discoveries, citing the long period of time required in the settlement of North America and recalling that it was 30 years from 1585, when 'the first colony was carried to Virginia', to 1616, when at last there were reports of a prosperous colony filtering back to Europe.[77]

In 1829, the area around the newly established Swan River Colony was being reported as fertile, with good soil and plenty of water. Sir John Barrow of the Admiralty, also one of the founders of the Royal Geographical Society, was an acknowledged expert on the southern hemisphere. In the *Quarterly Review* he wrote that 'with the exception of a few articles, such as oil from the whale and seal fisheries, wool, timber, acacia bark for tanning, and a few cargoes of hides and skins', there was as yet nothing of value to export. Barrow, arguing for a great link between the coastal settlements in Australia, including the Swan River Colony on the western coast, proposed a cordon that would protect British interests and gradually open up the interior from all angles.[78] Barrow embraced Captain James Stirling's glowing reports on the Swan River Colony, writing an article for the *Quarterly Review* in which he associated the new colony with 'Hesperia' (the Greek 'Isles of the Blest') and 'Goshen' (the biblical 'Land of Plenty').[79] Foreseeing a dense settlement in the interior, Barrow wrote that the extent of the territory 'is estimated to contain from five to six millions of acres, the greatest part of which...may be considered as land fit for the plough and fully capable of giving support to millions of souls'.[80] By that stage, however, Stirling had only explored 260 square kilometres of land.[81]

These glorious forecasts for Australia's west, heralding the further spread of British culture, were supported by prominent European writers and thinkers including Samuel Taylor Coleridge. In a conversation with John Frere on 10 December 1830, he is reported to have asked, rhetorically: 'Are we to beware of having two [sets] of men bound to us by the ties of allegiance and of affinity; two [sets] of men in distant parts of the world speaking the language of Shakspear and Milton, and living under the laws of Alfred?'[82] In the following year, inspired by the same kind of rhetoric, Barrow wrote: 'This extensive territory will, in all probability, in process of time, support a numerous population, the progeny of Britons, and may be the means of spreading the English language, laws, and institutions'.[83] Despite new discoveries in Australia's west, Barrow explained that 'a country which, though as large as Europe, is as yet represented on our maps nearly as a blank'.[84] The blankness of the map corresponded with and supported the concept of Australia as an emptiness waiting to be filled, and of *terra nullius*.[85] The effect of the publicity given to the Swan River Colony in the *Quarterly Review* was to dramatically raise the general interest in migration. 'Within a month...rapturous descriptions, far removed from that of Stirling or Barrow, were being circulated'.[86]

Pressing inland from the eastern coast, there were various explorations following Oxley, including those of Charles Sturt (in 1828–30) and Surveyor-General Major Thomas Mitchell (in 1831–2). Sturt, in particular, fuelled the belief that extensive inland waterways were yet to be discovered by finding the Murray and Darling Rivers, both of which seemed to point to a great source of water being located further west.[87] But even by 1835 the *Quarterly Review* was reporting that the only new land that had been named since Oxley's discoveries was the Liverpool Plains, to the north of Sydney.[88] In 1836, the *Journal of the Royal Geographical Society of London* acknowledged despondently that Mitchell had followed the Darling River for 300 miles without finding 'a single river or chain of ponds from either side'.[89]

The mythology of a fertile inland had been established firmly by Oxley and the believers before him. It was a mythology that was eventually discredited by explorers later in the nineteenth century. Paradoxically, there is now evidence suggesting that Australia's centre may once indeed have been a fertile – even tropical – landscape, following the finding of megafauna fossils at Riversleigh in 1999.[90] Commenting on the historical significance of

Australian exploration narratives, Paul Carter argues that the accounts are 'characteristically discontinuous' and 'also lack "plot"'. For Carter, they differ from classic Indian and African colonial travel narratives in two ways: Indigenous presence plays 'no determining role in the structure', and they 'do not culminate in major discoveries'.[91] These observations point to the special place that Australia's interior spaces occupy in the history of Europe's imagining of the antipodes. This was a final great unknown. Its exploration demanded a traversing of land rather than of sea. Because these expeditions did not yield the expected and hoped-for fulfilment of the myths of central Australia's fertility and plenty, they were reported negatively as *not* finding and as disappointment. For this reason, the Australian centre took on the powerful negative symbolism reflected in terms such as 'dead heart' and 'never-never'.[92]

Account of an Expedition to the Interior of New Holland (1837)

> The European and aboriginal races became in time completely blended together; for it appears to have been one of the principles most earnestly maintained and inculcated by their extraordinary leader, to allow of no hereditary degradation; – no subjection of one race of men to another on the ground of colour or caste, but to make all subjects of the State necessarily admissible to the rights of citizenship. Yet, on the other hand, he was well aware of the actual inferiority of the aborigines as individuals and as a race, and was fully alive to the evil of placing inferior men on a level with those morally and intellectually superior. The maxim, accordingly, which he continually dwelt on, and laboured to embody in practice, was, that it is not the colour of the skin, but the heart and head, that makes a man savage or civilized. Education, accordingly, was the means adopted for reclaiming and for preserving men from barbarism.
>
> – *Account of an Expedition to the Interior of New Holland* (1837)[93]

Australia's interior has been the setting for a long-established tradition of novels and books for young readers as well as drama, poetry, film and television programs. In the 1890s and in the early twentieth century, there was a proliferation of 'lost race' romances, to which the imaginary voyage discussed in this chapter was a precursor.[94] In J. W. Gregory's *The Dead Heart of Australia* (1906),[95] the heart was deemed dead perhaps because it had been so long imagined as alive and fertile. It was a powerful image and by the 1950s the identity of Australian space was often 'treated as synonymous with the inland'.[96] The mystical, barren interior, now captured by the term 'outback',[97] continues to be a feature of Australian iconography, both within Australia and as it is promoted and perceived elsewhere.

In contrast to the limited discoveries of contemporary explorers, the vision of Australia's interior in the imaginary voyage *Account of an Expedition to the Interior of New Holland* (1837) is of a nation of between 3 and 4 million people living in utopian isolation in the centre of Australia. Detailing this amazing purported discovery, the book is subtitled:

The late wonderful discovery of a civilized nation of European origin, which had, in so remarkable a manner, been kept separate hitherto from the rest of the civilized world.

Australia's centre offered an anonymous writer an opening to portray a fictional Europeanized society and to show the benefits brought to the Indigenous population by colonialism at the time that actual colonial settlement was well under way on both sides of the continent. It is a 'double' utopia in the sense that it reflects upon European society but also suggests comparisons with the colony of New South Wales. In traditional utopian fashion, the city of 'Bath' in this story is compared with the English town of Bath.[98] One of the purported founders of the colony was English, the other German. Germany, in fact, has an important literary connection with colonial Australia, having produced the first novel to utilize the Australian penal setting as a backdrop in 1793.[99] Although the authorship of *Account of an Expedition to the Interior of New Holland* remains unknown, it is sometimes attributed to Richard Whately, who was Archbishop of Dublin, Oxford University Professor of Political Economy and a commentator on Australian convict transportation.[100] The work is included in the multi-volume collection *Modern British Utopias 1700–1850* (1997), edited by Gregory Claeys.[101] Claeys suggests that, because of stylistic inconsistencies throughout, it is possible that there was more than one author involved; or, if the author was not Richard Whately, that it may have been Lady Mary Fox, who is named as an editor.[102] The text has had little attention paid to it since it falls outside of the period covered by the few major studies of imaginary voyages. Ross Gibson provides a discussion of the work in utopian terms as a commentary on European government and social reform.[103] John Dunmore also refers to it, describing the Victorian society that has developed in Australia's interior as 'almost genteel' and 'polished'.[104]

Published in 1837, *Account of an Expedition to the Interior of New Holland* is set in 1835. The writer was possibly inspired to imagine the world of the interior and its people by the presumed death of Richard Cunningham, colonial botanist, who was lost in the bush after apparently wandering off alone from Mitchell's expedition in 1835. In Mitchell's official letter to the Governor dated 4 September 1835, written from the camp where Cunningham disappeared and later printed in the *Journal of the Royal Geographical Society of*

London, Mitchell placed the blame on two groups of menacing Aborigines nearby.[105] According to reports from Sydney, dated 22 December 1835, police had been sent to ascertain Cunningham's fate. They found a shred of Cunningham's coat and met an Aboriginal clan who had bones that they said were those of a white man.[106]

I

> ...tho' the folks dont walk with their heads down & heels up in the air neither, as the old nurses used to tell us.
> – *Account of an Expedition to the Interior of New Holland*[107]

Account of an Expedition to the Interior of New Holland is 24 chapters in length. Breaking with earlier conventions, this work omits the customary assortment of introductory passages. As the *Quarterly Review* observed in 1828: 'The days are gone by when an author, to beget the serious attention of his readers, deemed it a matter of indispensable necessity to procure the meretricious aid of "laudatory epistles", or "commendatory verses", from his very good friends and patrons'.[108] The final chapter, however, makes up for the lack of introductory sections by adding another, more personal, voice to the book. The chapter takes the form of a letter purportedly written from Sydney by a member of the expedition party conveying the story of his adventures to a friend in England.[109] References to the new Swan River Colony help to lend additional historical realism.[110] The letter is said to be printed 'exactly from the manuscript', including spelling mistakes, making it seem even more authentic.[111] At times a slightly confusing narratorial voice makes it unclear if there is more than one narrator in the main account, and whether this indicates that there was more than one writer, although early references to 'our readers' and 'our travellers' may simply adhere to the convention of using the royal plural.[112]

Account of an Expedition to the Interior of New Holland begins as the story of a group of five settlers, led by a Mr. Hopkins Sibthorpe, who go in search of fertile regions in Australia's interior. Following closely in the footsteps of actual contemporary explorers, the expedition party leaves Bathurst, New South Wales, in early August 1835.[113] Detailed planning goes into the expedition because of the difficulty of seasonal flooding, a recognized obstacle to contemporary exploration in New South Wales. In order to carry all their supplies, the explorers construct a canoe, and they use it to paddle in a northwest direction through the marshes.[114] Here the 'waters abounded with fish and wildfowl'.[115] Progress is 'tediously slow' at first. However, in the narrator's words: 'After two days of troublesome navigation they found the water become deeper, and gained a sight of some elevated land towards the west, which they reached on the evening of the third day'.[116] The waterway was surrounded 'within narrow limits by hills, for the most part of a rocky, sterile, and uninviting character', but at length 'it became a broad river, flowing in a northerly direction, and serving evidently as a drain to the great expanse of lake they had passed'.[117] This discovery fires the explorers' hopes of reaching 'some large navigable river, which they might follow to the sea'.[118] After two days' navigation, the party comes to an 'expanse of water; so extensive that, in pursuing their adventurous course nearly in the same direction, they were, for the greater part of one day, out of sight of land'.[119] The waterway continues to change, becoming narrower within gorges, and then 'expanding itself at intervals into a chain of lakes, smaller but deeper than those they had passed, and surrounded by a much more agreeable country, which continued to improve as they advanced'.[120]

II

In the course of the expedition, the explorers land at several places. At one point they come across a 'party of natives, who were of a less savage aspect than those in the vicinity of our settlements, and shewed no signs of hostility, and much less of alarm and astonishment than had been expected'.[121] In the explorers' eyes, the character of the Aboriginal people they encounter seems to be changing along with the landscape, becoming calmer and less savage as the land becomes more fertile. They do not speak the language common around the area of Sydney that explorer 'Mr. Jones' is familiar with, but some of the natives have steel knives, and this is taken as a sign that they have visited the settlement on the coast.[122] However, although at first they find it implausible, the explorers gradually come to believe that they must now be in the vicinity of another settlement because they see wild boars, which they know are not native to Australia.[123] The land continues to improve as they navigate through a landscape 'continually improving in beauty and fertility, and presenting a strong contrast to the dreary rocks and marshes they had left behind'.[124]

The expedition had travelled for over a month when the narrator reports that they came across a startling scene (which recalls the first sighting of the Glumms and Gawreys in *The Life and Adventures of Peter Wilkins*): 'they were at length surprised and gratified, on entering a lake somewhat more extensive than the last, to see several fishing-boats, the men in which they ascertained by their glasses to be decently clothed, and white men'.[125] The explorers 'ventured to approach and to hail the men', and to their 'unspeakable surprise and delight, they received an answer in *English*'.[126] This English 'was, indeed, not precisely similar to their own, but not differing so much from it as many of our provincial dialects'.[127] Reflecting the lexicographical changes in the English language taking place in the real-world Australian colonies, these settlers have developed a modified language that has evolved over three centuries. However, as the narrator explains: 'in a short time the two parties were tolerably intelligible to each other'.[128] 'The reception they met with was most friendly and every way refreshing, after an anxious and toilsome journey'.[129] The tended landscape, although it features Australian plant and animal life, seems very similar to that of England, 'a rich and partially cultivated country, interspersed with cheerful-looking villages, having much of an English air of comfort'.[130] It becomes apparent to the travellers that their journey has been exceptionally successful, the party having not only found endless stretches of fertile land but also a welcoming Europeanized society already occupying the interior.[131]

The first moments of cross-cultural encounter are dealt with in a summary manner, as is typical in many imaginary voyages, creating a sense that the visitors' arrival is natural and welcomed. The narrator explains: 'We are compelled to pass over the interesting detail of the meeting',[132] '[w]e are compelled to pass over the particulars of the several steps by which the travellers arrived at the knowledge of the singular country in the midst of which they found themselves',[133] '[w]e have only space for a brief summary of the results',[134] and '[t]he curious and interesting particulars of their voyage, their various adventures, disappointments, and reiterated attempts, we are compelled to pass over'.[135] The explorers are 'the guests of the chief magistrate of a neat town of considerable size'.[136] Here everyone is exceptionally friendly, 'eager to obtain and to afford information', and 'with pressing invitations'.[137] The narrator summarizes the astonishing setting the explorers had discovered:

> They found themselves, then, in a nation of European, and chiefly, though not entirely, of English extraction, which had had no intercourse with Europe, or with any other portion of the civilized world, for nearly three centuries. Their numbers were estimated at between three and four millions; and they were divided into eleven distinct communities, existing in a sort of loosely federal union, or rather in a friendly relation, sanctioned and maintained by custom more than by any formal compact.[138]

The narrator reports that the governments and other institutions are 'agreeing in the manifestation of a high degree of civilization', that is, 'considering the disadvantage of labouring in their seclusion from the rest of the world'.[139] This nation is later compared to Britain and Ireland because it is equivalent in size.[140] An answer is also given to the question of why no Australian explorer had yet been able to find any great rivers pointing to the interior. The reason is that these people have developed gigantic dams to harness the abundant water supplies.[141]

When the residents of the interior learn about the penal colony at Sydney, of which they have no knowledge, they are shocked:

> To people a new settlement with convicted criminals, – to form a new nation of the scum and refuse of mankind, – appeared to them so preposterous, that for some time they could not help supposing they must have misunderstood their informants. "To bring together a number of villains," they said, "to a country where good character is not the rule, but the exception, allowing them free intercourse with each other, must be the most effectual mode of hardening and confirming them in wickedness, and entailing the same character on successive generations."[142]

In the unique setting of Australia as a continent that remained only partly known, *Account of an Expedition to the Interior of New Holland* reflected on the nature of society in New South Wales as well as on European society. Australia was large enough to be a setting for this kind of double utopian reflection. The book is also indicative of the direct impact that colonization in the antipodes was having on writers of utopian fiction in Europe.

III

The history of the settlers of the interior is narrated in the form of a second fictional journey within the first, this time involving the familiar devices of storm and shipwreck, and including a voyage by sea that precedes an overland journey to inland Australia. The visitors are told that the original colony was made up of a group of only three to four hundred people who fled Europe during the Reformation approximately three centuries earlier. Some were from England, others from Germany. By leaving for 'some distant region' they believed they 'should escape finally from strife and oppression, and establish a civil and religious community'.[143] Recalling utopian social schemes such as Coleridge and Robert Southey's pantisocracy in America, as well as the actual early settlement of Australia, this voyage is a large-scale undertaking rather than the experience of a lone traveller. In this story the original explorers had, in fact, deliberated about whether to go to America, but were lured by the power of antipodean myths, being 'induced by some glowing descriptions they had heard, but which proved to consist chiefly of fable or exaggeration, to seek for the long-famed southern continent, the "Terra Australis Incognita"'.[144] The leaders of the expedition were two Mullers, 'a German settled in England', and his nephew, 'the son of an Englishwoman'.[145] The senior Muller is described as being 'of enthusiastic wildness, brilliant genius, and sanguine credulity, which periods of great excitement – such as the commencement of the Reformation – are often found to call forth'.[146] He is presented as one who was called upon to colonize by some divine power. 'He possessed great eloquence', the narrator explains, 'and a power of exercising an unbounded influence over the minds of a certain description'.[147]

In the original voyage of discovery, a shipwreck provides the transitional point of entry into the imagined world. The arriving settlers are forced by a storm onto the coast of New Holland, 'somewhere, it is supposed, between lat. 10 and 20 south, and long. 130 and 140 east'.[148] One of the four ships is wrecked on a coral reef, and two others are 'driven ashore with a considerable damage'.[149] The narrator then gives an account of the initial cross-cultural contact between the Europeans and the Aboriginal inhabitants. On arrival, the party of original settlers were sick due to fever. They moved inland eight or nine miles where they rested and regained their health. They began to build a makeshift settlement, not knowing whether or not they would stay. Their decision to move 'was ultimately fixed by means of the intercourse they succeeded in establishing with a native tribe'.[150] However, as in the fictional journey of 1835, the narrator glosses over the details of the initial cross-cultural contact, '[m]utual good-will and confidence having been completely established between the settlers and the natives'.[151]

A significant point to make from a postcolonial perspective is that the Aboriginal people on the coast are presented as being responsible for actually inviting the Europeans to claim the centre of the continent. As the narrator explains, they made this gesture because they were once the rightful owners of the land there but were forced away by aggressive tribes from other interior regions:

> They were anxious to induce their European neighbours to settle there themselves, and enable them to reinstate themselves in their ancient abode. They easily perceived the vast superiority which European arts and arms would give to their new allies over enemies who had proved to be too powerful for themselves, and they hoped through their aid to re-establish themselves in a country which they had quitted with regret.[152]

The Europeans, '[m]oved by their representations', agreed to support this moral cause, which was also in their own best interests.[153] In contrast with the historical pattern of settlement in which British settlers drove the local Indigenous populations from the fertile coasts towards the arid interior, the first move inland the Europeans make in this story is by invitation and undertaken with the knowledge that the centre is more fertile than the coast. Since there is already routine conflict amongst the Indigenous people, it seems to the settlers

130   VIRTUAL VOYAGES

as though their needing to take sides is a natural way of life in the interior. It is presented as both a means of survival and of showing friendship.

The narrator goes on to describe the founding journey undertaken to reach the interior. As in the expedition of 1835, the land the settlers traverse becomes more fertile and welcoming as the group proceeds. They go in a direct line inland from the coast, over a mountain range, across an elevated plain 'of a most sterile character, extending for more than a three hundred miles in the same direction', to a chain of rocky mountains, before at last reaching their destination. They are 'rewarded by the view of a most extensive and delightfully fertile region', watered 'with numerous streams from these mountains, and interspersed with beautiful lakes'.[154] The narrator reflects that it had been a perilous journey, 'not without some narrow escapes from the hostility of some of the wandering native tribes'.[155]

At this stage, accompanying the 300-strong group of European settlers are 'a somewhat smaller number of natives', once scattered and 'subsisting by the chase', but now united.[156] In preparation for the expected battle to come, the Europeans teach their Aboriginal allies how to use bows and arrows instead of spears.[157] As predicted, 'they were attacked in spite of all their endeavours to preserve peace, by the native tribes of the interior, moved by their inveterate animosity against their ancient enemies'.[158] The combined European/Aboriginal forces 'gained an easy and complete victory in every encounter'.[159] The European firearms, 'though only old-fashioned, clumsy matchlocks of those days', were 'sufficient to strike terror into savages unacquainted with gunpowder'.[160] Remarkably similar expressions of colonial power-play can be found in descriptions of cross-cultural encounters that had been taking place in the real world of the antipodes in the early nineteenth century. In 1815, for example, the *Quarterly Review* had reported on American David Porter's exploits in the Pacific, writing:

> Captain Porter soon discovered, or pretends to have discovered, that the people of a neighbouring valley, at the head of Comptroller's bay, named the Happahs, were at war with those among whom he landed; though it was admitted that a friendly intercourse was still kept up between the two tribes. Anxious to shew his prowess among a people whose weapons were harmless when put in competition with fire-arms, and still more anxious to procure provisions without paying for them (for avarice is the ruling passion of this huckstering captain), he caused a message to be sent over the mountains "to tell the Happahs he had come with a force sufficiently strong to drive them from the island; and if they presumed to enter into the valley while he remained there, he should send a body of men to chastise them".[161]

In Porter's account, a scene of 'massacre and plunder' followed, which the reviewer could not condone.[162]

In *Account of an Expedition to the Interior of New Holland*, the European-led force had defeated the other tribes to successfully take over the fertile centre of the continent. Now there was relative peace, only 'interrupted from time to time by predatory incursions and irregular renewals of hostilities'.[163] The narrator refers to the bonding effect that fighting together in defence had for the Europeans and the Aborigines, explaining: 'This state of things, with all its inconveniences, appears to have had the advantage of cementing the friendship between the settlers and their native allies; each party feeling the other's importance for security against a common enemy'.[164] The Europeans teach their Aboriginal allies to cultivate the land and to shoot guns, as well as to speak the English language and follow their religion and social customs. As the narrator explains: 'The whites, accordingly, seem to have been assiduous and successful in civilizing these natives, with whom they were thus thrown into close contact'.[165] To symbolize the new bond, the colony adopts a crest of intertwined black and white swans,[166] later to become the arms of the kingdom, when the 'European and aboriginal races became in time completely blended together'.[167] Lending historical realism through a real-world comparison, the reader learns that the new colony's population seems 'to have advanced at about the same rate as those of some of the North-American settlements'.[168]

Back in the setting of the 1835 layer of the narrative, the explorers find most of the trappings of European civilization in the colony, but some things seem very different. A chapter on law and government describes the nation as being at a highly developed stage, with a state structure and no national debt. It accommodates 17 church communities, some of them devoted entirely to missionary ventures for Aboriginal education. The original settlement is called Mullersfield, after its founders. Another town, near Bath, is named Eutopia. As the narrator explains – not quite giving away the fictional nature of the text – the town was named 'probably with something of a covert allusion also to the well known fabulous Utopia (no place)'.[169] The colonists 'have a deep-seated and habitual contempt for every thing which, according to their notions, savours of barbarism'.[170] Most of them look very much like Europeans because the Aborigines were far outnumbered from the outset, 'tho' some of them', the narrator explains, have 'a lick of the Tar brush as they say in the West Indies'.[171] Big feasts are judged as barbaric because they are perceived as a 'practice of the savages'.[172] The children parody traditional native customs when they participate in a sport they refer to as '"playing at being savages"; the dances consisting in a ludicrous imitation of those of the aborigines'.[173] In fact, the people of the interior are surprised that European culture still promotes dancing of any kind because of the connection they make between dancing and savagery.[174] All people in the colony routinely cover every part of their bodies with clothing to avoid looking like 'the savages', and wear no jewellery for the same reason.[175] With such a mix of contrary customs to learn about and chronicle, two members of the European expedition party stay while the three others set off to return to Sydney with the news.[176] One of the few direct hints in the text of its fictitious nature comes in the appended letter at the back of the book. The writer explains: 'I hardly knew whether I was a sleep or a wake, it seam'd a kind of dream like'.[177]

Account of an Expedition to the Interior of New Holland engaged with contemporary colonial politics as well as with debates in Europe and in Australia relating to the opening up of the continent's interior. This interaction was made possible by the historical conditions in which the text was written. Physical barriers to Australia's interior meant that the continent was claimed but not fully known, mapped but only in outline, and settled but contested. This text capitalized on the anticipation and hope transferred to one of the last unexplored regions of the globe, where myth and fiction continued to flourish in the face of fact. Australia remained a place half-real, half-imagined.

CONCLUSION

The accounts of the first voyagers are mingled with fabulous tales of giants and monsters, that could only have existed in the imagination of the writer; or, what is more probable, they were introduced by artful and designing men, for the purpose of deterring other adventurers from exploring the same spot, and enriching themselves with the supposed treasure it contained…

– *Retrospective Review* (1824)[1]

In the closing years of the eighteenth century, the *British Critic* reported: 'Travellers continue to assert their privilege of telling their tales in their own way, "of hair-breadth escapes", and the public seems very indulgently disposed to give them audience'.[2] 'Curiosity will always make travellers, and a still more extended curiosity, produces readers for their narratives'.[3] Accounts of travels were so popular in 1798 that the editors suggested, humorously, that their own prefaces should be 'allied to that species of composition'.[4] They later explain: 'We are, however, kinder to our readers than the generality of travel writers' because 'the hardships they encounter are generally detailed at full length; frequently, perhaps, not without exaggeration'.[5] In 1799 the *British Critic* claimed that voyages and travels 'always were, and must be, popular' because 'they administer to a curiosity which is liberal and almost universal' and 'give the satisfaction of knowledge, without exacting the labour of serious study'.[6] Expressing succinctly the power of literary realism before critical conceptions of realism had developed, the editors wrote in 1799 that the literature of voyages and travels, of all forms of literature regularly surveyed, 'approaches more nearly to the character of the novel, than any other book of information'.[7] While readership of novels reached a new high point in Britain at the beginning of the nineteenth century, the *Monthly Review* noted that 'next to novels, voyages and travels constitute the most fashionable kind of reading'.[8] Compared with the often tortuous physical experience of months or years at sea in tentatively charted waters, virtual voyaging was a pleasurable activity which followed safe and well-defined routes.[9]

Despite this enthusiasm for accounts of travels and for novels, the imaginary voyage went out of vogue in the first half of the nineteenth century. The creative potential of the antipodes for writers of imaginary voyages was spent by the historical process of discovery itself, which slowly reduced the *terra incognita* aspect of the antipodes to which they had so creatively lent life. The prospect of trade and colonization there had now become a reality. More interesting than fictional portrayals of colonization in imagined locations were the numerous genuine reports of the progress of trading posts and colonies. Throughout the nineteenth century, imaginary voyages set in various locations continued to appear, but only occasionally. In 1812, Henry Weber's collection entitled *Popular Romances, Consisting of Imaginary Voyages and Travels* was published in Edinburgh. It included four English examples and one French text in English translation, together with a selection of romances and an introduction by Weber (who was assisting Walter Scott as an editor).[10] Announcing the new collection, Weber described a 'universal inclination for the marvellous' which, in earlier centuries, had 'pervaded almost every department of literature and science' but was now being superseded by an empirical kind of evaluation.[11] A rare mention of the imaginary voyage in generic terms is in an 1823 review of Charles Mills' *The Travels of Theodore Ducas* (1822).[12] The *voyage imaginaire* is described as:

> ...a difficult and most unprofitable class of belles-lettres; – unprofitable because such a work can only be a larceny from more authentic stores; – and difficult, because what is *invented* is so limited and straitened by the realities to which it is attached, that the liveliest fancy would be paralysed.[13]

The reviewer continues, complaining:

> We deny to the imaginary traveller the indulgence which we every day allow the poetical flights of real tourists; yet we require him to be lively and entertaining... We fly from the languid interest of his compilation to the *professed* dictionary of poets and painters which he has plundered; and prefer seeking for knowledge where it may be found stripped of the useless incumbrance of a fiction which neither fascinates nor informs.[14]

The heyday of the imaginary voyage was over. The very qualities that had intrigued and delighted earlier audiences now drove them away. Readers who had been willing to suspend disbelief to be carried by the wildest imaginative projections into undiscovered places, had lost their taste for such flights of fancy once it became clear that there was no longer even a flimsy possibility that they could be true. Voyage literature remained popular because its truths were validated by a belief, grounded in the emerging scientific vision, that impartial observation was possible. Imaginary voyages, by contrast, were increasingly dismissed as corruptions of the empirical project. It was the double game they had played with truth that had held audiences of imaginary voyages for so long.

One reason for the imaginary voyage's decline in popularity was that the mixing of fact and fiction in a single genre brought together two modes that were in the process of being separated. Referring to the split between empiricist and non-empiricist approaches to history writing in the *Quarterly Review* in 1832, historian and poet Henry Milman called this separation a 'division of labour'.[15] Modern historiography aimed at objectively determining the truths of the past. The historian's role, satisfying 'the unquestioned convention of the all-seeing spectator', was as 'an impartial onlooker, simply *repeating* what happened'.[16] Earlier frameworks for interpreting the past could not satisfy the new goals.[17] Consider the following passage written by J. J. Blunt, also taken from the *Quarterly Review*, in the same year:

> "Give me a liar" was the phrase which Charles the Fifth used to call for a volume of history; and certainly no man can attentively examine any important period of our annals without remarking, that almost every incident admits of two handles, almost every character of two interpretations; and that, by a judicious packing of facts, the historian may make his picture assume nearly what form he pleases, without any direct violation of truth.[18]

The newer belief was that, through the power of careful historical research, things could be described simply 'as they were', the activity of writing being merely a transparent means of conveying information.[19]

In literary works published in the early nineteenth century, a corresponding distinction was emerging between the eighteenth-century style of prose fiction and a newer, more modern form of the novel. In 1815, the *Quarterly Review* described the differences between earlier adventure writing and the current novels, recalling the predictable narrative structure of adventures in which a single traveller takes a chaotic voyage of discovery. As the reviewer explained it:

> Violent changes of time, or place, and of circumstances, hurry him forward from one scene to another, and his adventures will usually be found only connected with each other because they have happened to the same individual. Such a history resembles an ingenious, fictitious

narrative, exactly in the degree in which an old dramatic chronicle of the life and death of some distinguished character, where all the various agents appear and disappear as in the page of history, approaches a regular drama, in which every person introduced plays an appropriate part, and every point of the action tends to one common catastrophe.[20]

The reviewer summarized the changing trends in this way:

Accordingly a style of novel has arisen, within the last fifteen or twenty years, differing from the former in the points upon which the interest hinges; neither alarming our credulity nor amusing our imagination by wild variety of incident, or by those pictures of romantic affection and sensibility, which were formerly as certain attributes of fictitious characters as they are of rare occurrence among those who actually live and die.[21]

The difference between the novels old and new is in the 'conduct of the narrative, and the tone of sentiment attributed to the fictitious personages'. Claiming that the prevalent themes of earlier romances were annoyingly repetitive, the reviewer noted that now, 'the hero no longer defeated armies by his single sword...or gained kingdoms'.[22] The reader of the earlier style of prose fiction was expected to identify with the protagonist, 'since by incidents so much beyond the bounds of his ordinary experience, his wonder and interest ought at once to be excited'. But gradually, the reader 'became familiar with the land of fiction', the 'adventures of which he assimilated not with those of real life but with each other'.[23] In short, the *Quarterly Review* observed:

...the author of novels was, in former times, expected to tread pretty much in the limits between the concentric circles of probability and possibility; and as he was not permitted to transgress the latter, his narrative, to make amends, almost always went beyond the bounds of the former.[24]

The modern novel was being given a different thematic treatment, depicting more subtly the character of everyday life. In the reviewer's words, 'instead of the splendid scenes of an imaginary world', the novelist now aimed at 'a correct and striking representation of that which is daily taking place around him'.[25]

New stylistic considerations were also affecting writers of genuine travel accounts. In 1815, the *Monthly Review* complained of Matthew Flinders' account that there were too many navigational details included, recommending that 'it may have been advantageous to have kept them apart' from the 'descriptions of country and narrative of events'.[26] Such details, as this reviewer put it, continued to be 'useful to the mariner and geographer' but were now of less interest to most readers.[27] With the same desire to identify sources and separate out component narrative elements, Henry Brougham, reviewing John Turnbull's *Voyage Round the World* in 1807, set out a checklist of the kinds of information he would like to see in a voyage account. One of Brougham's main complaints, however, was that he suspected Turnbull had employed a professional writer, 'a fashion too prevalent among travellers of the present day' and a practice he did not support.[28] In cases where professional writers were used, Brougham asked that authorship be made clear, explaining: 'We must know the writer's name, as well as the traveller's. We must have the responsibility resting wholly upon known persons, and not shared between one who appears, and another who lurks'. Above all, Brougham asked that there be a clear distinction made between traveller and writer, insisting: 'We must not see the writer so entirely confounded with the traveller, as to deceive us respecting their separate existence'.[29]

Related transformations can be seen in the history of cartography. At the beginning of the early modern period, maps had been unashamedly speculative. They were canvasses for creative cartographers, many of whom were also engravers or painters. The less knowledge there was of the world beyond Europe's boundaries, the more scope there was for maps to be inventive, blending received knowledge with fictional projection. In time, as proto-scientific ways of seeing and measuring were adopted, cartographers' attempts to display the mythic imaginary alongside authenticated information were gradually superseded by the more pragmatic modern approach of exposing the remaining gaps in knowledge and filling them as accurately as possible.

While the same impulse to explore unknown parts of the world provided inspiration for voyages both real and imaginary, the actual voyages slowly but effectively erased the open fictional terrain that appealed to writers of imaginary voyages. Although changing European literary tastes were equally responsible for the demise of imaginary voyage literature in the nineteenth century, familiarity with the southern world meant that there was simply no longer a guaranteed market for stories of *imaginary* travel to the antipodes. By the late 1820s, Sydney Smith, in the *Edinburgh Review*, reported that the circumnavigation of the globe, 'once the boast of the greatest naval men', is 'in modern times a common trading voyage'.[30] At some point the balance had shifted. Travellers were no longer 'lone ethnographers' in worlds outside of the usual bounds of European knowledge.[31] The perceived heroism of penetrating unknown lands would now be associated not primarily with first discovery, but with successfully establishing imperial rule.

The demand for other kinds of speculative fiction, however, did not diminish. Writers of utopian literature, for example, continued to utilize the setting of the Pacific through the nineteenth and twentieth centuries, for 'utopias survived with less difficulty than imaginary voyages'.[32] However, the voyage into the unknown could no longer be a voyage into the antipodean *terra incognita*. More interesting and informative to nineteenth-century readers were the stories of real adventures within this new world, written by settlers and tourists, which incorporated and added to an increasingly complex, growing mosaic of general information about the region. The colonial guidebook genre, making recommendations to prospective emigrants and travellers, featured alluring descriptions of colonial society that suggested the realistic potential for alternative ways of life in the southern hemisphere. Despite the demand for authenticated information, the tradition of travel fiction masquerading as reliable documentary evidence continued in different forms. The history of Australian colonial literature, for example, includes a list of notorious books, published as factual accounts, which were actually written by people who had never set foot in Australia.[33] The Pacific too continued to be a setting for fictionalized or romanticized accounts of the adventures of travellers and tourists, but these no longer followed the predictable formula of the seventeenth- and eighteenth-century imaginary voyage.[34] Meanwhile, the ancient imagery of antipodal reversals retained its grip on the imagination. For example, Charles Rowcroft, in his novel *Tales of the Colonies* (1843), which by 1845 had run to three editions, invented bizarre oddities such as cherries with the stone on the outside and rivers running uphill.[35]

In the late nineteenth century, Jules Verne almost single-handedly re-popularized the narrative structure of earlier imaginary voyages.[36] However, the destination of Verne's fictional journeys was not usually the antipodes, although characters do occasionally pass through this part of the world.[37] Verne chose the centre of the earth, the moon, the depths of the sea, and other settings. Nineteenth-century science fiction and fantasy were both responses to the challenge of finding new kinds of locations for writers to explore and utilize. These included outer space and the untapped setting of the future. In today's globalized, information-rich society, the true successor to imaginary voyages may not be the fiction of space exploration, but the new world of virtual voyaging into the seemingly endless shifting maze of the World Wide Web and the distributed electronic spaces of the networked media environment, where fact and fantasy are able to mix and merge freely once more. These observations on the demise of imaginary voyage writing in relation to growing European knowledge of the antipodean space, and to the evolution of literary forms that utilized new imaginative settings, provide further evidence of the close, complex connections between fiction and history, virtual worlds and actual worlds, with which this book is concerned.

As a reference to physical space, the term 'antipodes' has been gradually superseded by newer words that are geographically more specific. Many of the nineteenth-century terms devised to describe divisions or regions within this vast area have been in continuous use since that time. They include the designations 'Melanesia', 'Micronesia' and 'Polynesia'. While general terms, such as 'Oceania', 'Australasia' and 'the Pacific' are now more frequently used, arguably none are ideal because they are either too regionally inclusive or are unspecific. 'The Pacific' cannot easily include Australia since it refers to an ocean rather than to land, and 'Oceania' and 'Australasia' refer to such large regions as to be best suited as headings on the pages of atlases. 'South Seas' is still used occasionally, but mainly in popular travel literature rather than in scholarly writing.[38] 'Oceania' is the broadest of these terms. First used in the mid nineteenth century and increasingly common today, 'Oceania' is 'a general name for the islands of the Pacific and its adjacent seas', covering 'the island-groups of the Pacific Ocean…including Melanesia, Micronesia and Polynesia, and sometimes also Australasia and the Malay archipelago'.[39] Sometimes, however, it only includes the region of Melanesia, Micronesia and Polynesia.[40] Like the term 'antipodes', 'Oceania' can seem exceptionally broad. But 'Oceania' does have the advantage of being a relatively neutral marker of space that does not indicate a historical relationship with Europe. Even so, as Greg Dening writes, it is 'a little too invented, the sort of place Gulliver might have visited or Jules Verne explored'.[41] The term 'Oceania', for Dening, lost some of its meaning with increasing competitiveness amongst nation states and splintered economic agendas in the region, but has nevertheless been adopted positively in the Pacific itself by island people who 'feel that invented though it might be, the name "Oceania" represents the "sea of islands" that it was their triumph to encompass'.[42]

The region of the antipodes exists in the historical shadow of colonization as a space defined in relation to Europe and influenced by a transformative mythic discourse. The antipodes had a double status prior to European contact: it was a space already occupied by Indigenous peoples with cultural systems of ownership that had continued unbroken in some cases for tens of thousands of years; and yet, at the same time, that space was steeped in Europe's own mythologies. Not surprisingly, the term 'antipodes' has become decreasingly relevant since the nineteenth century because it is based on a defining relation to the northern hemisphere that has been weakening since the first European settlers arrived and began to interpret and construct the antipodes from the vantage point of the place itself.[43] At the endpoint of the period that is this study's focus, the relationship between European colonizers and the Indigenous peoples of Australia and of New Zealand would take radically different paths following the signing of the Treaty of Waitangi in New Zealand in 1840, which acknowledged, in a way it never was in Australia, that settlement was an act of invasion that required negotiation.

The history of discovery that this book sketches was deeply influenced by European ideologies that were at the core of the interpretative process. The concept of the antipodes is significant not only because of the enduring influence of popular images of the southern hemisphere as a place of reversals and distortions, but because visions of a world opposite to Europe have been used, politically, in such a variety of ways and over such an exceptionally long period of time. Places and peoples of the antipodes were compared to those of Europe, measured against European expectations and, where possible, made to fit the spirit of those expectations. Their textual representation often relied upon narrative strategies that were employed routinely in all kinds of travel accounts, regardless of whether they were intended to be, or were received as, real or imaginary. Perhaps the most important lesson that the story of the rise and fall of imaginary voyages in the antipodes can teach us is not about genre, nor about the politics of colonialism, but rather something even more fundamental to literary and historical understanding. They provide an illuminating case study in the power of literature to participate in the invisible process of establishing and building assumptions and prejudices within a society. From one perspective, the sense of the rightness of discovery and colonization can be thought of as a moral core at the heart of each story, so obvious that it could be taken for granted as true. Whether the stories were read as truthful or otherwise did not matter. Either way, they continued to lay the imaginative foundations for Europe's political, as well as moral, conception of its role in the antipodes. Indeed, the deep interweaving of truth with fantasy assisted in this process. And yet, it is also important to recognize that these stories of colonial ambition are open to counter-colonialist readings, arguably exposing metropolitan insecurities about the rightness of imperialism. Literary critics may have dismissed examples of imaginary voyages on the grounds that they confusingly and misleadingly blurred fact and fiction. However, this very ambivalence illustrates the complex process by which ancient myths of the antipodes were overlaid with and interacted with empirical knowledge, producing a dynamic colonial epistemology that continues to exert its influence even now. More broadly, it shows how powerfully fiction and the imagination influence the real worlds that people create and inhabit.

CONCLUSION

There is a land in distant seas
Full of all contrarieties.
There beasts have mallards' bills and legs,
Have spurs like cocks, like hens lay eggs.
There quadrupeds go on two feet,
And yet, few quadrupeds so fleet:
And birds, although they cannot fly,
In swiftness with the greyhound vie.
With equal wonder you may see
The foxes fly tree to tree;
And what they value most – so wary –
These foxes in their pockets carry.
There parrots walk upon the ground,
And grass upon the trees is found.
On other trees another wonder,
Leaves without upper side or under.
There apple-trees no fruit produce,
But from their trunks pour cid'rous juice.
The pears you'll scarce with hatchet cut;
Stones are outside the cherries put;
Swans are not white, but black as soot.
There the voracious ewe-sheep crams
Her paunch with flesh of tender lambs.
There neither herb, nor root, nor fruit
Will any christian palate suit,
Unless in desp'rate need you'd fill ye
With root of fern and stalk of lily.
Instead of bread, and beef, and broth,
Men feast on many a roasted moth,
And find their most delicious food
In grubs picked out of rotten wood.
There birds construct them shady bowers,
Deck'd with bright feathers, shells, and flowers;
To these the cocks and hens resort,
Run to and fro, and gaily sport.
Others a hot-bed join to make,
To hatch the eggs which they forsake.
There missiles to far distance sent
Come whizzing back with force unspent.
There courting swains their passion prove
By knocking down the girls they love.

There every servant gets his place
By character of foul disgrace.
There vice is virtue, virtue vice,
And all that's vile is voted nice.
The sun, when you to face him turn ye,
From right to left performs his journey.
The North winds scorch; but when the breeze is
Full from the South, why then it freezes.
Now of what place can such strange tales
Be told with truth, but New South Wales?

– 'The Land of Contrarieties' (1850s)[44]

NOTES

Opening Quotation

1 Extract from Manfred Jurgensen, *Shadows of Utopia* (Rockhampton: University of Queensland Press 1994), 'Dirk Hartog's First Awakening', second canto, 17.

Editorial Note

1 'Flinders' Voyage to Terra Australis', *Monthly Review*, no. 76 (1815): 165.
2 John Dunmore, *Visions and Realities: France in the Pacific 1695–1995* (Waikanae, New Zealand: Heritage Press 1997), 6.
3 Hanno Beck, *Geographie* (Munich: Freier 1973), 197. Passage translated in Justin Stagl, *A History of Curiosity: The Theory of Travel 1550–1800* (Australia: Harwood Academic 1995), 204.
4 Frederic C. Lane, *Venice: A Maritime Republic*, 3rd edn (London: Arnold 1981), 275.
5 David Turnbull, '(En)-Countering Knowledge Traditions', *Humanities Research*, no. 1 (2000): 57.
6 See Simon Ryan, *The Cartographic Eye: How Explorers Saw Australia* (Cambridge: Cambridge University Press 1996), 23.
7 Matthew Flinders, *Observations on the Coasts of Van Diemen's Land, on Bass Strait and Its Islands and on Part of the Coasts of New South Wales*, ed. George Mackaness (Sydney: D. S. Ford Printers 1946), 16.
8 A debate over the status of the landmass as a continent or an island continued into the early nineteenth century. See 'Flinders' Voyage to Terra Australis', 152–67.

Introduction

1 R. D. Keynes, ed., *Charles Darwin's Beagle Diary* (Cambridge: Cambridge University Press 2001), 380.
2 'Behring's Strait and the Polar Basin', *Quarterly Review* 18, no. 36 (1818): 449.
3 Greek and Roman thinkers (such as Pythagoras, then Aristotle and later Pomponius Mela and Ptolemy) saw the earth as spherical; hence the theory that a great south land must exist to balance those of the northern hemisphere. See William Eisler, *The Furthest Shore: Images of* Terra Australis *from the Middle Ages to Captain Cook* (Cambridge: Cambridge University Press 1995), 9. New interest in Ptolemy's ideas about a great south land came with the invention of the printing press. Ptolemy's *Geography* was used to showcase large-scale printing processes.

4 Pythagoras imagined that the world was made up of five regions – two frigid and temperate zones north and south of a torrid equatorial central band. The equatorial region was seen as a physical buffer beyond which religion and civilization could not reach. See Eisler, *The Furthest Shore*, 9.
5 In keeping with Christian beliefs in the Middle Ages, Saint Augustine (AD 354–430) argued that ocean completely filled the southern world. Those who believed in a southern continent were often deemed to be heretics. See Eisler, *The Furthest Shore*, 9. In the seventh century, Isidore of Seville (c. AD 560–636) wrote of an inaccessible landmass of extreme heat in a fourth region of the globe in his *Etymologies*: 'Moreover [beyond] these three parts of the world, on the other side of the ocean is a fourth island part in the south, which is unknown to us because of the heat of the sun, within the bounds of which the *Antipodes* are fabulously said to dwell'. Quoted in the *Cartographic Images* archive, available at http://www.henry-davis.com/MAPS/EMwebpages/205mono.html (accessed 12 July 2009).
6 Eisler explains that *Terra Australis* then '"decomposed" into its "component parts" – Australia, New Zealand, New Guinea, the Pacific islands, the Antarctic'. Eisler, *The Furthest Shore*, 154.
7 While there is not scope for a detailed discussion in this study, it is important to note that the term 'antipodes' was applied at times to the northern 'opposite', that is, the region of the later-discovered Americas. Other classical terms such as 'Antoikoi' and 'Antichthones' were also sometimes applied to the southern hemisphere. For discussion of the conceptual and etymological complexities associated with the changing usage of the term 'antipodes', see Philippa Tucker, 'England's Antipodes: Early Modern Visions of a Southern World' (MA thesis, Victoria University of Wellington 2002), 21–2.
8 David Fausett, *Images of the Antipodes in the Eighteenth Century: A Study in Stereotyping* (Amsterdam: Rodopi 1995), 1.
9 Ryan makes a related point when he writes that imperial discourse acted 'not only as an instrumental construction of knowledge but also according to the ambivalent protocols of fantasy and desire'. Simon Ryan, *The Cartographic Eye: How Explorers Saw Australia* (Cambridge: Cambridge University Press 1996), 208.
10 See Tucker, 'England's Antipodes'.
11 For example, Joseph Marie Degérando, in *Considérations sur les diverses méthodes à suivre dans l'observations des peuples sauvages* [*The Observation of Savage Peoples*] (Paris: Société des Observateurs de l'homme 1800), proposed: 'The *voyageur philosophe* who sails till the end of the world actually travels in time; he explores the past; every step he makes corresponds to the course of an age'. Passage translated in Justin Stagl, *A History of Curiosity: The Theory of Travel 1550–1800* (Australia: Harwood Academic 1995), 289. Degérando's work, which can be thought of as an early methodology for anthropological fieldwork, set out the terms of the research to be pursued by French Captain Nicolas Baudin and crew.
12 See Rod Edmond, *Representing the South Pacific: Colonial Discourse from Cook to Gauguin* (Cambridge: Cambridge University Press 1997), 8. The physical distance between Europe and the antipodes that once defined these spaces as so very different should now, one would think, be of little relevance. The equator was once a vital halfway mark, imagined as the point where everything would change, where the familiar world would be turned upside down. Now, with fast air travel and instant computer linkups, the date line has become much more important than the equator. A set of vertical lines on a different axis has replaced the equator as the more significant influence on the way we perceive distant places. And yet, the myth of distance from Europe, as indexing an

ever-greater cultural otherness, continues to be reiterated. For example, internationally known travel writer Bill Bryson invokes a full range of exotic Eastern imagery when he reports that Australia, on arrival, did not match his highly imaginative preconceptions. Bryson explains:

> Every cultural instinct and previous experience tells you that *when you travel this far* [emphasis added] you should find, at the very least, people on camels. There should be unrecognisable lettering on the signs, and swarthy men in robes drinking coffee from thimble-sized cups and puffing on hookahs, and rattletrap buses and potholes in the road and a real possibility of disease on everything you touch – but no, it is not like that at all.
>
> Bill Bryson, *Down Under* (London: Doubleday 2000), 10.

While Bryson's vision can be read as keeping alive mythic notions of the exotic East, it can also be read as a parody of cultural determinism.

13 As Fausett puts it: 'the old mirror-image type of utopia, a sort of collective monologue, gave way to a dialogical avatar which took account of the fact that such places contained real societies'. Fausett, *Images of the Antipodes*, 199.
14 Daniel Defoe, *The Life and Strange Surprizing Adventures of Robinson Crusoe* (London: W. Taylor 1719).
15 Jonathan Swift, *Travels into Several Remote Nations of the World, in Four Parts, by Lemuel Gulliver* (London: Benjamin Motte 1726).
16 In particular, Gabriel de Foigny's *La Terre Australe connue* (Vannes [Geneva]: Jacques Verneuil 1676), discussed in Chapter Two, and also Denis Vairasse, *The History of the Sevarites or Sevarambi [L'Histoire des Sevarambes]* (first published London: For Henry Brome 1675, with extended versions published in French and in English in 1677, 1678 and 1679). Defoe's later work, *A New Voyage Round the World* (London: Printed for A. Bettesworth...& W. Mears 1724), was presented as a real voyage account of antipodal discoveries.
17 This imagery has a long history in the antipodean 'world turned upside-down' trope. However, as examples in the following chapters show, the notion was also used to opposite effect in literary satire, with Europeans depicted as distorted and 'upside-down' relative to their antipodean counterparts. These highly political portrayals were often presented in a humorous way. In Zaccaria Seriman's *Viaggi di Enrico Wanton alle Terre Incognite Australi [Voyages of Enrico Wanton to Terra Australis Incognita]* (Venice: Giovanni Tagier 1749), for example, the people of the antipodes are articulate, educated humans who dress in European clothes and live comfortably in houses. But they have the faces of monkeys and baboons.
18 Perera traces the enmeshing of British literature and empire back at least as early as Spenser's *A View of the Present State of Ireland* (1596). Suvendrini Perera, *Reaches of Empire: The English Novel from Edgeworth to Dickens* (New York: Columbia University Press 1991), 5.
19 Markley argues that Defoe's later novels offer complex critiques of colonialism and that they are far more significant as commentaries on cross-cultural relations than critics have generally acknowledged. He also makes the point that by focussing on colonialist imagery critics may run the risk of unwittingly perpetuating a Eurocentric version of colonial history. See Robert Markley, *The Far East and the English Imagination 1600–1730* (Cambridge: Cambridge University Press 2006), 177–210.
20 Hi Kyung Moon, 'Fictitious Travellers in French and English Literature: A Study of Imaginary Voyages from Cyrano de Bergerac to Oliver Goldsmith 1657–1762' (PhD thesis, University of Oxford 1989), v.
21 Ryan, *The Cartographic Eye*, 109.

22 These extracts offer a contextual framework, and yet it is beyond the scope of this study to comment specifically on issues related to patterns of production, reception and circulation, how the influence of fiction was felt for the actual readers of imaginary voyages, and to what extent that influence may have resulted in changing behaviours and attitudes.
23 In the late eighteenth century there was, for the first time, sufficient knowledge to imagine the earth as a whole and so to foresee the global outcomes of colonial programs. See Alan Frost, *The Global Reach of Empire: Britain's Maritime Expansion in the Indian and Pacific Oceans 1764–1815* (Melbourne: Melbourne University Publishing 2003).
24 David Fausett, *Images of the Antipodes in the Eighteenth Century: A Study in Stereotyping* (Amsterdam: Rodopi 1995), 25.
25 There were, however, differences between the two traditions of imaginary voyage writing, and especially in the late eighteenth century when romanticism in French literature took specific forms. In France, more than in Britain, the imaginary voyage was used as a mode of active philosophical propaganda. See Moon, 'Fictitious Travellers in French and English Literature', iv.
26 See, for example, the 'Australia on the Map' project – information available at http://www.australiaonthemap.org.au (accessed 8 September 2009) – marking 400 years since the Dutch discovery of the Australian continent. The Australian ABC TV documentary series *Captain Cook: Obsession and Discovery* (Film Australia 2007) attracted millions of viewers. There have also been ambitious museum exhibitions, in some cases the largest of their kind, such as the National Museum of Australia's 'Cook's Pacific Encounters' (2006) and the Western Australian Museum's 'Voyages of Grand Discovery' (2007).
27 These include *Duyfken* and *Endeavour*, both built in the past two decades in the port town of Fremantle, Western Australia, using traditional techniques. For a global listing of historic ship reconstructions and re-enactments, see http://gotheborg.com/links/links-index.htm (accessed 2 January 2010).

Chapter 1: Real and Imaginary Voyages

1 Raleigh stated plainly that 'imaginary voyages and travels cannot, for the most part, be regarded as pure romances' because 'they have generally some ulterior purpose in view, political or satirical'. Walter Raleigh, *The English Novel: Being a Short Sketch of Its History from the Earliest Times to the Appearance of* Waverley (London: John Murray 1895), 136. 'Pure' romances for Raleigh, it seems, would avoid contemporary political issues and would also be more likely to declare their fictionality than try to obscure it. Likewise, imaginary voyages were difficult to categorize unequivocally as novels. By following the conventions of genuine voyage accounts, writers rarely achieved the novelistic unity of construction expected by critics. See Phillip Babcock Gove, *The Imaginary Voyage in Prose Fiction: A History of Its Criticism and a Guide for Its Study, with an Annotated Check List of 215 Imaginary Voyages from 1700 to 1800* (New York: Columbia University Press 1941), 167. Reflecting on similar issues, Furst considers the early realist novel as a 'transgressive' genre, 'somewhere between romance and history'. Lillian R. Furst, *All Is True: The Claims and Strategies of Realist Fiction* (Durham: Duke University Press 1995), 13. See also discussion in Marian Hobson, *The Object of Art: The Theory of Illusion in Eighteenth-Century France* (Cambridge: Cambridge University Press 1982), 81.

2 On the roots of science fiction, see Paul K. Alkon, *Science Fiction before 1900: Imagination Discovers Technology* (New York & London: Routledge 2002) and David Seed, ed., *Anticipations: Essays on Early Science Fiction and Its Precursors* (Liverpool: Liverpool University Press 1995).
3 [Joseph Hall], *Mundus alter et idem siue Terra Australis ante hac semper incognita longis itineribus peregrini Academici nuperrime lustrata* (London: Printed by Humphrey Lownes 1605); [Joseph Hall], *The Discovery of a New World, or, A Description of the South Indies, Hitherto Unknowne, by an English Mercury*, adapted into English by John Healey (London: For E. Blount & W. Barrett 1609).
4 Gabriel de Foigny, *La Terre Australe connue* (Vannes [Geneva]: Jacques Verneuil 1676); Gabriel de Foigny, *A New Discovery of Terra Incognita Australis, or the Southern World, by James Sadeur, a French-Man Who Being Cast There by a Shipwreck, Lived 35 Years in That Country, and Gives a Particular Description of the Manners, Customs, Religion, Laws, Studies, and Wars, of Those Southern People; and of Some Animals Peculiar to That Place* (London: Printed for John Dunton 1693).
5 Gove, *The Imaginary Voyage in Prose Fiction*.
6 For example, see Derrick Moors, 'Imaginary Voyages', *La Trobe Journal*, no. 41 (1988): 8.
7 Hordern House acquisitions catalogue (Sydney: Hordern House July 2008), 9, available at http://www.hordern.com/hh/pdf/acquisitions/web_hordern_house_acq_072008.pdf (accessed 19 September 2009).
8 As Carter puts it: 'Voyagers carried their mental geographies with them, promiscuously mingling old and new worlds'. Paul Carter, 'Strange Seas of Thought', *Australian*, 14 June 1998, Review of Books, 31. The typical process by which both explorers and readers would comparatively interpret newly discovered places involved a practice that is arguably fundamental to the production of all knowledge. That is, to know something new is not to know it in an innate sense but rather to slot it into an existing knowledge system. The reality of the antipodes, while it may have seemed to be unfolding naturally, was being constructed in the very activity of gathering knowledge of the region and its people. In order to become comprehensible, unfamiliar places needed to be assimilated into established knowledge systems. The unknown, whatever form it took, was made familiar by being associated with what was already known and compared with what had already been imagined.
9 Jonathan Lamb, 'Reimagining Juan Fernandez: Empire and Pretence in the South Seas' (paper presented at 'Re-Imagining the Pacific: A Conference on Art History and Anthropology in Honour of Bernard Smith', National Library of Australia, 2 August 1996). The word 'pretence' (used in the title of Lamb's paper) is defined both as 'the action or an act of pretending' and 'an assertion of a right', defined in two ways, that is, which facilitate the twin interests of imagining and controlling (*OED*).
10 One of the important contributions of Bernard Smith's *European Vision and the South Pacific 1768–1850* (Oxford: Oxford University Press 1960) – a founding book in the field within which this study situates itself – is to show that imaginings, in all modes of representation, deserve attention because they were active in helping to construct and perpetuate ideas that generated an awareness of and support for particular expressions of colonialism in the antipodes. Smith describes the development of European visual representation in Australia and refers to the art produced during the first voyage of James Cook and Joseph Banks to the Pacific from 1768 to 1771.
11 On the writing of the account of Marco Polo's travels, see Francis Wood, *Did Marco Polo Go to China?* (London: Secker & Warburg 1995).

12 Accounts based wholly on interviews rather than on original descriptions would be fully compiled by an external editor. For example, see George Keate, *An Account of the Pelew Islands* (London: Printed for Captain Wilson 1788). For commentary on the text, see Nicholas Thomas, *In Oceania: Visions, Artifacts, Histories* (Durham: Duke University Press 1997), 121.
13 These include the German terms '*reiseroman*', '*reisemarchen*' and '*reisefabulistik*'. Gove, *The Imaginary Voyage in Prose Fiction*, 7–11.
14 Garnier, for example, includes in his major collection of *voyages imaginaires* a story that is widely accepted as a true narrative – Dubois-Fonatanelle's *Naufrage et aventures de monsieur Pierre Viaud* (1769). For further examples, see Gove, *The Imaginary Voyage in Prose Fiction*, 40–2. The practice of collecting together travel reports to publish as compilations became increasingly popular as more people travelled. One of the first collections may have been published in 1502 in Lisbon by the German printer Valentin Fernandez, but there was little interest in these kinds of compilations until the latter half of the sixteenth century. See Numa Broc, *La Géographie de la Renaissance 1420–1620* (Paris: 1980), 37. The best-known contemporary English collection was Richard Hakluyt's *The Principal Navigations, Voyages, Traffiques and Discoveries of the English Nation* (London: George Bishop, Ralph Newberie & Robert Barker 1598).
15 Mentioning factual and fictional accounts alongside one another was sometimes part of a romanticized discourse promoting the glory and heroism of discoveries. Despite obvious differences in truth value, texts that glorified empire could be grouped together. Giles, for example, wrote: 'I had ever been a delighted student of the narratives of voyages of discoveries, from Robinson Crusoe to Anson and Cook'. Ernest Giles, *Australia Twice Traversed: The Romance of Exploration* [1889], 2 vols (London: 1973), 1:lv.
16 See Percy G. Adams, *Travelers and Travel Liars 1660–1800* (Berkeley: University of California Press 1962).
17 The same determined impulse to separate out the real from the imaginary in maps has been described as a universal condition, related to 'cartophilia'. See P. Lewis, Presidential address, *Annals of the Association of American Geographers* 75, no. 4 (1985): 465.
18 John Dunlop, *The History of Fiction: Being a Critical Account of the Most Celebrated Prose Writers of Fiction from the Earliest Greek Romances to the Novels of the Present Age* [1814], 4th edn (London: Longman, Brown, Green & Longmans 1845), 389.
19 Ibid.
20 David Fausett, translator's introduction to Gabriel de Foigny, *The Southern Land, Known* [1676], trans. David Fausett (New York: Syracuse University Press 1993), xxxv.
21 Felipe Fernandez-Armesto, 'Spain's Quest for Australis', *Australian*, 17 May 2006, Higher Education Supplement, 43.
22 Mary Louise Pratt, *Imperial Eyes: Travel Writing and Transculturation* (London: Routledge 1992), 7.
23 Underscoring a growing interest in visual representation, in 1800 the *British Critic* noted: 'there is a very valid excuse for elegant and expensive works of Natural History', explaining that 'by the aid of fine engravings and painting, more accurate ideas can be given of the subjects represented than word can give'. 'Voyages and Travels', *British Critic*, no. 15 (1800): xv. However, as Thomas puts it, natural history can conversely be seen as creating merely an illusion of authority, through use of 'opaque images that attest more to insecurity…and to a disputed knowledge of the exotic'. Thomas, *In Oceania*, 100.

24 For related discussion of the narrative function of voyages in fiction, see Diana Loxley, *Problematic Shores: The Literature of Islands* (London: Macmillan 1990).
25 Steve Clark, ed., *Travel Writing and Empire: Postcolonial Theory in Transit* (London: Zed Books 1999), 2. Clark refers to Michael McKeon, *The Origins of the English Novel 1600–1740* (Baltimore: Johns Hopkins University Press 1987), 102–10. According to Raleigh, Defoe created the illusion of authenticity by limiting himself 'to the simplest facts' so as 'to avoid giving the reader anything at all to swallow'. In Raleigh's mind, it was the very absence of marvellous imagery and incidents in *Robinson Crusoe* that appealed to readers. Defoe, he wrote, 'makes the most barren parts of his subject interesting by the very sense of expectation that so unprecedented a monotony awakes'. In Defoe's works, 'the other world, described with statistical minuteness, is so like this one, that the reader finds himself wondering why there should be two'. See Raleigh, *The English Novel*, 135–6.
26 George Saintsbury, *The English Novel* (London: J. M. Dent 1913), 60.
27 Ross Gibson, *South of the West: Postcolonialism and the Narrative Construction of Australia* (Bloomington: Indiana University Press 1992), 95.
28 Likewise, in the prefaces to genuine travel accounts, editors or writers would often explain their social standing and give a detailed personal history so as to convince readers of their authority and ability to provide a balanced account.
29 Referring to oneself as an editor was a common means of disguising authorship. See Gregory Claeys, ed., *Modern British Utopias 1700–1850*, 8 vols (London: Pickering & Chatto 1997), 7:253. When an 'Author' and 'Reader' are referred to, these can be thought of as 'metacharacters emplotted within the novel'. See William Ray, *Story and History: Narrative Authority and Social Identity in the Eighteenth-Century French and English Novel* (Cambridge, Massachusetts: Basil Blackwell 1990), 15. Ray's book discusses the critical reception of early French and English novels. He cites a range of nineteenth- and twentieth-century thinkers who have contributed to the debate over eighteenth-century narrative truth and emerging concepts of realism. For Ray, eighteenth-century realist fiction focussed attention 'on the social practices of which it is itself an expression', meaning that the eighteenth-century novel arguably 'stands for the culture it depicts…it represents the system it represents'. Ray, *Story and History*, 5.
30 One of the very longest titles may have been that of an early nineteenth-century edition of Ralph Morris [pseud.], *A Narrative of the Life and Astonishing Adventures of John Daniel* [1751] (London: Fisher 1801), which takes up 41 lines.
31 Many of the invented languages were influenced by contemporary knowledge of Chinese characters and inspired by the continued search for a human origin language. See Paul Cornelius, *Languages in Seventeenth- and Early Eighteenth-Century Imaginary Voyages* (Genève: Libraire Droz 1965).
32 Richard Phillips, *Mapping Men and Empire: A Geography of Adventure* (London: Routledge 1997), 14.
33 Simon Ryan, *The Cartographic Eye: How Explorers Saw Australia* (Cambridge: Cambridge University Press 1996), 97.
34 Suvendrini Perera, *Reaches of Empire: The English Novel from Edgeworth to Dickens* (New York: Columbia University Press 1991), 3.
35 Preparing his famous world atlas of 1570, Ortelius revised *Terra Incognita* to *Terra Australis Nondum Cognita* (that is, 'southern land, not yet known'), suggesting that it will be discovered in the future, and so adding a further narrative dimension to the map.
36 Spate, for example, introduces the antipodean setting for utopian fiction in these terms: 'The heroic age of *Utopia* in Terra Australis or the South Sea ran from Gabriel de Foigny

in 1676 to Restif de la Bretonne in 1781; during this period eleven *imaginary voyages* to the Southland appeared in France alone' [emphasis added]. O. H. K. Spate, *Paradise Found and Lost*, The Pacific since Magellan series, vol. 3 (Sydney: Australian University Press/Pergamon Press 1988), 82. Similarly, Friederich uses 'utopia' and 'extraordinary voyage' (following Atkinson) interchangeably. See Werner P. Friederich, *Australia in Western Imaginative Prose Writings 1600–1900* (Chapel Hill: University of North Carolina Press 1967).

37 A common approach is to think of utopia as a theme that features in different ways in a variety of genres that act as hosts. Extending this analogy, Rees asks that we think of utopia as a literary theme that has been 'given a hospitable reception not only in the novel, but in other literary forms: satire, the imaginary voyage, the proto-feminist tract, the eastern tale, and the philosophical fable'. Christine Rees, *Utopian Imagination and Eighteenth-Century Fiction* (New York: Longman 1996), 3.

38 Georges van den Abbeele, *Travel as Metaphor: From Montaigne to Rousseau* (Minneapolis: University of Minnesota Press 1992), xiii.

39 Denis Vairasse's imaginary voyage *The History of the Sevarites or Sevarambi* [*L'Histoire des Sevarambes*] (first published London: For Henry Brome 1675, with extended versions published in French and in English in 1677, 1678 and 1679) is often included in histories of socialism. See M. Keith Booker, *The Dystopian Impulse in Modern Literature: Fiction as Social Criticism* (London: Greenwood Press 1994), 3. When David Hume wrote of the 'Idea of a Perfect Commonwealth', he paid particular attention to James Harrington's utopia, *The Common-Wealth of Oceana* (London: J. Streater 1656), which he considered 'the only valuable model of a commonwealth, that has yet been offered to the public'. Hume, incidentally, opposed 'extensive conquests', claiming that they 'must be the ruin of every free government' and that there should be 'a fundamental law against conquests'. David Hume, 'Idea of a Perfect Commonwealth', in *Essays: Moral, Political, and Literary*, ed. Eugene F. Miller (London: Printed for Cadell, Donaldson & Creech 1777), 513.

40 David Beers Quinn, Alison M. Quinn and Susan Hillier, eds, *New American World: A Documentary History of North America to 1612*, 5 vols (New York: Arno Press 1979), 1:79.

41 Ibid. See also Boesky, who writes: 'The "found" nature of the utopia is one of its most prized fictions, as the ideal commonwealth claims to have been discovered (often by chance) rather than built or conquered'. Amy Boesky, *Founding Fictions: Utopias in Early Modern England* (Athens: University of Georgia Press 1996), 2.

42 For discussion of More and colonialism, see Jeffrey Knapp, *An Empire Nowhere: England, America, and Literature from* Utopia *to* The Tempest (Berkeley: University of California Press 1992), 21–61.

43 Quoted in G. Arnold Wood, *The Discovery of Australia* (London: Macmillan 1922), 1.

44 Showing the continuing interest in utopian fiction in the more recent past, Viscount Samuel's *An Unknown Land* (London: Allen & Unwin 1942) is modelled on Francis Bacon's *New Atlantis* (1627), a utopia set in the Pacific region. In this work the author claims to have followed Bacon's directions to find New Atlantis.

45 Fausett, *Images of the Antipodes*, 27.

46 David Fausett, translator's introduction to Foigny, *The Southern Land, Known*, xxxiii.

47 Fausett, *Images of the Antipodes*, 27.

48 *OED*.

49 Ibid.

50 For discussion, see Philippa Tucker, 'England's Antipodes: Early Modern Visions of a Southern World' (MA thesis, Victoria University of Wellington 2002), Chapter 4.

51 Geoffroy Atkinson, *The Extraordinary Voyage in French Literature before 1700* (New York: Columbia University Press 1920).

52 Geoffroy Atkinson, *The Extraordinary Voyage in French Literature from 1700 to 1720* (Paris: E. Champion 1922).
53 Gove, *The Imaginary Voyage in Prose Fiction*.
54 Cornelius, *Languages in Seventeenth- and Early Eighteenth-Century Imaginary Voyages*.
55 David Fausett, *Writing the New World: Imaginary Voyages and Utopias of the Great Southern Land* (New York: Syracuse University Press 1993).
56 George Mackaness, *Some Fictitious Voyages to Australia* [1937] (Dubbo, New South Wales: Review Publications 1979).
57 John Dunmore, *Utopias and Imaginary Voyages to Australasia: A Lecture Delivered at the National Library of Australia, 2 September 1987* (Canberra: National Library of Australia 1988).
58 Hi Kyung Moon, 'Fictitious Travellers in French and English Literature: A Study of Imaginary Voyages from Cyrano de Bergerac to Oliver Goldsmith 1657–1762' (PhD thesis, University of Oxford 1989).
59 Lance Schachterle and Jeanne Welcher, 'A Checklist of Secondary Studies on Imaginary Voyages', *Bulletin of Bibliography* 31, no. 3 (1974): 99, 100, 106, 110, 116, 121.
60 Dunlop, *The History of Fiction*.
61 Arthur J. Tieje, *The Theory of Characterization in Prose Fiction Prior to 1740* (Minneapolis: University of Minnesota 1916).
62 William Eddy, *Gulliver's Travels: A Critical Study* (Princeton: Princeton University Press 1923).
63 Percy G. Adams, *Travelers and Travel Liars 1660–1800* (Berkeley: University of California Press 1962).
64 Friederich, *Australia in Western Imaginative Prose Writings 1600–1900*.
65 Ross Gibson, *The Diminishing Paradise: Changing Literary Perceptions of Australia* (Sydney: Angus & Robertson 1984).
66 Fausett, *Images of the Antipodes*.
67 Neil Rennie, *Far-Fetched Facts: The Literature of Travel and the Idea of the South Seas* (Oxford: Oxford University Press 1995).
68 Jan Basset, ed., *Great Southern Landings: An Anthology of Antipodean Travel* (Melbourne: Oxford University Press 1995).
69 John Dunmore, *Visions and Realities: France in the Pacific 1695–1995* (Waikanae, New Zealand: Heritage Press 1997).
70 Phillips, *Mapping Men and Empire*.
71 Des Crowley and Clare Williamson, *The World of the Book* (Melbourne: Melbourne University Publishing 2007).
72 Henry Weber, ed., *Popular Romances, Consisting of Imaginary Voyages and Travels, to Which is Prefixed an Introductory Dissertation* (Edinburgh: Printed by James Ballantyne 1812), xxi.
73 Dunlop, *The History of Fiction*, 53. See Lucian of Samosata, *True History; and Lucius or, The Ass*, trans. Paul Turner (London: J. Calder 1958).
74 Joseph Jacobs, ed., *The Book of Wonder Voyages* (London: D. Nutt 1896), 215. On the *Odyssey* as an archetypal travel narrative, see Abbeele, *Travel as Metaphor*, xxv–vi.
75 Fausett, *Images of the Antipodes*, 11.
76 In *cosmographies* information from travel reports was taken out of context and rearranged to form a pastiche of impressions. See Justin Stagl, *A History of Curiosity: The Theory of Travel 1550–1800* (Australia: Harwood Academic 1995), 56. The best-known work of its kind was theologian Sebastian Münster's *Cosmographia* (Basel: Getruckt durch Henrichum Petri 1544).
77 [Anon.], 'The Shipwrecked Sailor', in *Egyptian Tales, Translated from the Papyri*, ed. W. M. Flinders Petrie (London: Bendetto 1926), 81–96. Cited in Rennie, *Far-Fetched Facts*, 3.

78 See Gove, *The Imaginary Voyage in Prose Fiction*, 80.
79 See *The Travels of Sir John Mandeville* [c. 1357], facsimile of Pynson's 1496 edition (Exeter: University of Exeter 1980).
80 Charles Georges Thomas Garnier, ed., *Voyages imaginaires, songes, visions et romans cabalistiques*, 36 vols (Amsterdam: 1787).
81 Dunlop, *The History of Fiction*, 389.
82 Dunlop, although he drew directly upon many of Garnier's ideas on categorizing imaginary voyages, only briefly refers to him and does not acknowledge Garnier, *Voyages imaginaires*, as his primary source. He also borrows directly from Weber, *Popular Romances*. See Gove, *The Imaginary Voyage in Prose Fiction*, 27. As the editors of the *Quarterly Review* noted, Dunlop seemed to be 'somewhat ashamed of the companions he introduces' (they were either unaware of or overlooked his plagiarism). 'Dunlop's History of Fiction', *Quarterly Review* 13, no. 26 (1815): 408.
83 Gove, *The Imaginary Voyage in Prose Fiction*, 74.
84 Atkinson, *The Extraordinary Voyage in French Literature before 1700*, ix.
85 Eddy, *Gulliver's Travels: A Critical Study*, 12.
86 Ibid., 8–15.
87 Gove, *The Imaginary Voyage in Prose Fiction*, 13.
88 Ibid., 20. The first known example Gove identifies was the anonymously published *Voyages Imaginaires* in 1711.
89 Ibid., 5.
90 Ibid., 4.
91 Ibid., viii.
92 Ibid., vii.
93 Ibid., 178.
94 Weber, *Popular Romances*, xxii.
95 Dunlop, *The History of Fiction*, 419.
96 At least 11 texts have been identified as being full-scale imitations of *Gulliver's Travels* in the eighteenth century. See Jeanne K. Welcher and George E. Bush, eds, *Gulliveriana IV* (New York: Scholars Facsimiles & Reprints 1973), 7. For more on Gulliveriana, see Jeanne K. Welcher, ed., *Gulliveriana VIII: An Annotated List of Gulliveriana 1721–1800* (New York: Scholars Facsimiles & Reprints 1988).
97 Gove, *The Imaginary Voyage in Prose Fiction*, 124. One example is the Dutch imaginary voyage, Hendrik Smeeks, *The Mighty Kingdom of Krinke Kesmes* [1708], trans. Robert H. Leek (Amsterdam: Rodopi 1995).
98 Gove, *The Imaginary Voyage in Prose Fiction*, 112, 124–5.
99 See Fausett, *Images of the Antipodes*, 33.
100 Dunlop, *The History of Fiction*, 389.
101 [Robert Paltock], *The Life and Adventures of Peter Wilkins*, 2 vols (Dublin: G. Faulkner 1751).
102 Ralph Morris [pseud.], *A Narrative of the Life and Astonishing Adventures of John Daniel* (London: Cooper 1751).
103 [Anon.], *Voyages curieux d'un Philadelphe dans des pays nouvellement découverts* [*The Curious Voyages of a Philadelphian*] (Paris [or The Hague]: Aux dépens de la Compagnie 1755).
104 [Anon.], *Histoire d'un peuple nouveau, ou découverte d'une isle...par David Tompson* [*Captain Tompson's Island*] (Londres: Aux dépens d'une Socié té dé libraires 1757).
105 Robertson [pseud.], *Voyage de Robertson, aux Terres Australes, traduit sur le manuscrit anglois* [*Robertson's Voyage*] (Amsterdam: 1767).

106 Gove, *The Imaginary Voyage in Prose Fiction*, 151.
107 Ibid.
108 Dunlop, *The History of Fiction*, 420.
109 Weber, *Popular Romances*, xxii.
110 Tieje, *The Theory of Characterization in Prose Fiction*, 64.
111 Fausett, *Images of the Antipodes*, viii.

Chapter 2: Blank Spaces for the Imagination

1 Richard Brome, *The Antipodes*, ed. Ann Haaker (London: Edward Arnold 1966), Act 5, Scene 12, lines 15–16. In her editorial introduction, Haaker notes that the play was published in 1640, first performed in 1638 and was written some time between August 1636 and December 1637 (xii).
2 [Joseph Hall], *Mundus alter et idem siue Terra Australis ante hac semper incognita longis itineribus peregrini Academici nuperrime lustrata* (London: Printed by Humphrey Lownes 1605).
3 [Joseph Hall], *The Discovery of a New World, or, A Description of the South Indies, Hitherto Unknowne, by an English Mercury*, adapted into English by John Healey (London: For E. Blount & W. Barrett 1609).
4 Gabriel de Foigny, *La Terre Australe connue* (Vannes [Geneva]: Jacques Verneuil 1676).
5 Gabriel de Foigny, *A New Discovery of Terra Incognita Australis, or the Southern World, by James Sadeur, a French-Man Who Being Cast There by a Shipwreck, Lived 35 Years in That Country, and Gives a Particular Description of the Manners, Customs, Religion, Laws, Studies, and Wars, of Those Southern People; and of Some Animals Peculiar to That Place* (London: Printed for John Dunton 1693).
6 Gabriel de Foigny, *The Southern Land, Known* [1676], trans. David Fausett (New York: Syracuse University Press 1993).
7 O. H. K. Spate, *Paradise Found and Lost*, The Pacific since Magellan series, vol. 3 (Sydney: Australian University Press/Pergamon Press 1988), 83.
8 David Fausett, *Images of the Antipodes in the Eighteenth Century: A Study in Stereotyping* (Amsterdam: Rodopi 1995), 8.
9 Hartmann Schedel, *Liber Chronicarum* [*Nuremberg Chronicle*] (Nuremberg: Anton Koberger 1493).
10 Dante's *Divine Comedy*, written at the end of the thirteenth century, refers to similar monstrous variations of the human form in the *Inferno*. See the illustrations in Kenneth Clark, ed., *The Drawings by Sandro Botticelli for Dante's* Divine Comedy (New York: Harper & Row 1954), especially Canto XXVII.
11 For further discussion, see Fausett, *Images of the Antipodes*, 12.
12 Medieval maps typically included a mix of fact and fiction, fostering myths at the same time as recording accepted geographical knowledge. Labarge discusses the example of a fourteenth-century world map from Hereford Cathedral. Margaret Labarge, *Medieval Travelers: The Rich and the Restless* (London: Hamish Hamilton 1982), 11. A chronological list of extant medieval world maps, many of which feature antipodean imagery, is included in Lee Bagrow, *History of Cartography*, 2nd edn (Chicago: Precendent Publishing 1963), 45. In medieval times, European projections of unknown worlds, no matter where their location, tended to be based upon imagery drawn from ancient Mediterranean and Middle Eastern societies. These included Greek, Roman and

Persian models, as well as visions of Eastern legends of extravagances. Fausett, *Images of the Antipodes*, 2–3, 14.

13 J. M. R. Cameron, 'Western Australia 1616–1829: An Antipodean Paradise', *The Geographical Journal*, no. 140 (1974): 376.

14 Marco Polo, *The Travels of Marco Polo*, ed. Ronald Latham (Harmondsworth: Penguin 1958), 251.

15 Miriam Estensen, *Discovery: The Quest for the Great South Land* (St Leonards, New South Wales: Allen & Unwin 1998), 9.

16 For example, Denis Vairasse's *The History of the Sevarites or Sevarambi* [*L'Histoire des Sevarambes*] (first published London: For Henry Brome 1675, with extended versions published in French and in English in 1677, 1678 and 1679) is set in an earthly Paradise, which is said to have been transported to *Terra Australis* following the biblical Flood but was originally located in Asia.

17 Gonneville famously pretended to have landed on the west coast of the unknown land of *Terre Australe* on 6 January 1504 and have lived there for six months, claiming that all records of his visit were destroyed. For discussion, see Ross Gibson, *The Diminishing Paradise: Changing Literary Perceptions of Australia* (Sydney: Angus & Robertson 1984), 30–1.

18 Abraham Ortelius, *Theatrum Orbis Terrarum* [*Theatre of the World*] [1570] (London: 1606), 1. See also Clancy and Richardson, *So Came They South*, 20.

19 Ibid., 58.

20 Ortelius, *Theatrum Orbis Terrarum*, 1.

21 Ibid.

22 Justin Stagl, *A History of Curiosity: The Theory of Travel 1550–1800* (Australia: Harwood Academic 1995), 72.

23 See Cameron, 'Western Australia 1616–1829', 377.

24 Commanded by Francisco Pelsaert, the *Batavia* ran aground in the Abrolhos Islands.

25 See Cameron, 'Western Australia 1616–1829', 377.

26 The site of the wreck is approximately 100km north of today's city of Perth. *Vergulde Draeck* was commanded by Pieter Albertszoon.

27 On the history of early European exploration and cross-cultural encounters in the Americas, including contemporary views on cannibalism, see Peter Hulme, *Colonial Encounters: Europe and the Native Caribbean 1492–1797* (London: Methuen 1986). For discussion of the land of legends envisaged in the Americas, see Jorge Magasich-Airola and Jean-Marc de Beer, *America Magica: When Renaissance Europe Thought It Had Conquered Paradise*, trans. Monica Sandor (London: Anthem Press 2006). On the fictional literature inspired by European discovery in the Americas, see Jeffrey Knapp, *An Empire Nowhere: England, America, and Literature from* Utopia *to* The Tempest (Berkeley: University of California Press 1992).

28 See Helen Wallis, 'The Enigma of Java-La-Grande', in *Australia and the European Imagination: Proceeds from a Conference Held at the Humanities Research Centre, May 1981*, ed. Ian Donaldson (Canberra: Humanities Research Centre, Australian National University 1982). The Dieppe maps are also associated with the supposed presence of the remains of a 'Mahogany Ship' – a Portuguese caravel said to have been wrecked in the dunes near the Australian town of Warrnambool. Frank Broeze, *Island Nation: A History of Australians and the Sea* (St Leonards, New South Wales: Allen & Unwin 1998), 16. This mysterious ship was the inspiration for Australian author James Bradley's first novel, *Wrack* (Melbourne: Random House 1997).

29 Clancy and Richardson, *So Came They South*, 58.
30 The two de Jodes, father Gerard and son Cornelis, were known as rivals of Ortelius, the more well-recognized map-maker. See R. V. Tooley, ed., *Printed Maps of Australia* (London: Map Collectors' Circle 1970), 55.
31 [Hall], *The Discovery of a New World*, 'The Occasion of This Travell' [unpaginated].
32 Tucker discusses the changes in the English titles of the various editions of this work published over the seventeenth century in terms of what they reveal about historical developments during the period. Philippa Tucker, 'England's Antipodes: Early Modern Visions of a Southern World' (MA thesis, Victoria University of Wellington 2002), 145–9.
33 Joseph Hall, *Virgidemiarum* [1597], in *Works* [of Joseph Hall], *with Some Account of His Life and Sufferings* (Oxford: D. A. Talboys 1837), 45–156.
34 In his reading of *Mundus alter et idem*, Dunmore ponders what Hall would have thought of New Zealand's flightless giant moas and of the Hawaiian aristocracy, known for their obesity. John Dunmore, *Utopias and Imaginary Voyages to Australasia: A Lecture Delivered at the National Library of Australia, 2 September 1987* (Canberra: National Library of Australia 1988), 10.
35 'Laverna' was the Roman patroness of crime.
36 [Hall], *The Discovery of a New World*, 'The Epistle Dedicatorie' [unpaginated].
37 For more of Hall's ideas on travel, see Joseph Hall, *Quo vardis?: A Just Censure of Travel As It Is Commonly Undertaken by the Gentlemen of Our Nation* (London: Printed by E. Griffin for H. Fetherstone 1617).
38 [Hall], *The Discovery of a New World*, 'The Occasion of This Travell' [unpaginated].
39 Ibid.
40 Ibid.
41 Ibid.
42 Ibid.
43 Ibid.
44 Ibid.
45 Ibid.
46 Hall's narrator has been described as 'both messenger and deceiver'. His 'naturalistic geographical descriptions appear to tell the simple truth, but are really the medium of Hall's satirical, political argument'. Richard Phillips, *Mapping Men and Empire: A Geography of Adventure* (London: Routledge 1997), 141.
47 [Hall], *The Discovery of a New World*, 'The Occasion of This Travell' [unpaginated].
48 Ibid., 234.
49 Ibid., 1–2.
50 Ibid., 123. Swift makes use of the same associative device when Gulliver refers to 'my worthy friend Herman Moll' (the cartographer). Jonathan Swift, *Gulliver's Travels* [1726], ed. H. Davis (Oxford: Blackwell 1959), 13.
51 [Hall], *The Discovery of a New World*, 1.
52 Richard Hakluyt, *The Principal Navigations, Voyages, Traffiques and Discoveries of the English Nation* (London: George Bishop, Ralph Newberie & Robert Barker 1598).
53 [Hall], *The Discovery of a New World*, 88.
54 Ibid., 136.
55 Ibid., 54.
56 Ibid., 57.
57 Ibid., 2.

58 Ibid. Knapp cites Hall's imaginary voyage as a typical example of English utopias in the period after Thomas More, which are increasingly 'explicit about identifying their new worlds with England'. See Knapp, *An Empire Nowhere*, 31.
59 [Hall], *The Discovery of a New World*, 3.
60 Ibid., 57.
61 Ibid., 110.
62 Ibid., 141–2.
63 Ibid., 243.
64 This is reminiscent of the story of Caliban in Shakespeare's *The Tempest* (c. 1611), written shortly after Hall's work.
65 [Hall], *The Discovery of a New World*, 183.
66 Ibid., 151.
67 Heylyn's *Cosmography* was first published in 1652.
68 Peter Heylyn, *Cosmographie in Four Bookes: Containing the Chorographie and Historie of the Whole World, and All the Principal Kingdoms, Provinces, Seas, and Isles Thereof* (London: Printed for H. Seile 1657), 4.
69 [Hall], *The Discovery of a New World*, 134.
70 Ibid., 135.
71 Ibid., 135–6.
72 Ibid., 31.
73 Ibid.
74 Ibid., 45.
75 Ibid., 161, 164.
76 Ibid., 164.
77 Ibid., 162.
78 Ibid., 234. 'Marvels' were a medieval literary form that intentionally blurred boundaries between fact and fiction, merging the marvellous with the everyday. 'Islands of the Blessed' featured regularly. See Jacques Le Goff, *The Medieval Imagination*, trans. Arthur Goldhammer (Chicago: University of Chicago Press 1988), 36.
79 [Hall], *The Discovery of a New World*, 235.
80 Ibid.
81 Ibid., 244.
82 George Mackaness, *Some Fictitious Voyages to Australia* [1937] (Dubbo, New South Wales: Review Publications 1979), 9.
83 Foigny, *The Southern Land, Known*.
84 Ibid., 95.
85 David Fausett, translator's introduction to Foigny, *The Southern Land, Known*, xi.
86 Foigny, *The Southern Land, Known*, 98.
87 Geoffroy Atkinson, *The Extraordinary Voyage in French Literature before 1700* (New York: Columbia University Press 1920), 163.
88 George Seddon, *Landprints: Reflections on Place and Landscape* (Cambridge: Cambridge University Press 1997), xi–xiii.
89 Phillips, *Mapping Men and Empire*, 120.
90 David Fausett, translator's introduction to Foigny, *The Southern Land, Known*, xiii.
91 Ibid., xx.
92 Ibid., xxi.
93 Quoted in Frédéric Lachèvre, *Les Successeurs de Cyrano de Bergerac* (Geneva: Slatkine 1968), 35.

94 Quoted in Pierre Bayle, *Dictionnaire historique et critique*, 2 vols (Rotterdam: Reinier Leers 1697), 2:987. Passage translated by David Fausett, translator's introduction to Foigny, *The Southern Land, Known*, xxv.
95 David Fausett, translator's introduction to Foigny, *The Southern Land, Known*, xxi.
96 Ibid., xxi–ii.
97 Ibid., xxii.
98 Gabriel de Foigny, *Les Avantures de Jacques Sadeur dans la découverte et le voiage de la Terre Australe* (Paris: Chez Claude Barbin 1692).
99 David Fausett, translator's introduction to Foigny, *The Southern Land, Known*, xxiii.
100 David Fausett, preface to Foigny, *The Southern Land, Known*, viii.
101 Geoffroy Atkinson, *The Extraordinary Voyage in French Literature from 1700 to 1720* (Paris: E. Champion 1922), 36.
102 The 1692 version of the text was published in a combined edition in 1793. For a list of all known editions and translations, see David Fausett, translator's notes in Foigny, *The Southern Land, Known*, 141–5.
103 Foigny, *The Southern Land, Known*, 1.
104 Ibid.
105 Ibid., 1–2.
106 Ibid., 4–5.
107 Ibid., 5.
108 Ibid.
109 Ibid., 6.
110 Ibid., 6–7.
111 Ibid., 7.
112 Ibid., 8.
113 Ibid., 8–9.
114 Ibid., 11.
115 David Fausett, translator's introduction to Foigny, *The Southern Land, Known*, xxxv.
116 Ibid., xxxi.
117 Vairasse, *The History of the Sevarites or Sevarambi*.
118 Foigny, *The Southern Land, Known*, 27. As Fausett reads it, this is a parody of Christ's crucifixion. See David Fausett, translator's introduction to Foigny, *The Southern Land, Known*, xxxiv.
119 These flying creatures have a possible source in the Nordic Kraken or the 'rukh' reported by Marco Polo. See David Fausett, translator's introduction to Foigny, *The Southern Land, Known*, xxix. Hall's 'RUC' may have the same possible source.
120 Foigny, *The Southern Land, Known*, 28.
121 Ibid., 29.
122 Ibid., 33.
123 Ibid., 35.
124 David Fausett, translator's introduction to Foigny, *The Southern Land, Known*, xxxiv. Fausett sees the customary nudity in the Australian land as 'a parody of the "moral transparency" (sincerity, honesty, and equality) that primitivists associated with savage society'. Ibid., xxxvi–vii.
125 Foigny, *The Southern Land, Known*, 36–7.
126 Ibid., 37.
127 Ibid.
128 Ibid.

129 Ibid.
130 Ibid., 38.
131 Ibid.
132 Ibid., 40. To make a comparison with this figure, Australia's population only reached 20 million in the early twenty-first century.
133 Foigny, *The Southern Land, Known*, 40.
134 Ibid., 44.
135 Ibid., 46.
136 Ibid. Atkinson notes that this vision of an absence of venomous creatures shows Quirós' influence on Foigny (Atkinson, *The Extraordinary Voyage in French Literature before 1700*, 55). Quirós had reported:
    Wee have not seene any barren and sandie ground, nor any Thistles, or trees that are thornie or whose rootes doe shew themselves, no Marishes or Fennes, no Snow upon the Mountaines, no Snakes or Serpents, no Crocodiles in the Rivers, no Wormes that use with us to hurt and consume our Grayne, and to worke us so much displeasure in our houses, no Fleas, Cater-pillers, or Gnats. Pedro Fernández de Quirós, *Terra Australis incognita, or, A New Southerne Discoverie, Containing a Fifth Part of the World* (London: 1617, published in facsimile Amsterdam: 1970), 21–2. Quoted in Tucker, 'England's Antipodes', 67.
137 Foigny, *The Southern Land, Known*, 46.
138 Ibid., 47.
139 Thomas Artus, *Les Hermaphrodites* (Paris: 1605). Later editions were published with the title *Description de l'Isle des Hermaphrodites*.
140 Ciccarone's catalogue essay contains extensive research notes. See Julia Ciccarone, *Fictitious Voyages* [exhibition catalogue and essay] (Melbourne: Robert Lindsay Gallery 1996).
141 Foigny, *The Southern Land, Known*, 88–91.
142 Ibid., 39.
143 Ibid., 97.
144 Ibid., 48.
145 Ibid., 128.
146 David Fausett, translator's introduction to Foigny, *The Southern Land, Known*, xxxvii.
147 Ibid., xv.

Chapter 3: Exoticism and Romanticism

1 Jonathan Swift, *The Examiner and Other Pieces Written in 1710–1711*, ed. Herbert Davis (Oxford: Klough Knight 1957), 149. This quotation is from *The Examiner* 14, no. 9 (1710): XI.
2 See Glyn Williams, *Voyages of Delusion: The Search for the Northwest Passage in the Age of Reason* (London: Harper Collins 2002), xvii.
3 Denis Vairasse played on the contemporary suspicion that the Dutch were trying to hide wealthy discoveries for their own trade benefit in his imaginary voyage *The History of the Sevarites or Sevarambi* [*L'Histoire des Sevarambes*]:
    What account he [Siden] hath given of these rare People is not so Publick, I confess, as could be wished, because the Persons and the Nation, who have now a Correspondency in those Parts, have discouraged all others, by declaring these things to be fabulous, because they intend to ingross all the Trade to themselves. The Advantages many Dutch Families have received by them

already is incredible. The vast Treasure they have heaped up in a few years, is beyond all belief. They have met with some new Mines of Gold in this golden Country, and raised their Families to an extraordinary Grandeur.
Denis Vairasse, *The History of the Sevarites or Sevarambi* [*L'Histoire des Sevarambes*] (London: 1679), 'To the Reader' [unpaginated].

4 Edward Heawood, *A History of Geographical Discovery in the Seventeenth and Eighteenth Centuries* (New York: Octagon Books 1965), 180.

5 William Dampier, *A New Voyage Round the World* [1697] (London: Adam & Charles Black 1937), 312.

6 Banks' daily journal entry, 22 April 1770. Quoted in J. C. Beaglehole, ed., *The Endeavour Journal of Joseph Banks 1768–1771*, 2 vols (Sydney: Public Library of New South Wales/Angus & Robertson 1962), 2:51. Also available at http://southseas.nla.gov.au/journals/banks/17700422.html (accessed 22 August 2009).

7 Jonathan Swift, 'On Poetry: A Rhapsody' [1733], in *The Complete Poems* [of Jonathan Swift], ed. Pat Rogers (Harmondsworth: Penguin 1925), 523–35, lines 179–82.

8 See R. A. Skelton, *Decorative and Printed Maps of the 15th to 18th Centuries: A Revised Edition of Old Decorative Maps and Charts* [by A. L. Humphreys] (London: Staples Press 1952), 7.

9 Tucker has shown that while the concept of the antipodes was used in classical times to support theoretical over sensory-based modes of understanding, this concept was deployed, somewhat ironically perhaps, in the early seventeenth century as a symbol for 'progress' and the advance of knowledge. As she explains:

The Antipodes had featured strongly in early seventeenth century writings celebrating the advance of knowledge and a 'new' empiricism. Indeed, it had been held as a symbol of contemporary 'progress', illustrating both what contemporaries perceived as a break with tradition and all the possibilities that new methods of inquiry promised to yield, especially through geographical discovery. Despite this, the very use of the concept of the Antipodes reveals the continued debt to classical geographical models and literary forms. The use of the Antipodes in epistemological debates also had classical precedence. However, whereas in classical times the geographical concept of the Antipodes relied on theoretical modes of understanding, and was thus ridiculed by those Epicureans and others who favoured an empirical approach to knowledge, to these seventeenth century writers it represented the epitome of a world best known through direct experience.

Philippa Tucker, 'England's Antipodes: Early Modern Visions of a Southern World' (MA thesis, Victoria University of Wellington 2002), 174–5.

10 On the parallel development of legal practices in England from 1550 to 1720, see Barbara J. Shapiro, *A Culture of Fact: England 1550–1720* (Ithaca: Cornell University Press 2000).

11 Graham Huggan, *Territorial Disputes: Maps and Mapping Strategies in Contemporary Canadian and Australian Fiction* (Toronto: University of Toronto Press 1994), 8.

12 Guillaume de l'Isle's map 'Hémisphère Méridional' (1714) is reproduced, with accompanying discussion, in Glyndwr Williams and Alan Frost, eds, *Terra Australis to Australia* (Melbourne: Oxford University Press 1988), 24.

13 For discussion, see R. V. Tooley, ed., *Early Maps of Australia: The Dutch Period* (London: Map Collectors' Circle 1965), 12.

14 The southern continent, as Ryan puts it, was viewed as 'empty, unsettled, and inviting European inscription', part of the 'imaginative preparation for empire'. Simon Ryan, *The Cartographic Eye: How Explorers Saw Australia* (Cambridge: Cambridge University Press 1996), 105, 106.

15 A reproduction of John Senex' world map (1725) is in the digital collection of the National Library of Australia. Available at http://nla.gov.au/nla.map-nk4556 (accessed 19 September 2009).
16 Bernard Mandeville, *The Fable of the Bees*, 2 vols (London: 1729), 1:276.
17 Daniel Defoe, *A New Voyage Round the World* (London: Printed for A. Bettesworth...& W. Mears 1724).
18 'Adventures of Peregrine Pickle', *Monthly Review* 4 (1751): 356.
19 Ibid., 357.
20 Most discussions of literary deception refer to a man who called himself George Psalmanazar and claimed to be from the island of Formosa. His *An Historical and Geographical Description of Formosa, an Island Subject to the Emperor of Japan, Giving an Account of the Religion, Customs, and Manners of the Inhabitants* (London: Printed for D. Brown, G. Strahan, W. Davis & F. Coggan 1704) was an elaborate fabrication and the author's real identity remains unknown. All that we do know, by way of the people who reported that they knew him, is that the writer behind the persona of Psalmanazar was born around 1680 and came from the south of France. See Justin Stagl, *A History of Curiosity: The Theory of Travel 1550–1800* (Australia: Harwood Academic 1995), 199.
21 'Boscawen's Voyage to Bombay', *Monthly Review* 4 (1750): 63.
22 'Adventures of Peregrine Pickle', 355.
23 'Boscawen's Voyage to Bombay', 63.
24 Ibid.
25 See Henry Home (Lord Kames), *Elements of Criticism* [1761], ed. James R. Boyd (London: B. Blake 1863), 66–7.
26 Quoted in 'Alceste to the Yellow Sea', *Quarterly Review* 17, no. 18 (1817): 465.
27 Ibid.
28 F. M. Baculard d'Arnaud, *Oeuvres completes*, 4 vols (Amsterdam: 1775), 4:8. Passage translated in William Ray, *Story and History: Narrative Authority and Social Identity in the Eighteenth-Century French and English Novel* (Cambridge, Massachusetts: Basil Blackwell 1990), 3. Addressing related issues, Marthe Robert asks: 'What do "truth" and "fiction" signify in a sphere where even empirical data are not experienced but written and therefore interpreted? Is "novelistic truth" identical, similar, or simply analogous to "real truth"?' Translated in Lillian R. Furst, *All Is True: The Claims and Strategies of Realist Fiction* (Durham: Duke University Press 1995), 11.
29 John Hawkesworth, ed., *An Account of the Voyages Undertaken by the Order of His Present Majesty, for Making Discoveries in the Southern Hemisphere* (London: Printed for W. Strahan & T. Cadell 1773).
30 François de Salignac de La Mothe Fenelon, *The Adventures of Telemachus, the Son of Ulysses*, trans. John Hawkesworth (London: W. Strahan 1754). For discussion, see Bernard Smith, *European Vision and the South Pacific 1768–1850* (London: Oxford University Press 1960), 22.
31 See, for example, these publications: Jonathan Swift, *The Works of Jonathan Swift, with Some Account of the Author's Life, and Notes Historical and Explanatory*, ed. John Hawkesworth (London: 1754); Jonathan Swift, *The Life of the Revd. Jonathan Swift, D. D., Dean of St. Patrick's, Dublin* (London and Dublin: S. Cotter 1755); Jonathan Swift, *Letters Written by the Late Jonathan Swift, D. D., Dean of St. Patrick's, Dublin, and Several of His Friends, from the Year 1703 to 1740: Published from the Originals, with Notes Explanatory and Historical by John Hawkesworth*, ed. Thomas Wilkes (London: Printed for R. Davis 1766).
32 'Hunter's Historical Journal', *Monthly Review*, no. 12 (1793): 258. On the controversy over Hawkesworth's interpretation of the voyage accounts, see John Dunmore, preface

to *The Journal of Jean-François de Galaup de La Pérouse 1785–1788*, by Jean-François de Galaup de La Pérouse, trans. John Dunmore, 2 vols (London: The Hakluyt Society 1994), 1:vii.
33 Le Goff refers to parallels between medieval 'marvels' and modern surrealism and fantastic romantic art. Jacques Le Goff, *The Medieval Imagination*, trans. Arthur Goldhammer (Chicago: University of Chicago Press 1988), 32.
34 Kathryn Hume, *Fantasy and Mimesis: Responses to Reality in Western Literature* (New York: Methuen 1984), xii.
35 *OED*.
36 First published in French, the work was translated to English the following year: Jean-Jacques Rousseau, *The Discourse Which Carried the Præmium at the Academy of Dijon, in MDCCL* (Dublin: Richard James 1751).
37 [Robert Paltock], *The Life and Adventures of Peter Wilkins* (London: Printed for J. Robinson & R. Dodsley 1751). In this chapter I abbreviate the title to *Peter Wilkins*. Although the publication of *Peter Wilkins* was listed in the *Gentleman's Magazine* in November 1750, some copies are dated 1750 and others 1751. Tobias Smollett's *The Adventures of Peregrine Pickle*, Henry Fielding's *Amelia* and Thomas Gray's *Elegy* were published in 1751. '[T]here is no sense of incongruity in mentioning it in the same breath as these three', writes Edwards. Oliver Edwards, *Talking of Books* (London: Heinemann 1957), 38.
38 David Fausett, *Images of the Antipodes in the Eighteenth Century: A Study in Stereotyping* (Amsterdam: Rodopi 1995), 78.
39 Paul Baines, 'Able Mechanick: *The Life and Adventures of Peter Wilkins* and the Eighteenth-century Fantastic Voyage', in *Anticipations: Essays on Early Science Fiction and Its Precursors*, ed. David Seed (Liverpool: Liverpool University Press 1995), 13.
40 The theme of an aerial voyage was used in literature as early as Lucian's *True History* (c. AD 160), and by Francis Godwin and Cyrano de Bergerac in the seventeenth century. See Lucian of Samosata, *True History; and Lucius or, The Ass*, trans. Paul Turner (London: J. Calder 1958); Francis Godwin, *The Man in the Moone, or, A Discourse of a Voyage Thither, by Domingo Gonsales the Speedy Messenger* (London: Norton 1638); and Cyrano de Bergerac, *Voyage dans la Lune* (Paris: 1657). *Peter Wilkins* attracted new readers around the time of the first hot air balloon flights in 1783. See Fausett, *Images of the Antipodes*, 72–3.
41 Robert Paltock was only confirmed as the author in 1835 when original copyright agreements were found. His name was sometimes written as Poltock or Pultock. See A. H. Bullen, preface to *The Life and Adventures of Peter Wilkins* [1750], by Robert Paltock, ed. A. H. Bullen (London: Oxford University Press 1973), viii–ix.
42 Ralph Morris [pseud.], *A Narrative of the Life and Astonishing Adventures of John Daniel* (London: Cooper 1751).
43 See Fausett, *Images of the Antipodes*, 86.
44 For a list of literary works, see Fausett, *Images of the Antipodes*, 72–3. *Peter Wilkins* also inspired the drama *Peter Wilkins, or, The Flying Islanders: A Melo-Dramatic Spectacle in Two Acts* (London: Thomas Hailes Lacy 1827) as well as the writing and performance of other dramas.
45 See Fausett, *Images of the Antipodes*, 79. These illustrations are reprinted on pages 82–3 of Fausett's book.
46 Bullen, ed., *The Life and Adventures of Peter Wilkins*, xvi.
47 Ibid., x.
48 Christopher Bentley, introduction to *The Life and Adventures of Peter Wilkins* [1750], by Robert Paltock, ed. Christopher Bentley (London: Oxford University Press 1973), x.

49 Leigh Hunt, *A Book for a Corner, or, Selections in Prose and Verse from Authors Best Suited to That Mode of Enjoyment*, vol. 1 (London: Chapman & Hall 1849), 1:68.
50 Peter Fitting, ed., *Subterranean Worlds: A Critical Anthology* (Middletown, Connecticut: Wesleyan University Press 2004), 59.
51 Quoted in Christopher Bentley, introduction to *The Life and Adventures of Peter Wilkins*, xiv.
52 'Peter Wilkins', *Times Literary Supplement*, 7 May 1925, 312.
53 J. H. Alexander, 'Literary Reviewing in Five British Periodicals 1800–1808' (PhD thesis, University of Oxford 1968), 1–2.
54 'Peter Wilkins', *Monthly Review*, no. 4 (1750): ix.
55 Walter Raleigh, *The English Novel: Being a Short Sketch of Its History from the Earliest Times to the Appearance of Waverley* (London: John Murray 1895), 219–20.
56 George Saintsbury, *The English Novel* (London: J. M. Dent 1913), 145.
57 See Young on 'fantasmatic desire'. Robert Young, *Colonial Desire: Hybridity in Theory, Culture and Race* (London & New York: Routledge 1995), 161.
58 See Christopher Bentley, introduction to *The Life and Adventures of Peter Wilkins*, ix.
59 Robert Southey, *The Poetical Works of Robert Southey*, 8 vols (London: Longman, Brown & Green 1847), 1:231.
60 See Samuel Taylor Coleridge, *The Table Talk and Omniana of S. T. Coleridge*, ed. T. Ashe (London: Bell 1923), 331–2.
61 John Dunlop, *The History of Fiction: Being a Critical Account of the Most Celebrated Prose Writers of Fiction from the Earliest Greek Romances to the Novels of the Present Age* [1814], 4th edn (London: Longman, Brown, Green & Longmans 1845), 420.
62 'Peter Wilkins', *Retrospective Review* 1, no. 7 (1823): 122.
63 Rowland Prothero, *The Light Reading of Our Ancestors* (New York: Farrar & Rinehart 1927), 283–4.
64 Edwards, *Talking of Books*, 39. Some critics have argued that a 'proto-Romantic cult of sensibility' was an integral part of eighteenth-century thought. See Thomas de Zengotita, 'Speakers of Being: Romantic Refusion and Cultural Anthropology', in *Romantic Motives: Essays on Anthropological Sensibility*, ed. George W. Stocking (Madison: University of Wisconsin Press 1989), 77–8.
65 Christopher Bentley, introduction to *The Life and Adventures of Peter Wilkins*, xiv.
66 For further discussion on the connections between romanticism and imperialism, see my article, Paul Longley Arthur, 'From Politics to Pleasure: Coleridge and Romantic Imperialism', *Journal of the South Pacific Association for Commonwealth Literature and Language Studies*, no. 45 (1997): 73–87. See also Tim Fulford and Peter J. Kitson, eds, *Romanticism and Colonialism: Writing and Empire 1780–1830* (Cambridge: Cambridge University Press 1998).
67 On *Peter Wilkins* in relation to the history of science fiction, see Baines, 'Able Mechanick', 1–25.
68 In the case of *Peter Wilkins* the title accurately introduces the account to come. And yet, at the midpoint of the eighteenth century, the *Monthly Review* was particularly wary of the value of long titles as a failsafe indication of the published material in books, asking, rhetorically: 'How many productions do we see continually foisted upon the publick, under the sanction of deceitful title pages?' (in 'Adventures of Peregrine Pickle', 355). It continued to be a problem in 1815, when a reviewer in the *Quarterly Review* complained that the title page of David Porter's account of his travels to the Pacific made exaggerated claims, writing:

> ...[if] some English publisher should be desperate enough to reprint it, it may save him both expense and trouble to be apprised of the fallacies held forth in

the *lengthy* title-page. We can assure him that he will look in vain for the promised description of the Cape de Verd islands, – or for that of the coasts of Brazil, – or of Patagonia, no part of the two latter of which, in fact, did the writer even see.

'Porter's Cruize in the Pacific Ocean', *Quarterly Review* 8, no. 16 (1815): 352.
69 See Christopher Bentley, introduction to *The Life and Adventures of Peter Wilkins*, xix.
70 [Robert Paltock], *The Life and Adventures of Peter Wilkins*, 2 vols (Dublin: G. Faulkner 1751).
71 Ibid., 1:iii.
72 Ibid., 1:iv.
73 Ibid., 1:v.
74 Ibid.
75 Ibid., 1:vi.
76 Ibid., 1:vii.
77 Ibid., 1:ix.
78 Ibid.
79 Ibid., 1:ix.
80 Ibid., 1:viii.
81 Ibid.
82 Ibid., 1:xi.
83 Ibid., 1:73–4.
84 Ibid., 1:74.
85 Ibid., 1:75.
86 Ibid.
87 Ibid.
88 Ibid., 1:76.
89 Ibid., 1:78.
90 Ibid., 1:98.
91 Ibid., 1:92.
92 Ibid., 1:110.
93 Ibid., 1:111.
94 Ibid., 1:112.
95 Ibid., 1:114.
96 Ibid., 1:115.
97 Ibid., 1:116–7.
98 Ibid., 1:117.
99 Ibid., 1:133.
100 Ibid., 1:111.
101 Peter Hulme, *Colonial Encounters: Europe and the Native Caribbean 1492–1797* (London: Methuen 1986), 141.
102 [Paltock], *The Life and Adventures of Peter Wilkins*, 1:x.
103 Julia Ciccarone, *Fictitious Voyages* [exhibition catalogue and essay] (Melbourne: Robert Lindsay Gallery 1996).
104 [Paltock], *The Life and Adventures of Peter Wilkins*, 1:111. Later in the narrative the reader is provided with the gruesome details of this act of maiming: 'The Criminal is laid on his back with his *Graundee* open' and 'a sharp Stone, slits the *Gume* between each of the Filas of the *Graundee*, so that he can never fly more' (1:218).
105 Ibid., 1:127.
106 Ibid., 1:128.

107 Ibid., 1:134.
108 Ibid., 1:129–30.
109 Ibid., 1:130.
110 Ibid., 1:132.
111 Ibid., 1:189.
112 Ibid., 1:144.
113 Baines, 'Able Mechanick', 13.
114 [Paltock], *The Life and Adventures of Peter Wilkins*, 1:178.
115 Ibid., 1:177.
116 Ibid., 1:181.
117 Ibid., 1:185.
118 Ibid., 1:221.
119 Ibid., 1:229.
120 Ibid., 2:36.
121 Ibid.
122 Mary Louise Pratt, *Imperial Eyes: Travel Writing and Transculturation* (London: Routledge 1992), 7. See also my reference to Pratt in Chapter 1.
123 See Greg Dening, *Readings/Writings* (Carlton, Victoria: Melbourne University Press 1998), 126. Cook's reception was also the subject of contemporary pantomimes as well as ballet, painting and poetry.
124 [Paltock], *The Life and Adventures of Peter Wilkins*, 2:54.
125 Ibid.
126 Ibid., 2:67–8. The voyager is imagined as a saviour, bringing technological advancement to otherwise vulnerable people.
127 Ibid., 2:87.
128 Ibid., 2:92.
129 Ibid., 2:102.
130 Ibid.
131 Ibid., 2:121.
132 Ibid., 2:127.
133 Ibid., 2:133.
134 Ibid., 2:135.
135 Ibid., 2:215.
136 Ibid., 2:216.
137 This was the rationale cited by nineteenth-century missionaries in the Pacific.
138 [Paltock], *The Life and Adventures of Peter Wilkins*, 2:172.
139 Ibid., 2:174–82.
140 Christopher Bentley, introduction to *The Life and Adventures of Peter Wilkins*, xvii.
141 [Paltock], *The Life and Adventures of Peter Wilkins*, 2:21.

Chapter 4: Finding Paradise and Utopia in the Pacific

1 [Anon.], *Fragmens du dernier voyage de La Pérouse* [*Fragments from the Last Voyage of La Pérouse*] (Quimper [France]: Imprimerie de P. M. Barazer, Prairial [1797 an v de la République]). The edition I refer to in this chapter is a recent two-volume set that includes a facsimile of the original French publication (vol. 1) and the first English translation of the work, by John Dunmore (vol. 2): [Anon.], *Fragmens du dernier voyage de*

La Pérouse [*Fragments from the Last Voyage of La Pérouse*] [1797], trans. John Dunmore, 2 vols (Canberra: National Library of Australia 1987).
2 [Anon.], *The Life of La Perouse, the Celebrated and Unfortunate French Navigator, Including His Voyage, Shipwreck, & Subsequent Adventures in a Desolate Island, on the Northern Coast of Japan, Where He Was Discovered by Madame La Perouse* (London: A. Neil 1801).
3 A reproduction of Jacques Bellin's 1753 map of Australasia is in the digital collection of the National Library of Australia. Available at http://nla.gov.au/nla.map-t157 (accessed 19 September 2009).
4 On his second voyage to the South Pacific, James Cook tested a copy of John Harrison's 'H-4' chronometer. For a history of the challenge of measuring longitude, see Dava Sobel, *Longitude: The True Story of a Lone Genius Who Solved the Greatest Scientific Problem of His Time*, illustrated by William J. H. Andrewes (London: Fourth Estate 1999).
5 The continuing belief in the great south land theory was supported, most famously, by Charles de Brosses in France, John Callander in Scotland and Alexander Dalrymple in England. See Charles de Brosses, *Histoire des navigations aux Terres Australes*, 2 vols (Paris: Chez Durand 1756); John Callander, ed., *Terra Australis cognita, or, Voyages to the Terra Australis or Southern Hemisphere during the Sixteenth, Seventeenth, and Eighteenth Centuries*, 3 vols (Edinburgh: 1766); and Alexander Dalrymple, *An Account of the Discoveries Made in the South Pacifick Ocean, Previous to 1764* (London: 1767).
6 A series of notorious fictional works followed in the wake of the voyage of James Cook with Joseph Banks in the South Seas in 1768–9. See Bernard Smith, *European Vision and the South Pacific 1768–1850* (London: Oxford University Press 1960), 29.
7 Greg Dening, *Mr. Bligh's Bad Language: Passion, Power and Theatre on the* Bounty (Cambridge: Cambridge University Press 1992), 373.
8 For postcolonial assessments of Cook as explorer, leader and negotiator, see Anne Salmond, *The Trial of the Cannibal Dog: Captain Cook in the South Seas* (London: Penguin 2003), and Nicholas Thomas, *The Extraordinary Voyages of Captain James Cook* (New York: Walker & Company 2003). Another cautionary event was the killing, seven years before Cook's death, of Marion du Fresne by Maori in New Zealand's Bay of Islands. See Rod Edmond, *Representing the South Pacific: Colonial Discourse from Cook to Gauguin* (Cambridge: Cambridge University Press 1997), 9.
9 Charles de Brosses, 'Proposal for Establishing a Colony in the South Seas' [1756], rpt. in *Some Proposals for Establishing Colonies in the South Seas* [1943], ed. George Mackaness (Dubbo, New South Wales: Review Publications 1976), 29.
10 Alexander Dalrymple, *Scheme of a Voyage to Convey Conveniences of Life, Domestic Animals, Corn, Iron…to New Zealand, with Dr. Benjamin Franklin's Sentiments upon the Subject* [1771] (London: B. Marchant 1882), 4. A further mythology promoted by Dalrymple, if unwittingly, was the belief that Pacific islanders could not build ships, and did not travel. The history of Pacific islander migration is now recognized as one of the greatest navigational achievements of any of the world's cultures. See Greg Dening, *Beach Crossings: Voyaging across Times, Cultures and Self* (Melbourne: Melbourne University Publishing 2004), 1–9.
11 Dalrymple, *Scheme of a Voyage*, 5.
12 Burke wrote about images of Venus a decade earlier. See Edmund Burke, *A Philosophical Enquiry into the Origin of Our Ideas of the Sublime and Beautiful* [1757], ed. J. T. Boulton (London: Printed for J. Dodsley 1787), 195.
13 Symbolic imagery of male penetration of female virgin territory often featured in descriptions of Tahiti. See Georges van den Abbeele, *Travel as Metaphor: From Montaigne to Rousseau* (Minneapolis: University of Minnesota Press 1992), xxv.

14 See Louis-Antoine de Bougainville, *Voyage autour du monde, par la frégate du roi la Boudeuse, et la flûte l'Étoile; en 1766, 1767, 1768 and 1769* (Paris: Chez Saillant & Nyon 1771); and Louis-Antoine de Bougainville, *A Voyage Round the World, Performed by Order of His Most Christian Majesty, in the Years 1766, 1767, 1768, and 1769*, trans. John Reinhold Forster (London: J. Nourse & T. Davies 1772).

15 See Jean-Jacques Rousseau, *Discours sur l'origine et les fondements de l'inégalité parmi les hommes* [*Discourse on Inequality*] [1755], trans. Maurice Cranston (Harmondsworth: Penguin 1994). For discussion of Rousseau and his contemporaries, see O. H. K. Spate, *Paradise Found and Lost*, The Pacific since Magellan series, vol. 3 (Sydney: Australian University Press/Pergamon Press 1988), 83.

16 For further discussion, see John Dunmore, translator's notes in [Anon.], *Fragmens du dernier voyage de La Pérouse*, 2:8.

17 Denis Diderot, *Supplément au voyage de Bougainville* [*Supplement to the Voyage of Bougainville*], in *Opuscules philosophiques et littéraires, la plupart posthumes ou inédite* (Paris: Imprimerie de Chevet 1796).

18 For related discussion, see Pamela Neville-Sington and David Sington, *Paradise Dreamed: How Utopian Thinkers Have Changed the Modern World* (London: Bloomsbury 1993), 143.

19 From 1767 onwards, in Rod Edmond's words, 'western representations of the Pacific were to form important chapters in the history of the Enlightenment and Romanticism, of nineteenth-century Christianity, science and social theory, of modern painting, anthropology and popular culture'. Edmond, *Representing the South Pacific*, 7.

20 Quoted in Neville-Sington and Sington, *Paradise Dreamed*, 144.

21 *Travels of Hildebrand Bowman* (1778) is an imaginary voyage set partly in New Zealand (purporting to be the diary of an officer under Cook on the ship *Discovery*), which portrays the Maori as hostile and cannibalistic. See Hildebrand Bowman [pseud.], *Travels of Hildebrand Bowman, Esquire, into Carnovirria, Taupiniera, Olfactaria, and Auditant, in New-Zealand; in the Island of Bonhommica, and in the Powerful Kingdom of Luxo-Volupto, on the Great Southern Continent, Written by Himself* (London: W. Strahan & T. Cadell 1778). On representations of cannibalism in the Pacific, see Barbara Creed and Jeanette Hoorn, eds, *Body Trade: Captivity, Cannibalism and Colonialism in the Pacific* (New York: Routledge 2001).

22 Neil Rennie, *Far-Fetched Facts: The Literature of Travel and the Idea of the South Seas* (Oxford: Oxford University Press 1995), 174.

23 Edmond, *Representing the South Pacific*, 7.

24 The traditional reading of the 'rise of science' is that an unsubstantiated body of mythic knowledge was replaced by scientific evidence as a means of reliably and objectively describing the world as it was. Science claimed, deterministically, that knowledge could be impartial and that this should be a goal. The late eighteenth century was the period in which societies of knowledge flourished, such as the Royal Geographical Society of London and the French Academy, which took a scientific approach to language itself.

25 See John Dunmore, translator's introduction to [Anon.], *Fragmens du dernier voyage de La Pérouse*, 2:1.

26 See 'Dentrecasteaux', *Quarterly Review* 3, no. 5 (1810): 21.

27 Rpt. in Carrie Marshall and James Stirrat, eds, *Pacific Voyages: Selections from Scots Magazine, 1771–1808* (Portland, Oregon: Binfords & Mort 1960), 45.

28 'Perouse's Voyage Round the World', *Monthly Review*, no. 26 (1798): 522. The term 'completed' was often used in the sense of a 'comprehensive exploration'. Matthew Flinders used the term in 1799 when describing his voyage with Bass and a crew of eight

men at the end of 1798, which was intended to settle the question of whether or not a strait existed to the south of the Australian mainland. Flinders wrote: 'To the Strait which had been the great object of research, and whose discovery is now completed, Governor Hunter gave at my recommendation the name of Bass Strait'. Matthew Flinders, *Observations on the Coasts of Van Diemen's Land, on Bass Strait and Its Islands and on Part of the Coasts of New South Wales*, ed. George Mackaness (Sydney: D. S. Ford Printers 1946), 9.
29 Quoted in Marshall and Stirrat, *Pacific Voyages*, 46.
30 Four decades later the *Quarterly Review* reported that some of the convicts building the first hospital in New South Wales had likely 'run away to the ships of La Perouse'. 'New South Wales', *Quarterly Review* 37, no. 93 (1828): 17.
31 Frank Horner, *Looking for La Perouse: D'Entrecasteaux in Australia and the South Pacific 1792–1793* (Carlton, Victoria: Miegunyah Press 1995), 15.
32 Baudin is credited with having produced the first complete map of the Australian coast. See Frank Horner, *The French Reconnaissance: Baudin in Australia 1801–1803* (Melbourne: Melbourne University Press 1987), 8.
33 Matthew Flinders, *A Voyage to Terra Australis, Undertaken for the Purpose of Completing the Discovery of That Vast Country*, 2 vols (London: 1814), 2:143.
34 Jean-François de Galaup de La Pérouse, *The Journal of Jean-François de Galaup de La Pérouse 1785–1788*, trans. John Dunmore, 2 vols (London: The Hakluyt Society 1994), 2:266.
35 For a list of texts inspired by La Pérouse's loss, see John Dunmore, 'The Literature of Laperouse', in *Lapérouse in the Pacific: An Annotated Bibliography*, ed. Ian F. McLaren (Carlton, Victoria: Miegunyah Press 1993), ix–xi. A long French poem, J. Esmenard's *La Navigation* (Paris: Chez Giguet et Michaud 1805), was illustrated with catastrophic scenes of La Pérouse's presumed shipwreck. The second imaginary voyage, *Découvertes dans la mer du Sud* (Paris: Chez Everat [between 1795 and 1798]), has never been translated into English. Bernard Smith suggests that it is possible that August von Kotzebue, German author of the play *La Peyrouse* (Wien: 1797), was inspired by the enormous natural arch described in *Découvertes dans la mer du Sud*. See Smith, *European Vision and the South Pacific*, 18–19.
36 'Perouse's Voyage Round the World', 517, 522.
37 Louis Antoine Milet-Mureau, ed., *Voyage de La Pérouse autour du monde*, 5 vols (Paris: Imprimerie de la République 1797).
38 The *British Critic* reported their concern at the dubious quality of these translations, published quickly after the original, claiming: 'competition is certainly the soul of commerce; but, in a literary race, there are qualities more valuable than speed, which sometimes are forgotten in the contest'. 'Voyages and Travels', *British Critic*, no. 15 (1800): xiii–xv.
39 John Dunmore, translator's notes in [Anon.], *Fragmens du dernier voyage de La Pérouse*, 2:vii.
40 Julius S. Gassner, *Voyages and Adventures of La Pérouse*, ed. F. Valentin (Honolulu: University of Hawaii Press 1969), 137.
41 See George Bayly, *Sea-Life Sixty Years Ago: A Record of Adventures Which Led up to the Discovery of the Relics of the…Expedition Commanded by the Comte de La Perouse* (London: Kegan Paul 1885), 221. For recent commentary on the discovery of the remains of La Pérouse's expedition, with quotations from d'Urville's diary, see Danielle Clode, *Voyages to the South Seas: In Search of Terres Australes* (Melbourne: Melbourne University Publishing 2007).
42 See Gassner, *Voyages and Adventures of La Pérouse*, 141. The wreck of the *Boussole*, one of the two ships of the La Pérouse expedition, was finally located in 2005 at a site known as 'the fault' near Vanikoro. See http://www.cnn.com/2005/WORLD/asiapcf/05/10/laperouse.wrecked/index.html (accessed 16 September 2009).

43 The few extant copies of the original text suggest that the narrative was published privately by the author. See W. M. Horton, preface to [Anon.], *Fragmens du dernier voyage de La Pérouse*, 2:vi–vii.
44 'Dentrecasteaux', 22.
45 John Dunmore, translator's introduction and notes in [Anon.], *Fragmens du dernier voyage de La Pérouse*, 2:6, 45.
46 [Anon.], *Fragmens du dernier voyage de La Pérouse*, 2:16.
47 John Dunmore, translator's notes in [Anon.], *Fragmens du dernier voyage de La Pérouse*, 2:45.
48 [Anon.], *Fragmens du dernier voyage de La Pérouse*, 2:16.
49 John Dunmore, translator's notes in [Anon.], *Fragmens du dernier voyage de La Pérouse*, 2:45.
50 [Anon.], *Fragmens du dernier voyage de La Pérouse*, 2:17.
51 John Dunmore, translator's notes in [Anon.], *Fragmens du dernier voyage de La Pérouse*, 2:45.
52 Ibid., 2:6.
53 'Voyages and Travels', *Monthly Review*, no. 4 (1791): 346.
54 Historian Ernest Scott appears to have made the mistake of interpreting *Fragmens du dernier voyage de La Pérouse* as a genuine travel account. See W. M. Horton, preface to [Anon.], *Fragmens du dernier voyage de La Pérouse*, 2:vi.
55 The *Charlotte* left from Plymouth on 13 May 1787 with 108 convicts, including 20 women.
56 [Anon.], *Fragmens du dernier voyage de La Pérouse*, 2:13.
57 John Dunmore, translator's introduction to [Anon.], *Fragmens du dernier voyage de La Pérouse*, 2:6. See also Watkin Tench, *1788:* A Narrative of the Expedition to Botany Bay (1788) *and* A Complete Account of the Settlement at Port Jackson (1788) (Melbourne: Text Publishing 1996).
58 John Dunmore, translator's introduction to [Anon.], *Fragmens du dernier voyage de La Pérouse*, 2:6.
59 [Anon.], *Fragmens du dernier voyage de La Pérouse*, 2:13.
60 Ibid.
61 Ibid., 2:38.
62 Ibid.
63 John Dunmore, translator's notes in [Anon.], *Fragmens du dernier voyage de La Pérouse*, 2:9.
64 [Anon.], *Fragmens du dernier voyage de La Pérouse*, 2:38–40.
65 See 'Flinders' Voyage to Terra Australis', *Monthly Review*, no. 77 (1815): 52.
66 [Anon.], *Fragmens du dernier voyage de La Pérouse*, 2:15.
67 Ibid.
68 Ibid., 2:15–16.
69 The reference to black swans follows traditional antipodean inversion mythology. Black swans were mentioned, for example, in Brome's play *The Antipodes* (1640): 'Are not their swans all black, and ravens white?' Richard Brome, *The Antipodes*, ed. Ann Haaker (London: Edward Arnold 1966), Act 1, Scene 6, line 158.
70 [Anon.] *Fragmens du dernier voyage de La Pérouse*, 2:15.
71 Ibid., 2:17.
72 John Hunter, *An Historical Journal of the Transactions at Port Jackson and Norfolk Island, with the Discoveries…in New South Wales and in the Southern Ocean, since the Publication of Phillip's Voyage* (London: 1793), 205.
73 [Anon.], *Fragmens du dernier voyage de La Pérouse*, 2:19, 20.

74 Ibid., 2:19.
75 Ibid.
76 Ibid., 2:17.
77 Ibid.
78 Ibid., 2:21.
79 La Pérouse, *The Journal of Jean-François de Galaup de La Pérouse*, 2:248, 277, 287, 306, 394–5.
80 [Anon.], *Fragmens du dernier voyage de La Pérouse*, 2:21.
81 Ibid.
82 John Dunmore, translator's notes in [Anon.], *Fragmens du dernier voyage de La Pérouse*, 2:8.
83 Ibid.
84 Ibid.
85 Ibid.
86 [Anon.], *Fragmens du dernier voyage de La Pérouse*, 2:18.
87 Percy A. Scholes, *The Oxford Companion to Music*, ed. John Owen Ward (Oxford: Oxford University Press 1970), 855.
88 [Anon.], *Fragmens du dernier voyage de La Pérouse*, 2:35–7.
89 Ibid., 2:37.
90 Note that I use the anglicized version of La Perouse's name (without the acute accent) when referring to the character in *The Life of La Perouse, the Celebrated and Unfortunate French Navigator*, as this is the way it appears in the text.
91 [Anon.], *Bysh's Edition of The Voyages and Adventures of La Perouse, to Which is Added The Life of Hatem Tai, or, The Generosity of an Arabian Prince* (London: Printed for J. Bysh 1829).
92 [Anon.], *The Life of La Perouse*, iii.
93 Ibid.
94 Ibid., 34.
95 Ibid., 35.
96 Ibid., 58.
97 Ibid., 35.
98 Ibid.
99 Ibid.
100 Ibid.
101 Ibid., 36.
102 Ibid.
103 Ibid.
104 Ibid., 37.
105 Ibid.
106 Ibid.
107 Ibid.
108 Ibid., 38.
109 Ibid.
110 Ibid.
111 Ibid.
112 Ibid.
113 After being captured by a group of Powhatan hunters, Smith claimed that Pocahontas saved him from certain death by appealing to her father, the king, to spare his life. See W. C. Armstrong, ed., *The Life and Adventures of Captain John Smith* (New York: Dayton 1859), 88.

114 [Anon.], *The Life of La Perouse*, 38–9.
115 Ibid., 39.
116 Ibid.
117 Ibid.
118 Ibid.
119 Ibid.
120 Ibid.
121 Ibid.
122 Ibid., 40.
123 Ibid.
124 Ibid.
125 Ibid., 41.
126 Ibid.
127 Ibid., 42.
128 Ibid.
129 Ibid.
130 Ibid.
131 Ibid.
132 Ibid.
133 Ibid., 44.
134 Ibid., 45.
135 Ibid.
136 Ibid., 46.
137 Ibid.
138 Ibid.
139 Ibid.
140 David Fausett, translator's introduction to Gabriel de Foigny, *The Southern Land, Known* [1676], trans. David Fausett (New York: Syracuse University Press 1993), xxxv.
141 [Anon.], *The Life of La Perouse*, 48.
142 Ibid., 49.
143 Ibid.
144 Ibid.
145 Ibid.
146 Ibid.
147 Ibid., 50.
148 Ibid.
149 Ibid.
150 Ibid., 51.
151 Ibid.
152 Ibid., 52.
153 Ibid., 53.
154 Ibid.
155 Ibid., 54.
156 Ibid.
157 Ibid., 55.
158 Ibid.
159 Ibid.
160 Ibid., 56.
161 Ibid.

162 Ibid.
163 Ibid.
164 Ibid., 57.
165 Ibid.
166 Ibid.
167 Ibid.
168 Ibid., 58.

Chapter 5: Australia's Mythic Inland

1 'Slavery and Famine', *Monthly Review*, no. 14 (1794): 475.
2 'Australian Colonies', *Quarterly Review* 54, no. 64 (1835): 311.
3 See Donald Horne, *The Lucky Country* (Ringwood, Victoria: Penguin 1964), and Richard White, *Inventing Australia: Images and Identity 1688–1980* (Sydney: Allen & Unwin 1981).
4 Lewis Carroll, Alice's Adventures in Wonderland [1865]; *and* Through the Looking-Glass and What Alice Found There: *The Centenary Edition*, ed. Hugh Haughton (London: Penguin Classics 1998), 11.
5 Judith Wright, 'The Upside-Down Hut', in *The Writer in Australia*, ed. J. Barnes (Melbourne: Oxford University Press 1969), 332.
6 For example, New York author Douglas Kennedy, in his novel *Dead Heart* (London: Little, Brown & Company 1994), portrays a lawless, dystopian community occupying a remote town that is officially abandoned and no longer marked on maps. I discuss this work in my article, Paul Longley Arthur, 'Imaginary Conquests', *Journal of Australian Studies* 23, no. 61 (1999): 136–42.
7 [Anon.], *Account of an Expedition to the Interior of New Holland*, ed. Lady Mary Fox (London: Richard Bentley 1837).
8 The extracts are from major journals such as the *Edinburgh Review* (founded in 1802) and the *Quarterly Review* (founded in 1809), which came to represent a new critical genre. For discussion of the approach and reach of these journals, see Margaret Stonyk, *Nineteenth-Century English Literature* (London: Macmillan 1983), 7. The anonymity of many of the contributors had been a custom since the beginnings of periodical publication, when the practice of anonymity in newspaper publishing was adopted. See Walter E. Houghton, ed., *The Wellesley Index to Victorian Periodicals 1824–1900*, 5 vols (Toronto: University of Toronto Press 1966), 1:xviii.
9 Rudolph Erich Raspe, *The Surprising Adventures of Baron Munchausen* [1785] (New York: Peter Pauper Press 1944), 97.
10 William Dampier, *A New Voyage Round the World* [1697] (London: Adam Black & Charles Black 1937), 312.
11 Sydney Smith, 'New South Wales', *Edinburgh Review* 47, no. 93 (1828): 94.
12 *Mirror of Parliament* 4, no. 19 (1840): 3122.
13 This phrase was used repeatedly in the American CNN television coverage of the 2000 Olympic Games, broadcast from locations around the Sydney Harbour Bridge area and featuring interviews with expatriate Australians including Paul Hogan of *Crocodile Dundee* fame.
14 Brian Castro, 'Cultural Cringe', *Meanjin* 59, no. 3 (2000): 38.
15 Quoted in Peter Good, *The Journal of Peter Good, Gardener on Matthew Flinders' Voyage to Terra Australis 1801–1803*, ed. Phyllis I. Edwards (North Sydney: Library of Australian History 1981), 19.

16 Matthew Flinders, *Observations on the Coasts of Van Diemen's Land, on Bass Strait and Its Islands and on Part of the Coasts of New South Wales*, ed. George Mackaness (Sydney: D. S. Ford Printers 1946), 17.
17 See 'Ship News', *Sydney Gazette*, 12 June 1803, 4.
18 See 'Flinders' Voyage to Terra Australis', *Quarterly Review* 12, no. 23 (1814): 4–5, and Good, *The Journal of Peter Good*, 19.
19 'Account of the Loss of His Majesty's Armed Vessel *Porpoise*, and the *Cato*, upon Wreck Reef', *Sydney Gazette*, 18 Sept 1803, 3–4.
20 See 'Flinders on the Marine Barometer', *Edinburgh Review* 9, no. 18 (1807): 419–24, and 'Flinders' Voyage to Terra Australis', *Quarterly Review* 12, no. 23 (1814): 1.
21 David Collins, *An Account of the English Colony in New South Wales from Its First Settlement, in January 1788, to August 1801*, 2 vols (London: Cadell & Davies 1802), 2:14.
22 Ibid.
23 John Turnbull, *A Voyage Round the World in the Years 1800, 1801, 1802, 1803, and 1804*, 3 vols (London: 1805), 1:75.
24 Quoted in 'Collins' Account of the Colony of New South Wales', *Monthly Review*, no. 42 (1803): 13.
25 Ibid., 5–6.
26 On the history of the Aboriginal reconciliation movement, see Henry Reynolds, *Why Weren't We Told?: A Personal Search for the Truth about Our History* (Ringwood, Victoria: Viking 1999). In a significant gesture of reconciliation, on 23 November 2001 Pope John Paul II made an official apology – in a statement that was the first ever to be sent out worldwide via email by the Vatican – in which he acknowledged that Australian Aborigines had sometimes been subject to shameful injustices by members of the church in the past. In early 2008, soon after Australian Prime Minister Kevin Rudd was sworn in to office, one of his first major official acts was to make an apology on behalf of the Australian Government to the 'Stolen Generations' – Indigenous Australians who had been subject to the notorious government policy of forcibly separating families in the name of social integration and education. See http://www.aph.gov.au/house/Rudd_Speech.pdf (accessed 6 July 2009).
27 'Collins' Account of the Colony of New South Wales', 1.
28 Ibid.
29 Henry Brougham, 'Turnbull's Voyage Round the World', *Edinburgh Review* 9, no. 18 (1807): 339.
30 Turnbull, *A Voyage Round the World*, 3:77.
31 Ibid., 3:78. Turnbull reported that the changes in Tahiti were partly due to introduced liquor (3:27). More harmful was the introduction of European diseases, including venereal diseases.
32 Brougham, 'Turnbull's Voyage Round the World', 339.
33 'Inquiry into the Poor Laws', *Quarterly Review* 8, no. 16 (1812): 355.
34 'Flinders' Voyage to Terra Australis', *Quarterly Review* 12, no. 23 (1814): 20.
35 Matthew Flinders, *A Voyage to Terra Australis, Undertaken for the Purpose of Completing the Discovery of That Vast Country*, 2 vols (London: 1814), 2:228.
36 See also Judith Ryan, *Spirit in Land: Bark Paintings from Arnhem Land* (Melbourne: National Gallery of Australia 1990).
37 See Henry Reynolds, *The Question of Genocide in Australia's History: An Indelible Stain?* (Richmond, Victoria: Viking 2001).
38 'Flinders' Voyage to Terra Australis', *Quarterly Review* 12, no. 23 (1814): 22.
39 'Flinders' Voyage to Terra Australis', *Monthly Review*, no. 76 (1815): 156.

40 'Collins' Account of the Colony of New South Wales', 5.
41 'Flinders' Voyage to Terra Australis', *Quarterly Review* 12, no. 23 (1814): 34.
42 'Flinders' Voyage to Terra Australis', *Monthly Review*, no. 76 (1815): 164–5.
43 Ibid., 165.
44 Ibid., 166.
45 Ibid.
46 Sydney Smith, 'New South Wales', *Edinburgh Review* 47, no. 93 (1828): 92.
47 Ibid. The Aborigines of Van Diemen's Land continued to be reported as even more savage than their mainland counterparts.
48 'New South Wales', *Quarterly Review* 37, no. 93 (1828): 29. By 1833, the *Edinburgh Review*, in response to James Montgomery's account of missionary activities, was claiming that the inhabitants of the Marquesan islands were 'the most ferocious savages in these seas'. 'Montgomery's Missionary Voyages and Travels', *Edinburgh Review* 57, no. 140 (1833): 80–95.
49 'New South Wales', *Quarterly Review* 37, no. 93 (1828): 29.
50 See John Alexander Ferguson, *Bibliography of Australia*, 7 vols (Sydney: Angus & Robertson 1969), and John Alexander Ferguson, *Addenda 1784–1850 to Vols 1–4 of the Bibliography of Australia* (Canberra: National Library of Australia 1986).
51 Sydney Smith, 'Botany Bay', *Edinburgh Review* 38, no. 75 (1823): 85.
52 Jacques Arago, *Narrative of a Voyage Round the World...Commanded by Captain Freycinet...in 1817, 1818, 1819, and 1820* (London: Treuttel & Wurtz...1823), 163.
53 Ferguson, *Bibliography of Australia*, 1:282. This first work of general literature, published in Tasmania, was Michael Howe, *The Last and the Worst of the Bush Rangers of Van Diemen's Land* (Hobart: Printed by Andrew Bent 1818).
54 Jonah Raskin, *The Mythology of Imperialism: Rudyard Kipling, Joseph Conrad, E. M. Forster, D. H. Lawrence, and Joyce Cary* (New York: Random House 1971), 1.
55 Ibid., 20.
56 Sydney Smith, 'Oxley's Tour in Botany Bay', *Edinburgh Review* 34, no. 68 (1820): 422.
57 Quoted in *Historical Records of New South Wales*, 7 vols (Sydney: New South Wales Government 1893–1901), 3:382.
58 Ibid., 3:382–3.
59 'Flinders' Voyage to Terra Australis', *Quarterly Review* 12, no. 23 (1814): 15.
60 Ibid., 21, 41.
61 On this expedition and its discoveries, see Ross Gibson, *The Diminishing Paradise: Changing Literary Perceptions of Australia* (Sydney: Angus & Robertson 1984), 57.
62 Smith, 'Oxley's Tour in Botany Bay', 430.
63 John Oxley, *Journals of Two Expeditions into the Interior of New South Wales, Undertaken by Order of the British Government in the Years 1817–1818* (London: 1820), 18.
64 Ibid., 243. Sydney Smith, reviewing Oxley's journal, guessed that 'Twenty or thirty miles further would in all probability have determined the point'. Smith, 'Oxley's Tour in Botany Bay', 428.
65 Ibid., 422.
66 'Wentworth', *Quarterly Review* 24, no. 47 (1821): 55.
67 Ibid., 72.
68 See J. M. R. Cameron, 'Western Australia 1616–1829: An Antipodean Paradise', *The Geographical Journal*, no. 140 (1974): 373.
69 Thomas J. Maslen, *The Friend of Australia, or, A Plan for Exploring the Interior and for Carrying on a Survey of the Whole Continent of Australia, by a Retired Officer of the Honourable East India Company's Service* (London: Hurst & Chance 1830).

70 Ibid., 15.
71 'New South Wales', *Quarterly Review* 37, no. 93 (1828): 31.
72 Smith, 'New South Wales', *Edinburgh Review* 47, no. 93 (1828): 88.
73 Ibid., 91.
74 Ibid., 88.
75 Ibid., 89.
76 'New South Wales', *Quarterly Review* 37, no. 93 (1828): 3.
77 Ibid., 17.
78 John Barrow, 'New Colony on Swan River', *Quarterly Review* 39, no. 78 (1829): 322.
79 Ibid.
80 Ibid., 317.
81 Cameron, 'Western Australia 1616–1829', 382.
82 Samuel Taylor Coleridge, 'Appendix F: Conversations with Coleridge', in *The Collected Works of Samuel Taylor Coleridge*, ed. Carl Woodring, 20 vols (London: Routledge 1990), 1:575.
83 John Barrow, 'Royal Geographical Society', *Quarterly Review* 46, no. 26 (1831): 56.
84 Ibid.
85 *Terra nullius*, a Latin term meaning 'land belonging to no one', is a concept used in international law. In Australia, the application of *terra nullius* denied to Aboriginal people the granting of land rights based on sovereignty until the landmark 1992 legal case known as 'Mabo'. See http://www.austlii.edu.au/au/cases/cth/HCA/1992/23.html (accessed 25 November 2009).
86 Cameron, 'Western Australia 1616–1829', 382.
87 See Charles Sturt, *Two Expeditions into the Interior of Southern Australia during the Years 1828, 1829, 1830, and 1831, with Observations on the Soil, Climate, and General Resources of the Colony of New South Wales* (London: Smith & Elder 1833).
88 'Australian Colonies', 316.
89 'Latest Accounts from Australia', *Journal of the Royal Geographical Society of London*, no. 6 (1836): 436. Mitchell set out on a third expedition in March 1836, successfully tracing the Lachlan, Murrumbidgee and Darling Rivers to where they joined the Murray River.
90 Paul Pottinger, 'Secret Garden', *Australian*, 21 August 1999, Magazine, 25–9. South Australia's Lake Eyre rarely fills with water. However, in 1999 it did fill, for only the fourth time in over a century. The South Australian tourist agency used the image of the inland sea for its humorous advertising slogan: 'Australia's mythical inland sea. Now showing for a strictly limited time'.
91 Paul Carter, *Living in a New Country* (London: Faber & Faber 1992), 11, 12.
92 The term 'dead heart' does not appear to have been used until the nineteenth century. The term featured in the title of J. W. Gregory's book *The Dead Heart of Australia: A Journey around Lake Eyre in the Summer of 1901–1902, with Some Account of the Lake Eyre Basin and the Flowing Wells of Central Australia* (London: John Murray 1906). It was later popularized in the title of Australian explorer Cecil Madigan's book *Crossing the Dead Heart* (Melbourne: Georgian House 1946). The *OED* notes usage of the term 'never-never', meaning 'the desert country of the interior', from 1833.
93 [Anon.], *Account of an Expedition to the Interior of New Holland*, 21–2.
94 See Simon Ryan, *The Cartographic Eye: How Explorers Saw Australia* (Cambridge: Cambridge University Press 1996), 13.
95 Gregory, *The Dead Heart of Australia*.
96 Phillip Drew, *The Coast Dwellers: Australians Living on the Edge* (Ringwood, Victoria: Penguin 1994), 93.

97 The term 'outback' was coined in the late nineteenth century and used chiefly in Australia and New Zealand (*OED*).
98 [Anon.], *Account of an Expedition to the Interior of New Holland*, 83.
99 See Therese Huber, Adventures on a Journey to New Holland [1793]; *and*, The Lonely Deathbed, trans. Rodney Livingstone, ed. Leslie Bodi (Melbourne: Lansdowne Press 1966). Huber was Georg Forster's wife, recognized expert, with his brother, on the Pacific in eighteenth-century Germany. For discussion, see Leslie Bodi, preface to Huber, *Adventures on a Journey to New Holland*, 7.
100 Gregory Claeys, personal conversation with author, 16 December 1997. For Whately's views on convict transportation, see Richard Whately, *Thoughts on Secondary Punishments, in a Letter to Earl Grey* (London: Fellowes 1832). For his views on politics, see Richard Whately, *Introductory Lectures on Political Economy, Being Part of a Course Delivered in Easter Term, 1831* (London: Fellowes 1831).
101 Gregory Claeys, ed., *Modern British Utopias 1700–1850*, 8 vols (London: Pickering & Chatto 1997).
102 Ibid., 7:253. Fox was the eldest daughter of the Duke of Clarence, later to be William IV.
103 See Gibson, *The Diminishing Paradise*, 71–8.
104 John Dunmore, *Utopias and Imaginary Voyages to Australasia: A Lecture Delivered at the National Library of Australia, 2 September 1987* (Canberra: National Library of Australia 1988), 18–19. This is a daring vision of a southern world, Dunmore suggests, because citizens are permitted to keep vows simply out of love for one another, that is, without the need to marry. See Dunmore, *Utopias and Imaginary Voyages to Australasia*, 19.
105 See 'Latest Accounts from Australia', 434–5.
106 Ibid., 438.
107 [Anon.], *Account of an Expedition to the Interior of New Holland*, 231.
108 'New South Wales', *Quarterly Review* 37, no. 93 (1828): 2.
109 A famous contemporary example of imaginative reporting in the fictional letter genre is Edward Gibbon Wakefield, *A Letter from Sydney, the Principal Town of Australasia, Together with the Outline of a System of Colonization*, ed. Robert Gouger (London: J. Cross 1829). For discussion, see Gibson, *The Diminishing Paradise*, 63.
110 [Anon.], *Account of an Expedition to the Interior of New Holland*, 93.
111 Ibid., 221.
112 Ibid., 1, 7, 20.
113 Ibid., 2.
114 Ibid., 4.
115 Ibid.
116 Ibid., 5.
117 Ibid.
118 Ibid.
119 Ibid.
120 Ibid., 6.
121 Ibid.
122 Ibid.
123 Ibid., 7.
124 Ibid.
125 Ibid., 7–8.
126 Ibid., 8.
127 Ibid.
128 Ibid.

129 Ibid., 8–9.
130 Ibid., 8.
131 In the previous century, Charles de Brosses and following him John Callander had imagined a civilized nation in the continent's interior. Callander's published account of 1766 speculated that there was a chance of finding 'some civilized nation in the interiour parts of this country, who are as utter strangers to us, or our arts, as we can be to theirs'. Callander's account was a modified version of de Brosses'. The relevant passages are in Charles de Brosses, *Histoire des navigations aux Terres Australes*, 2 vols (Paris: Chez Durand 1756), 1:20–1; and John Callander, ed., *Terra Australis cognita, or, Voyages to the Terra Australis or Southern Hemisphere during the Sixteenth, Seventeenth, and Eighteenth Centuries*, 3 vols (Edinburgh: A. Donaldson 1766), 1:14.
132 [Anon.], *Account of an Expedition to the Interior of New Holland*, 8.
133 Ibid., 9.
134 Ibid.
135 Ibid., 12.
136 Ibid., 9.
137 Ibid.
138 Ibid. In utopias, by definition, it is isolation that allows projected societies to live by alternative social models.
139 Ibid., 10.
140 Ibid., 225.
141 Ibid., 230.
142 Ibid., 29.
143 Ibid., 11.
144 Ibid., 12.
145 Ibid., 10.
146 Ibid.
147 Ibid., 10–11.
148 Ibid., 12.
149 Ibid.
150 Ibid., 13.
151 Ibid.
152 Ibid., 14.
153 Ibid.
154 Ibid., 14–15.
155 Ibid., 15.
156 Ibid., 16.
157 Ibid., 17.
158 Ibid., 16.
159 Ibid.
160 Ibid.
161 'Porter's Cruize in the Pacific Ocean', *Quarterly Review* 8, no. 16 (1815): 65.
162 Ibid. See also Porter's published account, David Porter, *Journal of a Cruize Made to the Pacific Ocean by Captain David Porter*, 2 vols (Philadelphia: 1815); and commentary in Greg Dening, *Readings/Writings* (Carlton, Victoria: Melbourne University Press 1998), 159–63.
163 [Anon.], *Account of an Expedition to the Interior of New Holland*, 17.
164 Ibid.
165 Ibid.

166 Ibid., 121. As earlier noted, the imagery of the black swan was a symbol commonly associated with the antipodes.
167 Ibid., 21. A similar interrelationship developed between the settlers and Aboriginal people of *Terra Australis* in the anonymously published *A Description of New Athens in Terra Australis Incognita* (1720). In a passage from the text the narrator explains: 'In short, they soon made the old Inhabitants Christians; and by marrying and intermarrying among them, grew together into one People'. [Anon.], *A Description of New Athens in Terra Australis Incognita by One Who Resided Many Years upon the Spot* [1720], in *Utopias of the British Enlightenment*, ed. Gregory Claeys (Cambridge: Cambridge University Press 1994), 51.
168 [Anon.], *Account of an Expedition to the Interior of New Holland*, 25.
169 Ibid. 'Eutopia' can be defined as a place of 'ideal happiness' (*OED*).
170 [Anon.], *Account of an Expedition to the Interior of New Holland*, 20.
171 Ibid., 233.
172 Ibid., 211.
173 Ibid., 82.
174 Ibid., 83.
175 Ibid., 86–7. The association of jewellery with savagery was repeated later in the century in the futuristic utopia, H. A. Dugdale, *A Few Hours in a Far-Off Age* (Melbourne: Carron & Bird 1883).
176 [Anon.], *Account of an Expedition to the Interior of New Holland*, 233.
177 Ibid., 229.

Conclusion

1 'Anson and Byron's Voyages', *Retrospective Review* 10, no. 2 (1824): 286.
2 'Travels', *British Critic*, no. 7 (1796): x.
3 'Voyages and Travels', *British Critic*, no. 10 (1797): ix.
4 Preface, *British Critic*, no. 12 (1798): i.
5 Ibid.
6 'Voyages and Travels', *British Critic*, no. 13 (1799): x. The editors conceptualized travel accounts hierarchically as a family tree. 'Tours', they suggest, may be 'considered as the younger brothers of travels, and of course will obtain notice after the superior branches of the family' (x).
7 'Travels', *British Critic*, no. 14 (1799): ix–x. These editors explain that the similarity lies in the way that 'the adventures of the individual are there interwoven with the delineation of the objects'. Ironically, the editors are pondering the real-life story of Mungo Park, the well-known explorer of the African interior, as conveyed in a recently published account. They suggest that the subject matter stands up to the same kind of literary scrutiny as a novel because dramatic real-world adventures, if written up with enough skill, could have the same impact on readers as well-written novels. There was little factually based information about the African interior available in Britain prior to Mungo Park's expedition of 1795. Before that time, literary fiction had fulfilled a similar function for colonial Africa as it had for the antipodes. See Roxann Wheeler, 'Limited Visions of Africa: Geographies of Savagery and Civility in Early Eighteenth-Century Narratives', in *Writes of Passage: Reading Travel Writing*, ed. James Duncan and Derek Gregory (London: Routledge 1999), 14.

8 'Collection of Modern and Contemporary Voyages and Travels', *Monthly Review*, no. 51 (1806): 419.
9 There was a race to publish foreign voyage accounts. A contributor to the *British Critic* in 1800 observed that 'almost every foreign Voyage is the parent of two or three English works, which start as rival translations'. 'Voyages and Travels', *British Critic*, no. 15 (1800): xiv.
10 Henry Weber, ed., *Popular Romances, Consisting of Imaginary Voyages and Travels, to Which is Prefixed an Introductory Dissertation* (Edinburgh: Printed by James Ballantyne 1812). See also Phillip Babcock Gove, *The Imaginary Voyage in Prose Fiction: A History of Its Criticism and a Guide for Its Study, with an Annotated Check List of 215 Imaginary Voyages from 1700 to 1800* (New York: Columbia University Press 1941), 65.
11 Weber, *Popular Romances*, viii. On the simultaneous growth of science, travel and empire, see Margarette Lincoln, ed., *Science and Exploration in the Pacific: European Voyages to the Southern Oceans in the Eighteenth Century* (Greenwich: The Boydell Press/National Maritime Museum 1998).
12 Charles Mills, *The Travels of Theodore Ducas in Various Countries in Europe, at the Revival of Letters and Art* (London: Printed for Longman, Hurst, Rees, Orme & Brown 1822).
13 'Travels of Theodore Ducas', *Quarterly Review* 28, no. 56 (1823): 365.
14 Ibid., 366.
15 Henry Hart Milman, 'Annals and Antiquities of Rajast'han', *Quarterly Review* 48, no. 95 (1832): 1.
16 Paul Carter, *The Road to Botany Bay: An Essay in Spatial History* (London: Faber & Faber 1987), xv.
17 Accounts of travel would now be regarded as 'subsidiaries of history', that is, as original sources that 'preserve the memory of many things which history disdains to notice'. 'Evelyn's Memoirs', *Quarterly Review* 19, no. 38 (1818): 12. In this quotation the voyage account is conceived as though it were an appendix or an index of information yet to be sorted by the guiding hand of history.
18 J. J. Blunt, 'Life of Cranmer', *Quarterly Review* 47, no. 94 (1832): 366.
19 See Robert Young, *White Mythologies: Writing History and the West* (London: Routledge 1990), 46. As Barthes puts it, this approach allows the historian to become invisible. There is 'a systematic absence of any sign referring to the sender of the historical message: history seems to *tell itself*'. Roland Barthes, *The Rustle of Language*, trans. Richard Howard (Berkeley: University of California Press 1986), 131.
20 'Emma', *Quarterly Review* 14, no. 27 (1815): 191.
21 Ibid., 192–3.
22 Ibid., 189.
23 Ibid., 190.
24 Ibid., 191.
25 Ibid., 193.
26 'Flinders' Voyage to Terra Australis', *Monthly Review*, no. 77 (1815): 36.
27 Ibid., 35.
28 Henry Brougham, 'Turnbull's Voyage Round the World', *Edinburgh Review* 9, no. 18 (1807): 332.
29 Ibid.
30 Sydney Smith, 'New South Wales', *Edinburgh Review* 47, no. 93 (1828): 98.
31 Harry Liebersohn, *The Travelers' World: Europe to the Pacific* (Cambridge, Massachusetts: Harvard University Press 2006), 13.

32 John Dunmore, *Utopias and Imaginary Voyages to Australasia: A Lecture Delivered at the National Library of Australia, 2 September 1987* (Canberra: National Library of Australia 1988), 18.
33 For example, John Sherer, *The Gold-Finder of Australia: How He Went, How He Fared, How He Made His Fortune* (London: 1853), was received as a genuine report, and it inspired many people to try to emulate the fictional gold-finder's success.
34 Herman Melville's *Typee: A Peep at Polynesian Life, during a Four Months' Residence in a Valley of the Marquesas* (London: John Murray 1846) is usually referred to as a novel but is actually a fictionalized account. See Liebersohn, *The Travelers' World*, 289.
35 Charles Rowcroft, *Tales of the Colonies, or, The Adventures of an Emigrant* (London: 1843).
36 On Jules Verne's imaginary voyages as a commentary on contemporary science and technology, see Arthur B. Evans, *Jules Verne Rediscovered: Didacticism and the Scientific Novel* (New York: Greenwood Press 1988). For a comparison of Verne's writings with *Robinson Crusoe*, see Diana Loxley, *Problematic Shores: The Literature of Islands* (London: Macmillan 1990).
37 Jules Verne's *L'Île à Hélice* [*Propeller Island*] (Paris: 1895) is one example that is set mainly in the South Pacific.
38 See Nicholas Thomas, *In Oceania: Visions, Artifacts, Histories* (Durham: Duke University Press 1997), 144. On the history of the adoption of the term 'Pacific' over 'South Seas', see O. H. K. Spate, 'From South Sea to Pacific Ocean', *Journal of Pacific History*, no. 12 (1977): 205–11.
39 *OED*.
40 O. H. K. Spate, *Paradise Found and Lost*, The Pacific since Magellan series, vol. 3 (Sydney: Australian University Press/Pergamon Press 1988), xxii.
41 Greg Dening, *Performances* (Carlton, Victoria: Melbourne University Press 1996), 208.
42 Ibid.
43 Reflecting the way contemporary Australia seeks to define itself as separate from England and from the mythology of the antipodes that linked this part of the world so intimately with Europe, a postcard sold at Sydney airport during the 2000 Olympic Games featured the caption 'Australia: No Longer Down Under'. It pictures a kangaroo with paws up and head down, hanging, precariously, from a globe of the earth. Holiday brochures advertising exotic trips to Australia, New Zealand and the Pacific on the shelves of travel agents the world over testify to the continuing currency of antipodean imagery as a means of commodifying cultural difference in the world 'down under' by casting it in an ongoing anti-relation to Europe. Even the 'Australia: No Longer Down Under' postcard reiterates this mythology at the same time as it jokingly exposes its irrelevance.
44 [Anon.], 'The Land of Contrarieties' (1850s), rpt. in *The Land of Contrarieties: British Attitudes to the Australian Colonies 1828–1855*, by F. G. Clarke (Melbourne: Melbourne University Press 1977), appendix.

INDEX

Aborigines (Australian) 100, 110–11, 115–16, 123, 125, 131; Dampier's impressions of 48, 109; genocide of 112; recognition of rights of 112; and reconciliation movement 172n26; significance of Mabo ruling for 174n85; Stolen Generations of 172n26; treatment of 111
Account of an Expedition to the Interior of New Holland (Anon.) 108, 123–32
'Account of the Loss of His Majesty's Armed Vessel *Porpoise,* and the *Cato,* upon Wreck Reef' (Anon.) 110
Adams, Percy 12
Adventures of Baron Munchausen, The (Raspe) 108, 109
Adventures on a Journey to New Holland (Huber) 124, 175n99
Adventures of Peregrine Pickle, The (Smollet) 53
Africa xviii, 21, 22, 30, 39, 48, 61; Australia compared with 118; Mungo Park's exploration of 118; travel narratives of 123
America(s) 10, 21, 47, 80, 81, 128, 144n7, 154n27; Indigenous peoples of, compared with those of antipodes 19; as model for conceptualizing otherness 24; North, compared with Australia 121
Anson, George 80
Antichthones 144n7
Antipode 21, **21**
antipodes xx–xxiii, 5–6, 48–9; Australia in relation to 108–17; colonialism in 18, 82, 106, 113, 130, 139–40; as counterbalance xvii; dangers of cross-cultural contact in 81; duality, inversion and monstrosity imagined in 20, 21, 34, 41, 73; imperial discourse in relation to xix; Indigenous peoples of, compared with those of other regions 19, 24, 140; paradise in 22–4, 83, 116; role reversals in 20, 109; shifting boundaries of xix, 22, 80, 107, 134, 139; transformation of, from myth to reality 20, 79, 140; usage of term xv, xvii–xix; as utopia xix, 9–11, 18, 149–50n36
Antipodes, The (Brome) 19, 153n1, 168n69
Antoikoi 144n7
Arago, Jacques 116
Aristotle 143n3 (Introduction)
Arnhem Land 112
Artus, Thomas 158n139, 41
Asia xviii, 22, 30
Astrolabe (ship) 84, 88
Atkinson, Geoffroy 11–12, 13–14, 36, 150, 158n136
Australasia xvii, 11, 79, 108, 139
Australia 19, 22–3, 40, 47–8, 82, 83, 84, 89–90, 126, 127 (*See also* great south land; New South Wales; Swan River Colony; Tasmania; Van Diemen's Land); Aboriginal peoples of (*See* Aborigines [Australian]); convicts in 87, 109, 111, 112, 113, 116, 124, 167n30; dead heart of (*See* dead heart, of Australia);

Note: Numbers in **boldface** indicate figures.

Australia (*Continued*)
discovery of, by Dutch 24; discovery of, by Portuguese 24; as *Hollandia Nova* xvi, 51, **51**; identity of 109, 123; inland sea of, anticipated 118–19, 122, 174n90; interior of 108–21, 123, 132; as land 'down under' 107, 109, 179n43; literary traditions of 116–17, 138; mapping of 25, 26, 51, 52, 79, 92, 110, 112, 119, 167n32; name of xvi; as New Holland xvi; as *Nouvelle Hollande* xvi, 3, 51; population of 158n132; reconciliation movement in 172n26; seen as *terra nullius* 122, 174n85; stereotypes of 107, 145n12; as *Terre Australe* xvi, 36, 51, 154n17
Australia in Western Imaginative Prose Writings 1600–1900 (Friederich) 12, 150n36
Australian, first use of term 20

Banks, Joseph 48, 89, 110, 117, 147n10, 165n6
Barrow, John 117, 121–2
Basset, Jan 12
Batavia (ship) 24, 154n24
Bathurst, New South Wales 118, 125
Baudin, Nicolas 85, 112, 144n11, 167n32
Bell, John 55
Bellin, Jacques 79, 92, 165n3
Bentley, Christopher 57, 59, 60, 76
Bergerac, Cyrano de 12
Bibliography of Australia (Ferguson) 116–17
black swans, as antipodean imagery v, 90, 131, 141, 168n69
Blaxland, Gregory 118
Blemmyae 21, **21**
Bligh, William 82
Boitard, Louis-Philippe **65, 66, 67, 68**
Botany Bay, New South Wales 84, 86, 87, 100, 107, 108–9
Bougainville, Louis-Antoine de 80, 82, 84
Bourignon, Antoinette 37
Boussole (ship) 84, 167n42
Bowen, Emanuel 51–2, **52**
Britain 57, 98, 105, 109, 110, 112, 127, 133, 177n7; imaginary voyages published in xx, xxii–xxiii, 146n25; recognition of Australian literature in 117; rivalry of, with other European nations 47. *See also* England
British Critic 133, 148n23, 167n38, 177n6, 177n7, 178n9
Brome, Richard 19, 153n1, 168n69
Brougham, Henry 111, 137
Bryson, Bill 145n12
Bullen, A. H. 57
Byron, John 55, 80
Bysh's Edition of The Voyages and Adventures of La Perouse (Anon.) 98, **99**

Callander, John 165n5, 176n131
cannibalism 24, 81
Carstensz, Jan 24
Carter, Paul 123, 147n8
Carteret, Philip 55, 80
cartography. *See* maps
cartophilia 148n17
Cassini, Giovanni 92, **93, 94**
Charlotte (ship) 87, 168n55
chronometer 79, 165n4
Ciccarone, Julia 41–2, **43, 44, 45**, 65, **69, 70, 71, 72**, 158n140
Coleridge, Samuel Taylor 58, 122, 128
Collins, David 110–11
colonial guidebook genre 138
colonialism xvi, xvii, 10, 35, 42, 56, 81–2, 86, 95, 124, 145n19, 147n10, 150n42; theme of, in imaginary voyages xxii–xxiii, 3, 5–7, 18, 140
Columbus, Christopher 81
Comical History of the States and Empires of the Worlds of the Moon and Sun, The (Bergerac) 12
Commerson, Philibert 82–3
Cook, James xix, 3, 55, 74, 80–81, 82, 84, 87, 92, 98, 108–9, 111, 114, 165n8
Cornelius, Paul 12
Coronelli, Vincenzo 48, **50**
cosmographies 12, 34, 151n76
Critical Review 57
cultural determinism 145n12
Cunningham, Richard 124–5

INDEX

da Gama, Vasco 22
Dalrymple, Alexander 81, 165n5, 165n10
Dampier, William 40, 48, 109, 119
Danckerts, Justus 48, **49**
d'Arnaud, Baculard 55
Darwin, Charles xvii
dead heart, of Australia 117–23. *See also* outback, of Australia
Dead Heart of Australia, The (Gregory) 123
de Brosses, Charles 81, 165n5, 176n131
de Bry, Theodor 22, **23**
Découvertes dans la mer du Sud (Anon.) 167n35
Defoe, Daniel xx, 15–16, 40, 53, 57, 61, 145n16, 145n19, 149n25
Degérando, Joseph Marie 144n11
de Jode, Cornelis 26, **27**, 155n30
de Jode, Gerard 155n30
de l'Isle, Guillaume 51
Dening, Greg 80, 139
d'Entrecasteaux, Bruny 3, 84–5
Desceliers, Pierre 24, **25**
Description de l'Isle des Hermaphrodites (Artus) 158n139
Description of New Athens in Terra Australis Incognita, A (Anon.) 177n167
de Vaugondy, Robert 79, **80**, 92
Diaz, Bartolomeu 22
Diderot, Denis 82
Dillon, Peter 85
Diminishing Paradise, The (Gibson) 12
discovery 28, 36, 79, 89, 120, 124, 134, 137, 140; of Americas 24, 154n27; of Australia's interior 117–23; Dutch 146n26; era of xxi, xxii, 20, 117; heroism of 98; imagining prior to xvii; and Indigenous rights 114–15; Portuguese 24; romanticized discourse of 5; of southern continent 22, 24; Spanish 22; of Tahiti 82–3; usage of term xv, 114–15; of utopia 10–11; vicarious 1; voyages of xxii, 8, 20, 39, 47, 51, 55, 80, 84, 87, 103, 108, 119
Discovery of a New World, or, A Description of the South Indies, Hitherto Unknowne, by an English Mercury, The (Hall) 20, 28–36, **31**, **33**

Dream of Scipio (Macrobius) xviii, **xviii**
Duff (ship) 111
du Fresne, Marion 165n8
Dunlop, John 6, 12, 13, 15, 16, 59, 152n82
Dunmore, John 12, 86, 88, 89, 95, 124, 155n34, 175n104
d'Urville, Jules Sebastian Cesar Dumont 85, 167n41
Dutch East India Company 24, 52
Duyfken (ship) 23, 146n27
dystopia 9, 32, 36, 171n6. *See also* utopia(s)

East, the: exotic imagery of 145n12, 154n12; knowledge of, through trade 21; location of paradise in 21
Eddy, William 12, 14
Edinburgh Review 109, 111, 116, 117, 120, 137, 171n8, 173n48
empiricism and empirical knowledge xx, 8, 11, 14, 20, 21, 29, 34, 49–50, 83, 134–5, 140, 159n9, 160n28. *See also* hyper-empiricism, in imaginary voyages
Endeavour (ship) 48, 146n27
England 22, 110, 112, 127, 128, 159n10, 165n5, 179n43; imaginary voyages published in 15; recognition of imaginary voyages in 13; writers of utopian fiction in 11, 156n58. *See also* Britain
English Novel, The (Raleigh) 146n1, 149n25
equator 53, 144n12; as torrid zone xviii, 49, 144n4
Espérance (ship) 85
Espiritu Santo 24, 82
Europe xviii, xix–xxi, xxiii, 5–7, 46, 80–4, 108–9, 123, 132, 137, 139–40; compared with antipodes 19, 117–18, 122; 'geographic unconscious' of 36; reception of *Robinson Crusoe* and *Gulliver's Travels* in 15; usage of term xvi; utopian projections of 9–11, 32, 128
eutopia 131, 177n169. *See also* utopia(s)
evolutionary theories 83
extraordinary voyage 2. *See also* imaginary voyage(s)

Extraordinary Voyage in French Literature before 1700, The (Atkinson) 11, 13, 158n136
Extraordinary Voyage in French Literature 1700 to 1720, The (Atkinson) 12

Fable of the Bees, The (Mandeville) 53
fabulous voyage 2. *See also* imaginary voyage(s)
family robinsonade 56. *See also* robinsonade
fantastic voyage 2. *See also* imaginary voyage(s)
fantasy, as term denoting genre 55–6
Far-Fetched Facts: The Literature of Travel and the Idea of the South Seas (Rennie) 12
Fausett, David 11, 12, 20, 36, 37, 42, 104, 145n13, 157n118, 157n124
Fawcett, John 97
Fenelon, François 55
Ferguson, John Alexander 116–17
fictional letter, as literary device 8, 125, 132, 175n109
'Fictitious Travellers in French and English Literature: A Study of Imaginary Voyages from Cyrano de Bergerac to Oliver Goldsmith 1657–1762' (Moon) 12
fictitious voyage 2, 65. *See also* imaginary voyage(s)
Fictitious Voyages (Ciccarone) 41, **43, 44, 45**, 65, **69, 70, 71, 72**, 158n140
First Fleet (to New South Wales) 84, 87
Flinders, Matthew xv, 85, 89, 110, 112, 118, 136, 166–7n28
Foigny, Gabriel de 2, 11, 16, 20, 36–46, 145n16
Fox, Lady Mary 124, 175n102
Fragmens du dernier voyage de La Pérouse [*Fragments from the Last Voyage of La Pérouse*] (Anon.) 79, 85–97, 168n54
France 84–6, 160n20, 165n5; imaginary voyages published in xx, xxiii, 146n25, 150n36; recognition of imaginary voyages in 13–14; rivalry of, with other European nations 47
French Revolution 85–6, 89, 98

Freycinet, Louis de 116
Friederich, Werner 12, 150n36
Friend of Australia, The (Maslen) 119–20, **120**

Garnier, Charles 13, 148n14, 152n82
genocide, in Australia 112
Geography (Pinkerton) 2
Gibson, Ross 12, 124
Godwin, Francis 161n40
Gold-Finder of Australia, The (Sherer) 179n33
Gonneville, Binot Paulmier de 22, 154n17
Gove, Phillip Babcock 2, 5, 12–16
Great Southern Landings: An Anthology of Antipodean Travel (Basset) 12
great south land xv–xvi, xix, 79, 81, 108, 143n3, 165n5
Gregory, J. W. 123
Gulf of Carpentaria 23, 24, 85, 110, 112
Gulliveriana 15, 152n96
Gulliver's Travels: A Critical Study (Eddy) 12, 14
Gulliver's Travels (*Travels into Several Remote Nations of the World*) (Swift) xx, xxii, 1, 15, 36, 53, 55, 56, 57, 103, 152n96

Hakluyt, Richard 30, 148n14
'halfway house', as literary device 6, 39, 104
Hall, Joseph 2, 16, 20, 28–36, 38, 41, 155n32, 155n34, 155n37, 155n46, 156n58, 157n119
Hartl, Martin 112, **113**
Hartog, Dirck 24
Hawaii 47, 74, 81, 84, 86, 155n34
Hawkesworth, John 55, 160n32
Healey, John 20, 28
hermaphroditism 20, 36–7, 41–2
Heylyn, Peter 34, 156n67
Histoire des navigations aux Terres Australes (de Brosses) 165n5, 176n131
Histoire d'un peuple nouveau, ou découverte d'une isle...par David Tompson [*Captain Tompson's Island*] (Anon.) 16

Historical and Geographical Description of Formosa, An (Psalmanazar) 160n20
historiography 135
History of Fiction, The (Dunlop) 6, 12, 13, 59
History of the Sevarites or Sevarambi, The (Vairasse) 39, 145n16, 150n39, 154n16, 158–9n3
Hollandia Nova xvi, 51. *See also* Australia; great south land
Home, Henry 54–5
Houtman, Frederick de 24
Howe, Michael 173n53
Huber, Therese 175n99
Hulme, Peter 64, 154n27
Hunter, John 91
hyper-empiricism, in imaginary voyages 7–8

Images of the Antipodes in the Eighteenth Century (Fausett) 12
Imaginary Voyage in Prose Fiction, The (Gove) 2, 12, 14, 15
imaginary voyage(s): antipodean setting of xx; compared to maps xxii, 8, 49, 53; counter-colonialist readings of xxii, 29, 96, 140; definition of xxi, 13–14, 15; earthly paradise in 22, 46, 86; fact and fiction in xxi, 13–14, 15, 46, 53, 135, 148n14; fictional maps in 8, **32, 33**; genre of xvii, xxi, xxiii, 1, 10, 12–13, 15, 17, 19, 108, 135, 140, 150n37; 'halfway house' as literary device in 6, 39, 104; hyper-empiricism in 7–8; Library of Congress subject heading for 1; literary criticism of xxi, 1, 2, 3, 5, 10, 11–15, 59, 140; literary forms related to xx, 1, 12, 14; narrative conventions in xxi, 1, 2, 3, 56–7; preface of, as literary device 8, 28, 38, 149n28; published in Britain xxii–xxiii, 15, 146n25; published in France xxii–xxiii, 12, 15, 146n25, 150n36; readership of 146n22; as realist fiction xx, 10–11, 54; in relation to genuine accounts and discoveries xxi, 1, 2, 3, 7, 39, 53, 92, 108, 134; as robinsonades 15–16; satire and parody in xxii, 7; as social commentary xx, 2; theme of colonialism in xx–xxiii, 3, 5–7, 18, 140; theme of utopia in xx, 6–7, 9–11, 14, 17, 36, 40, 79, 82, 86, 89, 95, 103, 108, 124, 128, 156n58; themes in xxi, 2, 5–7, 42, 95; translations of xxiii; usage of term 2, 5, 9; verisimilitude in 6, 7–9
India 21; travel narratives of 123
Indian Ocean 28, 39
Indigenous peoples 4, 81, 139; as 'embryonic civilizations' xix; typical portrayal of, in imaginary voyages xxi; as uncivilized xix, 110; as uncontaminated xix. *See also* Aborigines (Australian); Maori
Investigator (ship) 110

Jansz, Willem xxiii, 23
Java-La-Grande 24
Journal of a Cruize Made to the Pacific Ocean by Captain David Porter (Porter) 176n162
Journal of the Royal Geographical Society of London 122
Jurgensen, Manfred v

Keate, George 148n12
King, John 117
Kotzebue, August von 167n35

Lamb, Charles 58
'Land of Contrarieties, The' (Anon.) 142
Languages in Seventeenth- and Early Eighteenth-Century Imaginary Voyages (Cornelius) 12
La Pérouse, Jean-François de Galaup de, 3, 79, 80, 84–9, 92, 100, 105, 167n30, 167n41; disappearance of 79, 84–5
La Perouse, or The Desolate Island (Fawcett) 97
La Peyrouse (Kotzebue) 167n35
Last and the Worst of the Bush Rangers of Van Diemen's Land, The (Howe) 173n53

La Terre Australe connue (Foigny) 2, 16, 20, 36–46, 145n16
Lawson, Henry 117
Lawson, William 118
Les Avantures de Jacques Sadeur dans la découverte et le voiage de la Terre Australe (Foigny) 37
Les Hermaphrodites (Artus) 41
Letter from Sydney, A (Wakefield) 175n109
Liber Chronicarum [*Nuremberg Chronicle*] (Schedel) 21, **21**
Life and Adventures of Peter Wilkins, The (Paltock) 16, 42, 56–77, **65, 66, 67, 68**
Life of the Celebrated Navigator La Perouse and Surprising Adventures in His Voyage to the South Seas, The (Anon.) 98
Life of La Perouse, the Celebrated and Unfortunate French Navigator, The (Anon.) 79, 97–106
Life of Perouse and His Surprising Adventures in a Voyage to the South-Seas (Anon.) 98
L'Île à Hélice [*Propeller Island*] (Verne) 179n37
literary deception 5, 13, 160n20, 162n68, 179n33
literary romance. *See* romance, literary
Locke, John 49
longitude 79, 165n4
Lucian of Samosata 12, 161n40

Mackaness, George 12
Macrobius, Ambrosius xviii
Madagascar 38, 39, 104
Madigan, Cecil 174n92
Magellan, Ferdinand 22, 38
Mandeville, Bernard 53
Man in the Moone, The (Godwin) 161n40
Maori 81, 83, 165n8, 166n21
Mapping Men and Empire: A Geography of Adventure (Phillips) 12
maps xvi, xviii, xix, 22–7, 30, 48–52, 79–80, 92–4, 112, 119–20, 137; annotated 51, 53; blank spaces on xviii, xx, 47, 49, 50, 51, 80, 122; classical geography informing xviii; compared to imaginary voyages xxii, 8, 49; fact and fiction in 8, 89, 137; fictional, in imaginary voyages xxii, 8, 30, **32, 33**; as form of imperial discourse 9; French 24; of the Gulf of Carpentaria 112; illustrations and decorative imagery on xix, 21, 48, 50; medieval 21, 153n12; naming the unknown on 9; narrative potential of 119; of Pacific 22, 47, 80; as supporting myths 21, 48; *Terra Incognita* on 9; as trustworthy 9
marooning 110; of Alexander Selkirk 40; in robinsonades 16
marvellous voyage 2. *See also* imaginary voyage(s)
marvels 35, 156n78, 161n33
Maslen, Thomas 119–20
Mauritius 84, 100, 110, 112
Mela, Pomponius 143n3 (Introduction)
Melanesia 24, 139
Melville, Herman 179n34
Mercator, Gerardus 22, 30
Mestrezat, Amy 37
Micronesia 139
Milet-Mureau, Louis Antoine 85–6, 92
Mills, Charles 134
Milman, Henry 135
missionary work 81, 116, 131, 164n137, 173n48
Mitchell, Thomas 122, 124–5, 174n89
Montanus, Benito Arias 25, **26**
Montgomery, James 173n48
Monthly Magazine, or British Register 56
Monthly Review xv, 53–4, 55, 57, 84, 87, 107, 111, 113–14, 133, 136, 62n68
Moon, Hi Kyung 12
More, Thomas 10, 11, 32, 36, 150n42, 156n58
Mundus alter et idem (Hall) 2, 16, 20, 28–36, **32**, 41, 155n32, 155n34
myths and mythology 8, 19–20, 34, 73, 80, 108–9, 139–40, 145n12, 165n10, 168n69, 179n43; of Australia's inland sea 119–22, 174n90; consolidation of, in imaginary voyages 46; generated by maps 21–2, 26, 29, 137, 153n12; as

gesture of control xix; of land 'down under' 107; relationship of, with reality xx, 3–4, 11, 49–50, 132; relationship of, with science 166n24; of savagery in Australia 116; of Tahiti 81–3

Narrative of the Life and Astonishing Adventures of John Daniel, A (Morris [pseud.]) 16, 56, 149n30
native types. *See* noble savage; primitivism, soft and hard
natural history 148n23
neo-classical style xix, 92
never-never, of Australia 123, 174n92. *See also* dead heart, of Australia
Neville, Henry 11
New Caledonia 47
New Discovery of Terra Incognita Australis, or the Southern World, A (Foigny) 20, 36, 38
New Guinea 22, 110, 144n6
New South Wales 109–13, 115, 116–17, 121, 124, 125, 128, 142
New Voyage Round the World, A (Dampier) 48
New Voyage Round the World, A (Defoe) 53, 145n16
New Zealand xix, 19, 47, 92, 96, 107, 109, 115, 144n6, 155n34, 175n97, 179n43; Maori of 81, 83, 165n8, 166n21; Treaty of Waitangi 139
noble savage 82–3, 95
Norfolk Island 90–1
Northwest Passage 47
Nouvelle Cythère 82. *See also* Tahiti
Nouvelle Hollande xvi, 3, 51. *See also* Australia; great south land
novels and novelists xvii, 134, 138, 179n34; Australian interior as setting for 123; British 117; French 13, 36; historical truth in relation to 55, 160n28, 177n7; nineteenth-century literary style of 54, 59, 135–6; realist 3, 55–6, 135–6, 149n29; voyage accounts as model for 133. *See also* romance, literary
Nuremberg Chronicle. See *Liber Chronicarum*

Oceania xvii, 139
Odyssey (Homer) 12, 57
Ortelius, Abraham 22, 149n35
outback, of Australia 124, 175n97. *See also* dead heart, of Australia
Oxley, John 117, 118, 119, 121, 122

Pacific (Ocean) xix–xx, 39, 55, 130, 165n10, 175n99, 179n43; exploration of 19, 79–85, 109; maps of 22, 47, 80; as setting for utopian fiction 138; usage of term 139, 144n6, 179n38
Paltock, Robert 56–60, 63, 65, 66, 67, 68, 161n41
pantisocracy 128
paradise xx, 21–2, 24, 41, 46, 81, 103, 108, 111, 116, 154n16; in the East 21; Tahiti as 83
Park, Mungo 118, 177n7
parody xxii, 7, 32, 42, 131, 145n12, 157n118, 157n124
Phillips, Richard 12, 36
Pieter Nuytsland 52
Pinkerton, John 2
Plato 10
Pocahontas 101, 168n113
Polo, Marco 4, 13, 22, 24, 147n11, 157n19
Polynesia 139
Porpoise (ship) 110
Porter, David 130–1, 162–3n68, 176n162
Port Jackson, New South Wales 84, 88, 110
Portuguese: explorers 22, 24, 35, 154n28; empire 47. *See also* discovery
postcolonial attitudes and approaches 3, 42, 77, 95, 129, 165n8
Pratt, Mary Louise: 'anti-conquest' in work of 7, 74; 'seeing-man' in work of 7
pre-robinsonade 16. *See also* robinsonade
primitivism, soft and hard 83, 103. *See also* noble savage
Psalmanazar, George 160n20
Ptolemy 143n3 (Introduction)
Pury, Jean Pierre 52
Pythagoras xviii, 143n3 (Introduction), 144n4

Quarterly Review xvii, 55, 86, 107, 111–15, 118–22, 125, 130, 135–6, 152n82, 162n68, 167n30, 171n8

Quirós, Pedro Fernández de xxiii, 23, 39, 82, 158n136

Quo vardis? (Hall) 155n37

Raleigh, Walter 58, 146n1, 149n25
Raspe, Rudolph Erich 108, 109
realism 8, 11, 39, 54, 55, 57, 89, 96, 100; historical 125, 131; literary 3, 11, 133; usage of term 56, 149n29
Recherche (ship) 85
Rennie, Neil 12
Retrospective Review 59, 133
Reynolds, Henry 172n26
robinsonade 5, 15–17, 101; family robinsonade as form of 56; pre-robinsonade as form of 16
Robinson Crusoe (*The Life and Strange Surprizing Adventures of Robinson Crusoe*) (Defoe) xx, 1, 15–16, 40, 53, 56, 57, 58, 61, 148n15, 149n25, 179n36
Roebuck (ship) 40
romance, literary 1, 4, 13, 17, 54–5, 123, 134, 136, 146n1. *See also* novels and novelists
romanticism 54, 56, 58–9, 146n25, 166n19
Rousseau, Jean-Jacques 16, 56, 59, 82
Rowcroft, Charles 138
Royal Geographical Society 121, 122, 124, 162n66, 166n19
Ryan, Simon xxii, 144n9, 159n14

Samoa 47, 87
satire xix, 5, 6, 7, 16, 28, 32, 35, 42, 106, 145n17, 150n37
savagery, myth of 81, 116
Sciapod 21, **21**
science xvii, xxi, 117, 134, 166n19, 166n24, 178n11, 179n36
science fiction 1, 59, 138, 147n2, 162n67
Schedel, Hartmann 21
Scott, Ernest 168n54
Scott, Walter 58, 134
scurvy 4, 90
Selkirk, Alexander 40. *See also* marooning

Senex, John 51, 160n15
Seriman, Zaccaria 145n17
Shadows of Utopia (Jurgensen) v
Shakespeare, William 156n64
Shelley, Mary 58
Shelley, Percy 58
Sherer, John 179n33
Smith, Bernard 147n10, 167n35
Smith, John 101, 169n13
Smith, Sydney 109, 115–21, 137, 173n64
Smollet, Tobias 53, 161n37
societies of knowledge 166n24
Society Islands 47. *See also* Tahiti
Some Fictitious Voyages to Australia (Mackaness) 12
Southern Land, Known, The (Foigny) 20, 36–46
Southey, Robert 58, 128
South Pole 61, 104
South Sea Bubble (collapse of South Sea Company) 53
South Sea(s) xv, 47, 60, 79, 83, 84, 88, 98, 111, 139, 149n36, 165n6, 179n38
Spanish explorers 22, 23. *See also* discovery
Stirling, James 121–2
Stothard, Thomas 56
Sturt, Charles 122
Supplément au voyage de Bougainville [*Supplement to the Voyage of Bougainville*] (Diderot) 82
Surprising Adventures of Baron Munchausen, The (Raspe) 108, 109
Swan River Colony 121–2, 125
Swift, Jonathan xx, 15–16, 36, 40, 47, 48, 53, 55, 57, 155n50, 160n31
Swoboda, Franz 112, **113**
Sydney 109, 110, 111, 116–17, 118, 122, 125, 126, 128, 132, 171n13, 179n43
Sydney Gazette 110

Tahiti 82–3, 86, 111, 165n13, 172n31
Tales of the Colonies (Rowcroft) 138
Tasman, Abel xvi, 24
Tasmania 79 (*See also* Van Diemen's Land); Indigenous population of, eradication of 111

Tempest, The (Shakespeare) 156n64
Tench, Watkin 88
Terra Australis 19, 28–9, 34, 114–15, 128, 154n16, 177n167; maps of 9, 22, 24–5, 149n35; usage of term xv–xvi, xix, 144n6. *See also* Australia; great south land
Terra Australis cognita, or, Voyages to the Terra Australis or Southern Hemisphere during the Sixteenth, Seventeenth, and Eighteenth Centuries (Callander) 165n5, 176n131
Terre Australe xvi, 36, 51, 154n17. *See also* Australia; great south land
Theatrum Orbis Terrarum (Ortelius) 22, 149n35
Theopompos of Chios 10
Theory of Characterization in Prose Fiction prior to 1740, The (Tieje) 12
Thévenot, Melchisédech 51, **51**
Tieje, Arthur 12, 17
Times Literary Supplement 57
Torres, Luis Váez de xxiii
travel, arguments against 22–3
Travelers and Travel Liars 1660–1800 (Adams) 12
Travels from St. Petersburg in Russia to Various Parts of Asia (Bell) 55
Travels of Hildebrand Bowman (Bowman [pseud.]) 166n21
Travels of Sir John Mandeville, The (Anon.) 13, 34
Travels of Theodore Ducas, The (Mills) 134
True History (Lucian of Samosata) 12, 161n40
Turnbull, John 110–11, 137, 172n31
Typee (Melville) 179n34

Ulysses, voyage of, in the *Odyssey* 12
unknown, imagery of the 49, 147n8
'Upside-Down Hut, The' (Wright) 171n5
Utopia (More) 10, 11, 32, 36
utopia(s): antipodean setting of xix, 9, 10, 11, 137–8, 149n36, 150n44; classical 40; colonialism in relation to xx, 10, 18, 128, 150n41; 'double' 124, 128; and dystopia 9, 32, 36, 171n6; English 156n58; Golden Age references in 10; idealistic 17;

'negative' 9; as 'no-place' 18; portrayal and projection of, literary 1, 5, 9–11, 82, 101; 'positive' 9, 14; rebirth in 40; Tahiti as 83, 111; theme of, in imaginary voyages xx, 6–7, 9–11, 14, 17, 36, 40, 79, 82, 86, 89, 95, 103, 108, 124, 128, 156n58; usage of term 9, 11, 18, 150n36, 176n138. *See also* eutopia; *Utopia* (More)
Utopias and Imaginary Voyages to Australasia (Dunmore) 12

Vairasse, Denis 11, 39, 145n16, 150n39, 154n16, 158–9n3
van Diemen, Anthony 24
Van Diemen's Land 79, 92, 107, 110, 114, 173n47. *See also* Tasmania
Venus 64, 165n12; transit of 82
Vergulde Draeck (ship) 24, 40, 154n26
Verne, Jules 138, 139, 179n36, 179n37
Vespucci, Amerigo 10, 22
Viaggi di Enrico Wanton alle Terre Incognite Australi [*Voyages of Enrico Wanton to Terra Australis Incognita*] (Seriman) 145n17
Virgidemiarum (Hall) 28
voyage, imaginary. *See* imaginary voyage(s)
voyage accounts, genuine: literary conventions of xxi, 6, 55, 137, 146n1; nautical details in 54, 136–7; popularity of 2; quality and reliability of 2, 4–5, 160n32; in relation to imaginary voyages 6, 14, 53, 55; as 'subsidiaries of history' 178n17; translations of 178n9
Voyage autour du monde (Bougainville) 82
Voyage dans la Lune (Bergerac) 161n40
Voyage de La Pérouse autour du monde (Milet-Mureau) 85
Voyage de Robertson, aux Terres Australes, traduit sur le manuscrit anglois (Robertson [pseud.]) 16
voyage extraordinaire 2. *See also* imaginary voyage(s)
voyage imaginaire 2. *See also* imaginary voyage(s)
Voyage Round the World, A (Turnbull) 111, 137

Voyages curieux d'un Philadelphe dans des pays nouvellement découverts [*The Curious Voyages of a Philadelphian*] (Anon.) 16
Voyages imaginaires, songes, visions et romans cabalistiques (Garnier) 13

Wakefield, Edward Gibbon 175n109
Wallis, Samuel 55, 80, 82
Weber, Henry 12, 15, 16, 134, 152n82
Wentworth, William Charles 118

Whately, Richard 109, 124, 175n100
wonderful voyage 2. *See also* imaginary voyage(s)
World Wide Web 138
Wright, Judith 108
Writing the New World: Imaginary Voyages and Utopias of the Great Southern Land (Fausett) 12

Yirrkala bark petition 112. *See also* Aborigines (Australian)

www.ingramcontent.com/pod-product-compliance
Lightning Source LLC
Chambersburg PA
CBHW021827300426
44114CB00009BA/357